T0367022

THE

PUBLICATIONS

OF THE

SURTEES SOCIETY

VOL. CLXXXIX

Filmset in Great Britain by
Northumberland Press Limited
Gateshead

THE

PUBLICATIONS

OF THE

SURTEES SOCIETY

ESTABLISHED IN THE YEAR

M.DCCC.XXXIV

VOL. CLXXXIX

FOR THE YEAR MCMLXXIV

At a COUNCIL MEETING of the SURTEES SOCIETY, held in Durham Castle on 7 June 1976, Mr C. R. Hudleston in the chair, it was ORDERED—

"That the edition of Sir Christopher Lowther's Commercial Papers by Dr D. R. Hainsworth should be printed as a volume of the Society's publications."

A. J. PIPER
Secretary.

COMMERCIAL PAPERS
OF
SIR CHRISTOPHER LOWTHER
1611-1644

EDITED BY

D. R. HAINSWORTH

PRINTED FOR THE SOCIETY BY
NORTHUMBERLAND PRESS LIMITED
GATESHEAD
1977

CONTENTS

INTRODUCTION

Sir Christopher Lowther of Whitehaven, first baronet, was born at Skirwith, Cumberland, on 19 April 1611, and was buried at St Bees on 24 April 1644. He was the second son of Sir John Lowther of Lowther and Lady Eleanor, née Fleming, the grandson of Sir Christopher Lowther of Lowther[1] and the great grandson of Sir Richard Lowther, twice Sheriff of Cumberland, and Deputy Lord Warden of the West March for most of Elizabeth's reign. Christopher had an elder brother, John (subsequently Sir John Lowther of Lowther, first baronet), a younger brother William, and a sister Agnes who was married to Roger Kirkby of Kirkby-in-Furness, M.P. for Lancashire in the Long Parliament. At the time of his death (the cause of which is nowhere stated) Christopher was a royalist officer commanding the first brigade of foot to be raised in Cumberland and Westmorland under the Marquis of Newcastle, and had a few weeks previously been appointed governor of Whitehaven and of Cockermouth Castle.[2]

Both Christopher and his younger brother William seem to have been apprenticed to commerce, although not for the full term of an apprenticeship. John, the elder brother, was educated at the Inns of Court, and was briefly a member of parliament in the 1620s. Their father, Sir John Lowther of Lowther the Elder, who was member for Westmorland in four parliaments between 1623 and 1630, was a supporter of the Duke of Buckingham, and in 1629 was appointed to the Council of the North, a position he probably still held at his death in 1637. He devoted much of his formidable energy and ability to rebuilding the Lowther fortunes and estates which had decayed under the indifferent though brief stewardship of his father, Sir Christopher. From the profits of land and trade, supplemented by the fruits of office and law, he launched his posterity on the road that led to that empire of land and industrial wealth, the estates of the nineteenth century Earls of Lonsdale.

A very important element in that Victorian "empire" was the West Cumberland estates, based on Whitehaven, with their heavy rent rolls and substantial coal fields. A share in these properties, the core of which was the old monastic manor of St Bees, was first acquired by Sir John from the Irish branch of the Lowther family, which owned them jointly with Thomas Wibergh of Clifton, a distant kinsman. Lowther bought out Wibergh, a

---

[1] With whom he is sometimes confused, for e.g. J. E. Williams, "Whitehaven in the 18th century", *Economic History Review*, viii, 1956.

[2] Newcastle's warrants to Christopher are dated February, 1643/4.

transaction which later led to half a century of litigation for his grandson, and placed them in the stewardship of his second son Christopher, and directed in his will that they should pass to Christopher as his inheritance. This wish was reluctantly honoured by the eldest son in 1639 (see Appendix B).

The present collection of papers covers firstly, the period from 1632 to 1637 when Christopher was both acting for his father at Whitehaven and playing the chief role in the Lowther family's commercial speculations in conjunction with his brother William; and secondly, the period from 1639 until his death in 1644, when he was developing the Cumberland estates in his own behalf. During this period he founded the Whitehaven branch of the family which became extinct with the death of his grandson, Sir James Lowther, fourth baronet, in 1755. To this later period also belongs Christopher's brief public life, on which his papers throw little light. He was appointed Sheriff of Cumberland in 1641, was given a baronetcy in 1642, and was a royalist commander at his early death at the age of thirty-three. He left a son, John Lowther of Whitehaven, aged two, who was member for Cumberland for most of the period 1664–1698, a Fellow of the Royal Society, a Commissioner of the Navy under William III as an "Orange Tory", and died in 1706. Shortly after Christopher's death his widow Frances gave birth to a daughter, also Frances, who married Richard Lamplugh of Ribton.

Throughout the dozen years of Christopher's adult life the foundations of Whitehaven's prosperity were laid. Salt making and coal mining were launched, the first pier was constructed, and trade with Ireland and northern Europe exploited. The St Bees–Whitehaven estates were increased through purchases, and through his long matured marriage settlement with Frances Lancaster, which Sir John the elder negotiated when Frances was a child, Christopher acquired in 1639 the valuable Westmorland properties of Sockbridge and Hartsop.

The papers reproduced here are not a complete archive but a collection preserved rather by chance than conscious selection. Christopher's chief books of account and ledgers are missing. Basically the surviving papers consist of (i) a letter book containing letters written from Dublin in 1632–1633, and then used again in the period 1639–1642; (ii) four very small notebooks, in the first three of which Christopher jotted down rough copies of accounts, letters, memoranda and instructions, occasionally public records or documents of interest to himself or to the family's commercial activities, and also brief journal entries recording his travels and business dealings in England and Ireland in the period 1632–1637, until he embarked at Hull for Hamburg whereupon this type of record most unfortunately ceases. The fourth notebook belonged to his father, and Christopher simply made a series of notes about his estate in 1643 and his plans for the future (see below p. 208); (iii) finally there is a selection of documents, letters and agreements, including a draft will, which cover the period from 1637 to 1644.[3]

Although fragmentary and incomplete the papers enlarge our knowledge not merely of the Lowther family, but of the early history of Whitehaven and its coal industry, Irish economic history, the history of English internal and overseas trade in the 1630s, including trade with France, the Canary Islands, Germany, Scandinavia, Scotland and Ireland. They also throw light on early industrial developments, coal mining, salt making, rope making, iron smelting, and milling, and sidelights on the West Riding clothing industry. There are interesting sidelights also on the commercial interests of Sir Thomas Wentworth, Earl of Strafford, and his secretary Sir George Radcliffe, and other members of the Council of the North. Finally these papers contribute to our knowledge of the role of the gentry in commerce and manufacturing, and particularly the part played by the younger sons of gentry families with the financial backing of their father's capital.

I am greatly indebted—as will be generations of historians to come—to James Lowther, seventh Earl of Lonsdale, who did a magnificient service to historical scholarship when he decided to make his family's archives available to scholars, a decision which led to the formation of the present Joint Archives of Cumberland, Westmorland and the City of Carlisle. I should also like to thank him for permitting me to publish this selection of his family's papers. I must also warmly thank Bruce Jones, the Archivist, and the members of his staff, for much patient assistance in the early stages of this work.

A note on the editing

The editing has been governed by the principles set out in the British Records Association's *Notes for the Guidance of Editors of Record Publications*, London, 1946. The spelling of the original has been retained except for well-known place names which have been modernised (e.g. Bristol for Bristoe) and for common surnames where a modern version is sometimes employed by the seventeenth century writer. Here the name is standardised on the modern version (e.g. Batty for Battie, Battey, etc). Capitalisation and punctuation are modernised save where the meaning of the sentence is ambiguous and the insertion of a comma could arbitrarily determine the sense. Editorial interpolations are in square brackets. Contractions are usually expanded, with modern spelling, in the letters and documents in Sections One, Six and the appendices, but are commonly retained in the notebooks, Sections Two to Five, in order to retain something of the brief, random jotting flavour of the original. Numerals and figures are usually given as in the original, except for the omission of intrusive naughts before figures. The editor has indicated blank pages, gaps in the text,

[3] All the papers referred to are located at the reference D/Lons/W Sir Christopher Lowther.

interpolations in the original, damaged pages and smudged, overwritten or otherwise illegible words, and other words whose reconstruction has had to be conjectural.[4]

N.B. The copyright of these documents is retained by Lord Lonsdale.

[4] N.B. Every attempt has been made to present the papers in chronological order within individual volumes or sets. Thus the letters in Section One are in strict date order not in the order in which they were written in the letter book, which can be determined by the page numbers in italics in the left-hand margin.

Abbreviated family tree of the Lowthers showing the relationships of Lowthers referred to in the text

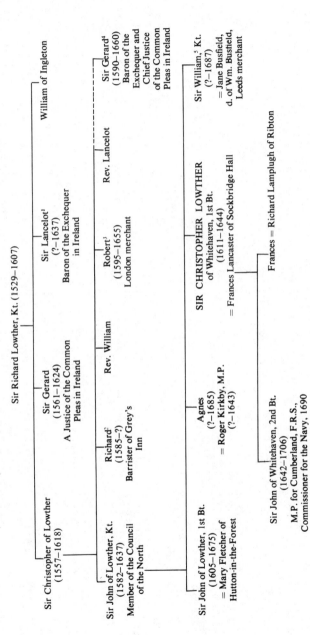

Sir Richard Lowther, Kt. (1529–1607)

Sir Christopher of Lowther (1557–1618) — Sir Gerard (1561–1624) A Justice of the Common Pleas in Ireland — Sir Lancelot[1] (?–1637) Baron of the Exchequer in Ireland — William of Ingleton

Sir John of Lowther, Kt. (1582–1637) Member of the Council of the North — Richard[2] (1585–?) Barrister of Grey's Inn — Rev. William — Robert[3] (1595–1655) London merchant — Rev. Lancelot — Sir Gerard[4] (1590–1660) Baron of the Exchequer and Chief Justice of the Common Pleas in Ireland

Sir John of Lowther, 1st Bt. (1605–1675) = Mary Fletcher of Hutton-in-the-Forest — Agnes (?–1685) = Roger Kirkby, M.P. (?–1643) — SIR CHRISTOPHER LOWTHER of Whitehaven, 1st Bt. (1611–1644) = Frances Lancaster of Sockbridge Hall — Sir William,[5] Kt. (?–1687) = Jane Busfield, d. of Wm. Busfield, Leeds merchant

Sir John of Whitehaven, 2nd Bt. (1642–1706) M.P. for Cumberland, F.R.S., Commissioner for the Navy, 1690 — Frances = Richard Lamplugh of Ribton

[1] "Uncle Lancelot", actually Christopher's great-uncle.
[2] "Uncle Richard".
[3] "Uncle Robert" of the letters, briefly Christopher's partner, and onetime his master in apprenticeship.
[4] Sir Gerard was a bastard, and that Sir Christopher was his father is generally assumed by genealogists, but is unproven. He is naturally often confused with his uncle (e.g. D.N.B.).
[5] Sir William, who spent much of the Civil War period in the Low Countries, founded the Swillington (Yorkshire) branch of the family from whom the present Earls of Lonsdale derive.

SECTION ONE

LETTER BOOK 1632–1642

To Robert Lowther, Merchant in London

Much I woonder that never since my departure from yow I had not any letter I expectinge here what your instructions weere for proceadinge, and but onley that my father showed us in a letter from yow that yow intended not to sende any wares over untill yow had advice from me in Ireland, it may be I had yet stayed longer, but now intend within this 14 dayes to be over in Ireland, if I can possiblely which I thinke I shall. Rowland Jackson and I this day have sealed indentures the same as I with yow onely he added in for him if any difference shoulde happen, Mr Anthony Hutton of Penrith to my father, and Mr Anthony Beddingfeilde for disscision of the same, which I hope we shall never neede, and another clause that was not clerely enough expressed, viz: and for proceading theirein to be done by advice one from another which wee have thought fitt ratther thus to expresse (our intention being all one in effectt) viz: and wee do agree and give full pooer to each other to buy, sell and make bargains for the advancing of ower stocke as each shall thinke fitt, unlesse the one advise the other to the contrary which you approving of may bee pleased to write by your letter to him and me.

And in respect his shipp (beeing about 40 tonne) is returned aboutt 10 days sence from France and now within 14 daies will have[6] unloaden all her wines, vineger, prunes and her sallett oyles and bee redy for Ireland and that yett your stock cometh nott in. Rowland Jackson intendeth for Leeds presently to buy some northern dozens; about 100^l worth; and aboutt 30^l of them for mee for Dublin; and the 100^l worth he intendeth for Belfast and Carrecfargas and there presently to fournish himselfe with what Irish comodities he cann gett, as tallow, hogshead staves and butter; which butter if I cann gett him better att Dublin he will take itt in there; and carry 50^l worth of Kendall Cottens, which hee sould in France att reasonable good prices, and leade yf at reason. Sir Phillip Musgrave will deliver itt at Milthrop[7]; beeing now worth in France about 15^l per tonne, in which voiage Rowland and I ar halves. And I have halfe his shippe which will come too aboutt 200^l, and yf before she make for France you write you may bee a quarter part, both for the shippe and her loading, and Row. will

---

[5] Page numbering added by the Archives staff.
[6] "redie for Ireland" crossed out.
[7] I.e. Milnthorpe.

bee one other quarter part; and yf you doe nott send word before then he and I will have all betweene us this voiage and att her rettorn out of France againe, yf you please wee may bee all in and you may stay for your London wares till I ore Rowland advise you out of Ireland.

Your faithfull and ever trusty parteners,
Christopher Lowther[8]
Rowland Jackson.

Dublin the 23th September 1632

To Miles Bateman,
Miles Bateman,

I ame glade you are safe reterned from France. Some dirrections my partner Rowland Jackson and myself lefte with Mr Tompson of Dublin how you observed them I know not, for wee had not leasure to copie your letters out, but we intended some 20 tons of the salt to be left at Dublin for sale, and yf yt would not have sould now, with sellering it upp afterwards I would not have dowbted to have sould it to reasonable proffitt. On Saterday the day you went away came I to Dublin about 5 of the clock at night, and hearing that you were come that night, on Sunday in the morninge when I was sending to you, I staid wondring that I heard noe word from you by anie letter lefte behind you of what you had done with the overplus of the salt which you will not use. I know not what you can doe with yt now. But about yt I pray you advice with Mr Tompson and doe according as he thincketh fitt, whether to leave yt there or carry it to the fishing, and tak the adventure of selling yt ther, or if a good fishing happen at Dublin and at the Ile of Man it haith failed, to make it upp all with fish, and fraight some other bark, or to carry some other with you alonge, but then I doubt you want cask, or what other way you thinck fitt.

My partner and I have purposlie bought 5 packs of Yorkshire cloth for Belfast and because I could not get yt conveied to Belfast from Whitehaven I brought it alonge with mee, intending to have put it aboord of you when you were come to Dublin that you might have caried yt, and now unlesse Mr Tompson's bark which is to come shortlie from Rochell[9], as I perceave, to touch at Dublin with Bay salt come that I may send it with him, I thinck I must make sale of yt hear as I can. I purposlie brought 8 tons of white salt to have mixed with your Bay as we weer advised, which being as you knowe fallen to that ebbe hear, I must doe as well as I can. But howsoever I thinck it best for you to hould on your herring fishing, in the North Iles, or where you hear it is better, for I perceave there is a fisherman hired, and

[8] The first letter appears to be in Christopher's handwriting. The letters dated 1632–3 which follow are not. They may have been copied by Richard Wibergh.
[9] I.e. La Rochelle.

leave you some ten or 12 tons of salt at Belfast and intereat Mr Tompson to lett you have some money if you need and I shall pay yt his sonne hear as by his letter he shall directe, for I brought moneys for you; and if John Boyd have not money for our slaughter, let him be spoken to to make some reddie against that tyme. Write to me by sea and land, or either or both if you can, an account of your voyedge and retorne, and what happened to you, and of your purposes now, and soe to you Miles I referr all, but advice withall whom you know discreat in aniething you interprise. I myself ame busie hear in great businesses, or els I would have bene with you. My partner Rowland Jackson went for Sturbedg[10] fair to London by Bristol, and he bringeth traine [oil] with him to Kendal. I gave him 400^l for these things, but onely 133^l which he sent in Yorkshire cloth which I have hear. About Michaelmasse or presently after he intendeth to be at Belfast, and soe comitting you and your company to God with my prayers for you all I rest,

Your loveing master,
Christopher Lowther.

Dublin the 24th September 1632   *Page 8*

To my uncle Robert Lowther
Uncle,

Since I wrote unto you by my partner Rowland Jackson from York I received some letters uppon Thursday next after at night being then retorned to Lowther from York, which my father had received the night before, and imediatelie uppon the receight of them the same night I wrote to you answer, and the next day without anie stay wrote[11] to Whitehaven. But the wind serveing not till the 20th day of the same, I came with the goods you sent, the Yorkshire cloth my partner bought in his comeing to you to London, with cole for ballast and some 8 tons of white salt. For both the Yorkshire cloth and the wares you sent I paid but 30^s costome, for I entred them but in grosse to 30^l, and I did not troble myself to make use of Mr Charlmley for it.[12] The crowen rashes and some of the Norrige[13] stuffs I packed upp, bought canvas and rope and I perceave none of these goods aile aniethinge. All I did not unpack soe I doe not know whether any thinge doe want or noe, but in good sooth I thinck not and but for the tusseling   *Page 9* them in packing and unpacking befor they came to my hands I perceave litle or noe hurt at all.

I remember I wrote to you of sending a rate of the comodityes as they ruled in Ireland by my partner, thincking when I wrote it I had had it in

---

[10] I.e. Stourbridge, Warwickshire.
[11] I.e. "rode", copying error?
[12] A. Charmley was a custom's official at Carlisle in 1636.
[13] I.e. Norwich.

my papers at York, but I had lefte it at Lowther, but I will send you the same now and another as neer as I can gett the rate knowne after a while, but at present I cannot doe it.

This day I have procured a bill of vewe to prevent a censure, for if I should have entred all that is hear such hard usage not a wrapp wil be allowed but to a farthing must be paid, and to enter short ther ar now new waiters, and trust them I durst not if they should goe to search soe I hope in a while I shall seek them out and gett some curtesie showen. Till this they lye on boord safe and well without anie dainger at all by sea as yet for, God be thanked, although we had a rough passedge and could bear noe saile yet we are gott well over.

The herringe fishing hear ar quite failed, and all those who made provision for herring turne it to mak beefe. The butchers saye beefe is at $\frac{1}{4}$ far [things] per lb, hide and tallow about 1^d and beef, hide and tallow altogeather about $1\frac{1}{4}^d$ the pound; runded tallow 27^s the hundereth, candles 3^s 6^d per dol',[14] cotton week; ould wheat 14^s and some sels for 16^s the Bristol barrell, and it is nott clensed from blacks as you wrote me to have it, neither is it very good but far worse then I have seene wheat this somer before, soe I thinck the wheat I buy, if I have tyme before the shipp come, I must hier wemen to skreene it and riddle it in a parchment sive and as soone as I have gott the goods from aboard the bark I will goe about the buying of the wheat. I have spoken to Mr Baddelow for his helpe and advice and factoredg. His businesse will not give him leave to discourse of yt yet to any purpose, yet semeth to imbrace it, of which when I know more I will write you. I have not yett delivered the 3 letters of creddit you sent; your other letter you sent I have not received, and though the letter I sent from Lowther in answer of your last may seeme to answer this to[o], yet will I presentlie after these in my next letter touch them all. I have received noe news hear at all but much wishing for the Deputy and praying for his comeing by all the Protestants, and fear of him and the cuntry by the Papists.

Our barke is come out of France hither last Wednesday and went out of Saterday at night last for Belfast before I could goe to make anie meanes to speak to her, they not knowing of my comeinge. The Biskauers[15] tok from them their best cabell, their flags and victualls, and a cople of samon but nothing els. They brought Bay salt but it growe soe dear they would not bringe there full ladeinge—from 400 to 800 lyvres the hundereth. They have a fishinge boat, a Scotchman at Belfast, reddie to goe with them to the North Ilands and ther cask is reddie, for I had letters from thence and I wrote to them this day to goe forward with haist and if they prove well I thinck they need never goe almost for France, they[16] will be soe dear

[14] I.e. doleum or cask or tun.
[15] I.e. "Biscayers", Biscay pirates.
[16] I.e. herring.

hear at Dublin, being now worth 25^s the barrell and that but 28 gallons, where ours is 30 gallons; and soe haveing not els at this tyme I rest,

> Your lo[ving] partner and as faithfull
> to you as to himself who would as
> gladlie have things goe all well as
> yourself and kynder tearmes betwixt
> my father and you and in all love,
>
> Christopher Lowther

With the first conveyance I shall
send this.

Page 9 ends

Dublin the 25th of September 1632

Page 8 top

To my father

Kynd father,

My humble duety promised, yt may please you to tak notise that on Saterday the 22th of this instant I and all the goods arived safe at Dublin, since which I casually spok to Mr Baddelow, and this day are we further to entreat for he was then rideing out of the towne. I hope wee shall come to some good conclusion. I ame now about to get the goods entred but now things ar soe narrowlie loked unto as I expecte in entring them noe favor. The *Georg* our bark is come over out of France, and in her goeing was pillaged uppon the coast of France, the mareners clothes, some of ther vitualls and ther best cable to the valew as I suppose of about XX marks or more, but she went on Saterday at night to Belfast and is now in her way for the herring fishing. I hear of noe place in the Channel that proveth well. Dales ar hear worth 7^l per cent, and used but to be at 4^l 10^s, soe that I know not whether I send any or noe or but a few. Bay salt and Spanish is hear in abundance, the fishing failing that now salt is worth litle but about 8^s the barrell. I hear nothing yet of the shipp my Uncle Robert spoke of sending yet. Hear is 2 or thre dais of good weather, which if it hould wheat is expected cheap, but as yet it is 14^s the barrell ould. Soe haveing not at this present more to write I rest desiring your blessing, with my prayers for you,

> Your obedient sonne and servant,
>
> Christopher Lowther

Dublin the 25th September 1632

Page 8 contd.

[To Rowland Jackson]

Kynd partner,

Soe it is that the 22 of this month being Saterday and being the first wind, which I a fortnight had waited for, came [I] to Dublin, and your bark as your sonne can tell you, came on Wednesday at night before. I purposlie brought the northren cloth with me to Dublin because I intended to put it abord the *George* for Belfast but soe it happened that on Saterday at night tyde, they lying a litle below Bullock,[17] before I scarce knew that they were come were they gone, soe that I intend if sales come not before Mr Tompson's shipp come out of France, which is to touch at Dublin in her way to Belfast and is every houer expected, to send the Yorkshire cloth and maybe some Spanish too by hir. Yet I have writt to Miles who I doubt not but is at Belfast, to haisten to the herring fishing for ther is a fisher prepared. I referr the rest to your sonne George with whom I have spoken my mynd to tell you, who telleth mee (as I perceave soe much) [he] haith his French[18] tonge perfectlie, and for tryall I had him in companie with some Frenchmen. So desiring to hear from you and my uncle Robert I rest,

Your loveing partner Christopher Lowther

Page 10

Dublin the 7th October 1632

To my uncle Robert Lowther

Uncle,

Since I last wrote being the 24th September with noe wind yet served, I have delivered the letters of creddit; that to Mr Champion being for 100*l*; Mr Barry for 200*l*, but after I saw a letter from Mr Darley lessoning it to 164*l*; to Mr John Standley 50*l*, soe that all is but for them 314*l*, which I ame to have uppon the letters[19] which by your letters I thought at least had bene 1,000*l*, and neither was Champions nor Standleys reddie but Barries is, and of him it may be I shall gett more 100*l*. There is 2 shipps hear which hath bene anie tyme this fortnight hear in loadeing of wheat. They give 14*s* a barrell the least as I hear and some 16*s*. My partner Rowland Jackson came hither uppon Thursday last but I had bargained before he came with 2 men for 260 barrells and all they can gett besides within one fortnight which will be 10 dayes hence. They thinck to gett 100 barrells more which wil be 300 barrells at least as they say at 13*s* 6*d* per barrell ould wheat, but at the same rate noe more to be gott. You now write for 600 quarters and but 500 before and I ame affraid wee shall not gett past 600 barrels of ould wheat but that we must have the rest new, but doubt you not but that wee shall gett hir ladeing, for if I had had noe directions at all againe by my partner, yett should the wheat have bene gotten reddie. The new wheat is about 12*s* the barrell. The ship is not yet come to us.

The goods since are all landed, none wantinge nor noe harme done, but the Yorkshire wrappers which had bene a litle wett in carieing by horse from Newcastle. On Thursday next I intend chapmen to come and buy them. I have taken a house uppon the ryver in the Cytye at the foot of the Wood Key of Mr Jacob Newmans at 20*l* per annum, and I dyet with them

---

[17] Fishing village, south shore of Dublin Bay, 7 miles from Dublin.

[18] "Spanish" crossed out.

[19] "of criddit" crossed out.

in their house the next dore and pay for myselfe 12^l per annum; and for each man I shall keep 6^l 13^s 14^d. When you write to me direct yt to Mr Jacob Newman's near the Wood Key. He haith the office of the Roules under my lord Angier, Baron of Langford.[20] I have very good contentment of yards and garneringe which may save us duble the rent in one year yf yt were but in porteredg being that wee may receave everything into it from the river, and the comliest house for a merchant in all the cytie. Neither could I gett 2 poor romes to lye in under the same rate elswhere, and have wanted all the convenience, and to have had garnering, yards and sellering, and hear I have selleredg for 40 butts of sack, yards for 500 tons of coles and for makeing of herrings and beefe, garnoringe for 1,000 barrels of wheat, and warehouse, studdies and chambers.

The costome of the wares you sent with gratutyes about 4^l. I got the rest entered but to 121^l 6^s 1$\frac{1}{2}^d$, the whole costome conveiance I wrought costome 6^l 1^s 1$\frac{1}{2}^d$ which we may thank God of; the costomers would not abate the odd 1$\frac{1}{2}^d$. I have made some merchants knowne I have some goods and I hope reasonable proffitt, but to trust Baddelow or anie other, they ar soe duble handed all of them; as yet I darr whether to make tryall of him in ayding me to sell these or not I am not yet resolved.

All the letters I received of yours are first: 2 of the 20th July and 21st Julie and 25th of August and per my partner of the 18th of September.

Whether the 2 ships that are now ladeing with wheat whether for London or Dunkirk as some tymes they say and other some tymes they say for Flanders or Germany in ther way I know not, but rather thinck for Spaine. The London ships you wrote of that were come from London for pilcherds in Ireland I hear are come by Mr Burre and that ther is noe store of fish for them, but if hearafter we follow that, we must bargaine for them before the fishinge begin alwais of which at leasure I will further enquire.

My partner Rowland Jackson is gone downe on my horse to Knock- *Page 11 begins* fergus[21] to sett our bark away to the north Iles fishynge; I ame of your opinion a greater is better for us. Coles I sould for 14^s the tonn, the barrell being 40 gallons at Dublin ours but 30 at Whitehaven as it is everywhere els, at Chester, and by us but 4 at Whitehaven with this new Dublin measure will make 3 at Dublin, but wanteth some; coles this year haith bene at 16^s and 14^s ton, ever since August, soe coles I thinck would be our best trade, for as much stock as they would require if we had Flemish bottoms to carry them, but our owne cuntry barks are soe litle they carry nothinge at a tyme, and yet will have[22] dear by reason they are comenly only about 7 or 8 men to one of 30 tons which eateth upp the proffitt.

[No signature or closure]

---

[20] Lord Angier, Master of the Rolls, obit 1632, see below p. 20.
[21] I.e. Carrickfergus, Belfast Lough.
[22] I.e. "prove", copying error?

Page 11 contd.

Dublin the 7th of October 1632

To my father,

There was noe passedg hence for the enclosed before this tyme since which I have reasonably after above a week's workinge the matter of the Costome House gott the goods entred at reasonable rates, under 20 nobles but in gratuityes they came to in all with the costome about 10¹, which if I had gone the comon way 20¹ would not have excused. The goods are all safe and nothing wanting. I spoke with Mr Baddelow afterwards who professeth all kyndnes and furtherance but he was soe busied with his owne affaires, or at least but onely verball to me, and not willing to come to anie conclusion of factoredg, as otherwise that I had noe helpe of him at all. Yet he would have lett me have had lodgeinge for me and Richard[23]; I 14¹, Richard 10¹, but noe rebatement if absent lesse then one month at a tyme. Neither had he rome for anie shifte that I would hould the cloth I brought onely but if I had bene with him I either might have taken another house within the cyty or by hireing roomes and selleredg at excessive rates continually and neither was ther anie neer him but within the cyty, and his house without the gates which inconvenie[nce] could never have done well; and therfor since I have taken the house I was telling you of by the ryverside and ame dyeted at the owner of the said house, into which I can goe into, myne being the next house, at 12¹ per annum myself, and each man I keep 6¹ 13ˢ 4ᵈ, where I am alreadie in the house. The house is Mr Jacob Newman's who haith the office of the Rowles under the Lord Angier, who kepeth a knight's table and of a very good estate, and soe kyndly used am I as may be. The house I have taken with the advice of Mr Bamber, a merchant which my partner wished me to before I went over, whom I am most beholden to. The house may save us duble the rent in a year. Mr Bamber him[self] is a Catholick but a very honest man if there be anie in towne to trust to, who will advise of things and meet either I with him or he with mee every day. He knoweth all the Irish wayes of trade and is a Freeman of the towne and of his name in aniethinge I may mak use to buy or sell as if I weer free. His trading is for England, France or Spain; is now sending 2 for France and he promiseth mee anything in his power to doe it for me, and he will informe me of all. Neverthelesse with Baddelow

Page 12 begins

I keepe fair and I doubt not but to know his waies alsoe err long. What I have writt to my Uncle Robert you may perceave for I send you the letter to send him unsealed, and the same I send by Chester. Your letters and the hooke I received as sone as I came hither and I send you the copie of Giles his account for the cattle that you may perfect with him. I perceave my uncle and Row[land] haith agreed with the London salter I spoke of.

Soe in haste the wind soe sodainley chainged with the tyde, I rest,

Your obedient sonn,
Christopher Lowther

[23] Wibergh.

Dublin the 7th October 1632

To Wm. Atkinson,

William Atkinson,

I received your letter by Tubman's bark and send you on the other side that ther are noe greater tymber yet to be gotten for money. Firr dales ar worth 7^l per C. but I have spoken to one Mr Bamber who will lett me have 150 or 200 at 5^l per C. which ar not yet gotten upp from Bullock, but as soone as I can gett them I will send them, and 7 dozen of sparrs. Let the wrights cast there work for them, for they shall come with the dales. My partner telleth me of sending iron wheales, but I cannot yet gett them.

I send the[e] a barrell of apples, 7^s and the cask 2^s, for thyself to sell; there is about 700 at 6 skoir to the 100 in the barrell, thou cannot but gett by them, but lett not the selling of them hinder thy busines.

I have a barrell of candles which will come unto about 50^s which I shall send the[e]. They cost $3\frac{1}{2}$ per lb, cotton weeks; if thou sell for $4\frac{1}{2}$ they will sell the faster and there will be gain enough. They ar most of them smale candles which sell to our pitts for the colliers, for thou may as well fynd candles as Tubman.

Write me as the peer and pann doe goe forwards and what you want, and when I send the candles thou shalt write how the 3^l ys bestowed. About those candles I have had more truble then thou thinckest of, but to doe the[e] good I weye it not. You must provide tarr for ther is but a last in towen. Direct thy letters to Mr Newman's.

Thy maister to doe the[e] good as thou deservest,

Christopher Lowther

Dublin the 20th of October 1632

To my uncle Robert Lowther,

Uncle and Partner,

My kyndest respecte and love remembred yt may please you to take notice that about the 7th of September last I intercepted some letters being then imediatly come from you and being about corne busines. I imediatly wrote unto you from Lowther, of which letters intended to be sent me into Ireland I was my owne carier, and in truth I staied not at Lowther in my comeing from York 15 houres till I went to Whitehaven and soe came over with the first wind, thoughe a tempest, and that others being reddie would not venture; and being come I found a Spanish ship fraighted as said, and then ladeing wheat for Dunkirk which the last week set fourth. But if I had bene then in Ireland yet could I have had the letters noe sooner which I *Page 13 begins* received at Lowther and being come into Ireland being about the 22nd/7 the harvist, as said being never later, was not in which took away much ould wheat for the cuntryes provision, and that other ship for Dunkirk and the shipeing of yt in the Spring and summer last away. Soe that ould wheat is scarce and not 1,000 barrell to be gotten in all the 4 next countyes as I perceave by the market, the wheat masters in towne and others which I employed abroad. Neither was there one corne of ould wheat in the towne then or is now but what is for us which is about, and wil be 700 barreles; onley one 40 barrels which Peter Wiburre a Dutchman who will not [sell] under 16ˢ the barrell. I haveing bought one 700 of ould wheat,[24] and for the same the Dutchman would have given 15ˢ the barrell but it costs not us one with another but about 14ˢ; for more ould noe hope yet. Of kylne-dryed new wheat I can procure enough but it is at 13ˢ the barrell undryed, besides our chardges in drying and the wast therein, and troble in removeing soe ofte, but fear not—nay I ame rather affraid that the ship you wrote of which you have fraighted will not be hear byfore that I be reddie for hir for as yet I hear nothinge of hir, but howsoever I will not fail to be reddie for hir, God willinge. If you hould it fitt to have anie more corne in store either for London or els where, lett me knowe, for now is the tyme to bargaine for it, and wee can have it delivered in any tyme before March next or when wee please.

I have received noe letters from you since those I received at Lowther that bear date the 25th August saveinge the copie of one of the 24th and under it one of the last of August by which you write for candles more then was in the others before, which are at 3ˢ 6ᵈ the dozen lbs, and soe I can have enough for wax, pilchards and salmon. My partner saith you intend not that I should provide them, soe in them I doe nothinge, neither for pipestaves, hear being none nerer then Wexford.

For wheat hear is noe prohibition nor for tallow, hides, beefe nor pipestaves yet that I can hear of, but it may be when the Deputy cometh there wilbe for his owne advantage in granting lycenses. But if you intend to send for wheat over presently, for London or els where, I perceave if one enter 1,000 barrels or more or lesse and pay the costome before it be caried away if it be half a year or soe and that in the meane tyme betwene the costome paid and the shipping away the same corne, a prohibition should come, yet might the same at leasure be transported, which is without behoulding to any for a lycence. And if a prohibition doe come yet fear not but I shall as reasonably gett lycense, I hope, as anie one. Wee could gett pipestaves att Belfast if you hould it fitt to send for anie or at Wexford, for in August when I was there divers would have sould us pipestaves. But the staves about Belfast are stronger and better to look uppon and they say that the Eniscorfee[25] staves at Wexford ys fyner wood but slender me thinck.

The letters you sent by the way of [Lowther erased] Chester and Bristol for takeing upp money are not come to my handes, and there is scarcely 1,000ˡ stirring in all this Citye till the tearme come, soe that I must be glad to take upp moneys of others and for as much as I take up for 3 fourths of
Page 14 begins   the corn I chardge it onely uppon Mr Batte and his compenye and what for

---

[24] "at 14ˢ the barrell, 220 at 13ˢ 6ᵈ 100, 13ˢ 7ᵈ 100," crossed out.
[25] I.e. Enniscorthy, 12 miles from Wexford on the Dublin Road.

our fourth uppon you onely, which you may take notice of, and for all the moneys I receave of Mr Edward Barry, which is 165^l, for the which I give my bills of exchange to him, Mr Batty and his companie is to pay it, as alsoe Champions 100^l and Standleys 50^l. When the bills come unto them Mr Barry haith this day promised me to pay it which if he doe the bills come uppon him.

Tallow is hear 27^s per cent.

Our bark I hope is in the north Iles of Scotland for herring with the Red Shanks[26] fishermen waiting on them, who came to Belfast to goe with them. They say herringe there great store; hear they fayled.

New wheat this market day I have offered for 13^s the barrell. Butter is at 3^d ob. per lb; beefe hide and tallow, taking them togeather at Belfast we bye for 1^d per lb and so have bargained 100 beasts. Dearer hear at Dublin by 6^s in a beast of 36^s price, weinge in all about 374 lbs or therabouts. Wax noe quantitye and dear, 14^d per lb. My partner Rowland Jackson haith seene 20,000 pipe staves at Belfast which ar about 6^l per m [thousand]. He intendeth to bargaine for them.

White plates is worth 8^s per dozen, duble plates of which 3 weye 2 pound and single half the price. About 50^l worth at a tyme wil be vented.

Noe letters did I ever receave either from Chester or Bristol but from Whitehaven onely which is the surest way of conveiance.

The goods you sent are not yet sould but towards Tearme I thinck they will. Since I wrote this letter I had forth Mr Edward Barry's 165^l.

To have the assistance of any merchants hear ys to very small purpose for aniething I see. Neither Burre nor Baddela are two dayes togeather in the town, Baddelas imployment being altogeather in the cuntry into the Countie of Fermanagh, and therabouts, and Mr Barre with an imployment of tanning houses and other particulars of his owne at Wickloe. The rest of the Duch are but all retailers, and now and then for a voyadge. Noe quantity of sackes vented hear, and about 14^l or 15^l thought extraordinarye good, for forreners cloye the towne with them,

Your loveing nephew,
Chr. Lowther

Dublin the 20th October 1632

To Mr John Battie,

Mr Battie,

I received this day 165^l sterling of Mr Edward Barry for which I send my bills of exchainge to be paid by you to Mr Richard Darley or his partner Tempest Milner which I pray you doe, and be sure you pay not the same to anyone but to one of them two, for other three bills of the same tenner was lost betwene my partner Rowland Jackson, Mr Barry and

---

[26] Scots?

myself, which yet cannot be found. The wheet I provide but the shipp is not yett come; in haste I rest,

Your Loveing ffrend,
Christ. Lowther

[Enclosure:]
Laus deo adi[uvante].   20 October 165[1]

At tenne dayes after sighte hereof pay this my firste bille of exchainge, my second or thirde not beinge payed, of one hundred and sixty five pounds sterling to Richard Darley or Tempest Millner for the value hearof receaved of Edward Barrie by me, for the use of your selfe and companie as etc.

To Mr John Battie, merchant in London   Chr. Lowther.
Pa: 2 other of the same effect
Viz: 2[d] and 3[d]

In Dublin the 22nd of October 1632

To my father;
Kynd father,

My humble duety remembred to yourself and my mother. My last being of the 7th instant, it may please you to take notice that since I heard noe news of the shipp from London for wheat. The wheat is bargained all but 300 barrells, of which there is 700 barrels and odd of ould wheat and wee pay for it as it is delivered in, and 150 of kyln dryed, in all about 900. The other 300 I can have tyme enough if that she were alreadie come, but for it I haild of til I hear further of the shipp or that in the meane tyme a good penyworth fall. For the money I was to receave by the letters of creddit being 315[l] I have receaved of it 185[l] and the rest can have when I call of them. Towards Tearme if yt were 1,000[l] they say they will help me to it. As far as $\frac{3}{4}$ parts goeth in the wheat I chardge uppon Mr Battie and his companie on and in the bills of exchange, and I make the receight for ther use and so with my letters of advice to them.

My partner Rowland Jackson haith bene at Belfast and haith sent his bark to the north Iles fishinge and haith bene hear at Dublin since. Tomorrowe wee send most of the Yorkshire cloth and some of the London wares which ar spoken for to my partner. He and his sonne goeth down to Belfast for the slaughter intending it for Bristol and soe to retorne traine oyle to Kendal for which he fraighted a bark when he was in England.

Dyvers merchants haith seene the London wares and the other but wee were but bidden litle more than they stand in with chardges. Yet [it] may be better, as advised, in Michaelmasse Tearme, and this trading may come to somthing which maybe shortly we may knowe.

The salt I brought would give at first but 7[s] a barrel and I have sould it for 8[s] 6[d] per barrel. Mr Angier who was Master of the Rowells is dead

Page 15

and some say one Mr Emanuell Gifford a courtier at London haith the reversion; it is a good place and as they say better than either my Lord Chefe Justice's place. Sherley,[27] the Lord Chefe Justice is gone to lyve in England and haith left his place and report goeth Sir William Reave the King's attorney shall have it and Mr Radcliffe to be in his place.[28]

I can gett noe great tymber yet for the saltpans for none cometh yet, nor dales at present. Alexander will come over to Whitehaven now so that for those things which Ralf is faultie in I pray you make an end with him of them as you best think fitt, soe haveing not els to troble you withall I rest,

Your obedient sonn,
Ch. Lowther

Dublin 22nd October 1632

To William Atkinson,
William Atkinson,

I received thy letter from William Wilkinson dated the 18th of October which I like well of. I send thee by this bark i barrel candles for thyself, the cost the first peny 2^l 12^s 6^d. There is 15 dozen, the cask 9^d, cariedg 3^d. John Nychelsons man 6^d for to carry it, and I send thee 7 dozen of sparrs; hear haith no great tymber more that I can gett for money, but if you must needs have any you must get it from Irton or Millom or Chester. Neither can I gett the fur dales for they are at Balliack and cannot be gotten upp, but when they come I shall send them. I thinck ther wil be but about 100. I cannot yet gett any wheales made.

Lett the key below the [salt] panhouse be made as highe as noe sand by any overflow be wasted. Alexander saieth he will come over. I see not things with him soe extraordinary as is there talked if that Ralf performe not better than he writt I hould best to stop of the coles. You writ not whether Ralfe pay the workmen half wages as wee agred nor what of that work is done, neither what thou thinck best of it. Let me know as things goe,

Thy loving master,
Chr. Lowther

Laus deo 29th October 1632 Dublin   *Page 16*

To Mr John Battie, merchant in London,
Mr Battie,

I formerly wrote unto you of the 20th instant and chardged uppon you on hundereth sixty fyve pounds to be paid to Mr Rich. Darley or Tempest Millner, which money I received of Mr Edward Barry and now I chardge more uppon you one hundereth pounds which this day I received of Mr Arthur Champion to be paid to the one of aforesaid men as my former bills

---

[27] He was to be replaced by Sir Gerard Lowther.

[28] Mr later Sir George Radcliffe, friend and assistant to Sir Thomas Wentworth.

wer, all which money by Mr Darley's letters was to be chardged uppon you, and by my uncle Roberts letter I was to chardg it both uppon you and him, in others 2/3 upon you and the rest for us, and then he writeth that I may chuse whether we will have 1/3 or 1/4, but I advise of one fourth onely, soe expect for 3/4 that I chardge it uppon you and your company and for 1/4 yf I need I will chardge it uppon my uncle, but I doe advise you, Mr Battie, that noe letter 8/8[29] of creddit to take upp moneys for your 3/4 fourth 8/8 but onely for 315^l and that my uncle writeth me of providing 1,200 barrels of wheat when that 900 of it will amount nere unto 650^l. My uncle writeth of letters of creddit and other letters to come by way of Chester and Bristol but in truth I never received anie word at all either from him, you or anye other which came that way, for all I hear is from the north of England by my owne tenants from Whitehaven, which way, when you send, chuse rather.

The shipp is not yet come. I have bought 900 barrels and have had it reddy a good while agoe; 700 barrels of it is ould, and as good if not much better than any ould which as yet haith bene shipped. Noe more ould now under 16^s the barrell and new at 13^s and 14^s the barrell. For the new I kilne dryed it all, which is done hear very neatlye without any alteration in smell, collor or tast.

There is noe money in towne now till Tearme tyme but 100^l which Champion haith and he will not passent[30] under 6^d a pound, so I forbear for your good yet to tak it unless I cannot better doe, and for the bills I now send you I will not fetch the money before the very day they bear date. Money is soe scarce hear with them Mr John Standley's 50^l could I not yett gett, so scarce is it hear but as soone as he haith it I shall not want it if money were to be had I could have it as soone as any one I thinck, for soe they doe professe; but att this tyme Peter Wiburre and Daniell and others haith bene all over the towne and cannot gett anye soe till the Tearm money will not be stirring, which beginneth this day sennit.

If you advise for more wheat against March or before lett me know but one month before and it shal be reddie. Corne wil be litle under 14^s the barrel and I thinck not much above unlesse store of shipeing come in. I hear that Mr Quoyman, a Dutchman, and some other will have a ship comeinge from Waterford, and is to goe for the Canaryes, but it will not be this month; soe in haist, with my service to Mr Captaine Lee and my love and best respects unto yourself I rest,

Your loveing friend,
Christo. Lowther

[Enclosure: a bill of 100^l dated 29 Oct 1632 in favour of R. Darley or Tempest Millner for 100^l received of Arthur Champion by C. Lowther.]

[29] Inserted.
[30] Could be copying error for "part with" or "assent".

The $\frac{29}{8}$(31) 1632 Dublin   *Page 18 lower*

To my uncle Robert Lowther,

Uncle,

My last unto you was of the $\frac{20th}{8}$ since which I have received Champion's 100^l and doe chardge the same uppon Mr Batty; and since my partner is gone for Belfast to make upp beef, and so to carrye it along to Bristol, and then to return the traine oyl for the north, his son Georg is with him. I have sent along with him 20 Yorkshires, 4 fryzes, 3 bayes, 1 kersey, 2 Spanish cloths, 2 serges, 1 carroll, 1 figuranay, 1 mohear, 4 crown rashes, 2 Carthages, because that they had sent upp for of them. They goe by sea with his sonne George, in my Ladie Hill's bark and my partner by land.

You doubted much of my performance of your commission and may if not that I know how to have money for to performe it, but I suppose that you imagine money is alwais be be had hear, but quit contrary for it was verie scarce with Champion, Barry and Standley, nay Standley's cannot yet be gott; therefore I pray you hearafter in the like cases, send not your commission without bills of exchange, or letters of credit, and doubt not you hearafter but that I will with as much trust and to as much advantedg and haist if need be, as anie one perform it.

I have had 900 barrels reddie a long tyme and the rest I can have reddie uppon an instant and now I begin to fear that you have sent noe ship at all but if you have not advise me whether I should send that I have alreadie provided.

Noe alteration of our Irish comodityes hear in there rate, from what I have formerlie writt. I fynd that new corne dryeth in upon 3 in the skow and that being dried it standeth to 15^s the barrel which methincks nevertheless it loketh far better then ould; for the rest I referr you to Mr Batties letter of the same date,

Y[ou]r Lo[ving] Co[usin],

Christ. Lowther

Laus deo in Dublin the 1/9 1632   *Page 17*

Kynd Father,

My duty remembred it may please you to take notice that my last was on the $\frac{22}{8}$ since which I have received noe letters from you save one by Robert Adney this weeke which bear date the $\frac{18}{7}$ by which you seeme angry that I spoke not with Mr Attorney[32] at York, for which both by cossen Lancaster and Mr Marris knoweth I was severall tymes to see him but could not. For the desiring letters of credit it was with directions I had from you; neither doe I conceave as yet any hurt in it, for say that I had returned our whole stock for London in comodityes, in the meane tyme my uncle adviseth for another comodity cheaper hear and very dear with him and that

---

[31] I.e. 29 October.
[32] I.e. Radcliffe.

our stock is come then to his hand and I want money, must not I take it up hear by exchange upon him or that he chardged bills of exchange upon me while our stock weer out of my hand, I have then noe other way but to take upp money and charge it againe uppon him, and therefore out of the tearme tyme what money in the City ys not to be had by exchange to have it at the farmers' hands it were a great benefitt for us, for then elswhere it is scarce to be had hear, for even now 6^d in the pound which is 50^s per cent is given to receave money, and in the tearme tyme 6^d wil be given uppon payinge money for then ther is more money to be exchanged than anie merchants comenly take, soe that difference of tymes maketh grease losse and gaine in exchange, soe that if I had the comand of money from the Costome House you see I might possibly now and then get 50^s in the hundreth without any danger or adventures by takeing it upp myself and letting others have it againe. But for my owne part, God willing, I will never take upp more, or in anything, further than my owne stock will answer.

You write alsoe of Mr Marris. His nephew cometh to me at candlemass which if you thinck fitt, and that by meanes thereof we may purchase the more curtesie from my lord, as in now and then to have lysence before another when any prohibition uppon comodityes are fourth, or that notwithstanding prohibitions to others yet that my lord would suffer us to be free at all tymes, or to ayde us now in an intended plott by my uncle of pipestaves, if otherwise without him it cannot be as that none may have the exportation of hogshed or pipe staves but ourselves then which wee neded no more, but otherwyse, unless wee could be better in that respect by my lord, John Barton or George Jackson were as good for mee, both which I am offered. Richard Wibergh I like well as yett. He haith a reasonable good forecast being put uppon it and is willing.

Besides 150 pounds worth of comodityes which my partner haith now at Belfast I have not sould above 50 pounds worth hear yet, but when the Tearme cometh I will if God please, quitt them of[f], for I have not yet bidden[33] 10 per cent above chardges.

Hear was some great timber of 20 foot long fitt for the pannes but the barks that were hear could not take it in for the length of yt.

The Lord [Deputy] is expected hear before Christmasse. I cannot yet enquire aniething of the pattent for salt, but if it be at Boudon Bridge[34] it may well doe good for the south of Ireland but I cannot perceave that it will doe anie good to the east coast hear. So you may see by the mapp that Banden Bridge, which is 7 [miles], up the river from Kingsale,[35] whether it is not navigable neither doth the salt water come into the towne as I remember, is worse to come from to Dublin than from France, soe if

---

[33] I.e. been bidden.
[34] Banden Bridge, a town founded in James I's reign, 14 miles from Cork.
[35] I.e. Kinsail.

hat be the onely place fear not that it can doe us anie harme for the vent
t Dublin if Banden Bridge be the place onely.

For harte chock plants Mrs Newman will give enough of them.[36]

I hear yett nothing of the London ship soe for the wheat yet I proceed
oe further then before.

Your obedient sonne,

Chr. Lowther

1 November [1632]

To Rowland Jackson at Belfaste   *Page 18 top*

1. Taylor played knave about the black Yorkshire [cloth].
2. Balle wente back of the 100 barrels of wheat of 14^s the barrel for he
   denieth it.
3. A London ship without the bar but knows not what she is, the wind
   contrary to bring her in.
4. I goe not about to b[u]y above 900 barrels wheat for want of money
   and noe certainty of the shipp comeinge.
5. Cloth sould since: 2 Yorkshire of 3^l 14^s pec. for 8^l 15^s, the kersey 3^l;
   one French grene parapus 3^l 14^s 6^d.

   > 100 barreis more in Portford castle; 14 barrels new wheat bought
   > in the market under 12^s 6^d per barrel; it loseth 3 in the skow in the
   > kilne dryinge but is very swete and white.

6. I have letters from my father this day desireth to see you in Christmasse
   or before.
7. Letters I have from my Lord Deputy[37] to my Lord Mountnorris[38] in
   our behalf.
8. Write to me what you did in England with the 400^l you had for I must
   make my father answer of yt, and whether that you wil be with him at
   or before Christmasse for after he goeth to York and stayeth Lent
   quarter.

Your Loveing frend Christo. Lowther

Sent per Mr Stafford's man.

Dublin the 5th November 1632

To my uncle Robert Lowther,   *Page 19*

My kynd uncle and partner,

1.   My last was $\frac{29}{8}$ to you since which I have received none from
   you, nor since the $\frac{8}{7}$ which is nothing but an incitation of me to procure the wheat, for which your first letter was sufficient, but yet
   for all your forwardnesse I doe not see anie such shipp, neither can I hear
2. any word of her. My Lord Deputy writt a long letter

---

[36] Artichoke plants.

[37] I.e. Lord Wentworth.

[38] Francis Annesley, Lord Mountnorris, Vice-Treasurer and Receiver-General of Ireland.

3. in my behalf from York to my Lord Mountnorris for to countenance me, and stand my frend in what I shall be occasioned to need or use him, which he maketh a protestation to doe and saith when he haith any moneys for exchange for London, I shall have the first preference of them which may doe us good.

4. I this day received a letter from my partner in the north who writeth me of the sale of 17 dozens, Spanish cloth; 8 peeces of stuffes, 2 fryzes, 3 bayes, but it semeth for tyme [payment] soe that he haith not yet reddie money for any, but writeth me he haith taken upp 100^l and chardged it uppon mee at 3 dayes sight, a very short tyme knoweing I have not one peny to pay for the wheat which I have bought but the 315^l which you sent letters for by Lowther and is all paid now and chardged uppon Mr Batty, but Standley's 50^l. Soe that I yet want at least 600 pounds, and biddeth me to chardg it uppon you, and he will send it from Bristol

6. when he cometh thither with the beefe he is now in makeing, which I thinck I must for yet doth not any cloths sell. They will not give one peny almost above what they stand to, such store is mad hear.

Ch. Lowther

Dublin the $\frac{5}{9}$ 1632

To my partner Row[land] Jac[kson],
Partner,

1. I received your letters of the $\frac{31}{8}$ this day from one Mr
2. Washer as I take his name to be. I wrote to you before by one who was toward Mr Stafford and amongst other things my father writeth what you did with the 400^l you had which I pray you particularlie doe, for you tould but me about 300^l of yt, viz: cloth about 133^l, or therabouts, hopps 98^l 12^s 5^d with the Mayor of Belfaste 80^l, in your owne chardgs 5^l which is not 320^l.
3. The shipp is not yett come.
4. Ned Blennerhassett in prison at Trym. He writeth me but not materiall to speak of.
5. I have bought noe more corne.
6. You chardge me with one hundereth pounds but I cannot get one peny to pay for the wheat I bought and did you thinck it good to chardge it upon [me?] If it had beene immediately on my uncle I could have convayed the bills of exchange, but to take it up upon me, I know not what discredit I may sufer by it. You tould me being hear you could have money enough there for London and why did you not then take it upp for London, but upon me, nay, and but three days to pay it in! The like short tyme haith not bene heard. For God's sake advise of other courses then these unlesse you would quit discreddit me. Yet

for this tyme thinck not but I will doe my best though I cannot assure you.

7.   I have sould noe more cloth or stuffs yet nor any letters have I yet from my uncle.

8.   You writ not to me when our bark went away for the Islands. If in the comeing back she touch at Dublin it may be she may make a better voyedge than for France for now they are 27^s a barrel and thought wil be worth 30^s.

Your loveing partner,
Chr. Lowther

Dublin the 11th November 1632   Page 20

To my partner Rowl[and] Jackson

Loveing partner,

I commend me unto you. Your letter I received as alsoe a bill of exch[ange] of the 6th of this instant wherein you charge me to pay 100^l to Mr Lyndon his use at 3 dayes sight. I doe much marvelle that you would charge yt uppon me knowing that I ame not provided of money, and yf I were, you know that I must provide the wheat with it and to charge it uppon my uncle, from whom I have this day received a letter of the 27th October wherein he writeth that he must charge moneys uppon me, soe that you see and know what want I have of moneys. I have spoken to my Lord Mountnorris for 100^l who did once promise me to helpe me with it and afterwards would not lett me have it. Notwithstanding I ame in hope to gett it of Mr Hull, my Lord's man, to pay your bill of exchange withall and hereafter I pray you charge me not by exchange unlesse you knowe I be better provided of moneys.

My uncle Robert writeth unto me that Captaine Lee is dead, who had a p[ar]te adventure in the shipp which was to come from London, and that others haith taken that p[ar]te which he should have had in the voyadge to the Canaryes. I entend to send Thomas downe to you shortly to goe about the business you have for him to doe in Scotland.

The shipp is not yet come the which I doe expect daylye and hourly, by reason of my uncle's letters now confirming the same. I should have had use of Tom hear when the shipp cometh but I know you expect him there. The hopps are come and tomorrow I fetch them upp from abord. I have sent you hear inclosed a copie of the contents of the wax and ryce which I have sent inclosed in my uncle Robert's letter.

Ned Blennerhasset is not yet out of prisson. That money I gave him I count it but lost.

Sales of cloth is nought as yet. I am offered for them but as they stand in with chardges[39] and if I should sell them soe, yet can I not get them

---

[39] I.e. Only as much as their prime cost plus the charge of bringing them to Dublin.

all sould of[f] at that poor rate, for they offer but that rate for some peces of them.

Write me how your business goeth and what moneies you carry with you to Bristol for provideing of traine oyl, as alsoe writte unto me answer of my other letters which I wrote unto you. I received a letter concerning your hopps and your wine the copie whereof is thus:

"Mr Jackson, I understand you are in Ireland. I have sent you the 7 baggs of hopps, which your man left with me and one litle p[ar]cel which I saved out of one of the baggs which was broken. I have agreed with Edward Nicolson to bring them to Dublin, God permitting. You are to pay for every bagg 3^s. Your man left the wine with me, but one ton[40] he sould. The price I doe not know, and I have sould one ton and $\frac{1}{2}$ for 26^l 10^s which is reddie and if either Thomas Britton or anie of his neighbours had come to Liv[er]pool before I had gone to sea I had sent to your wife this money, and if anie come from your wife or yourself I have left directions with my uncle Roger for the payment of it and I have lefte the key of the sellar dore with him. There is one ton of wine left and two h[ogs]h[ea]ds which was broken for ullage.

Thus committing you to the Almightie, being bound to sea, I rest, Liverpool this 29th of October 1632,

Your loveing frend,
Joseph Rose."

Page 21   Since yesterday I disch[arged] the 100^l you received. I received it from my Lord Mountnorris and have by bill of exch[ange] chardged it on my uncle this day. I received a letter from Mr Lyndon this day writt by George, but not any from you. You writ me not whether you received all the debts for cloth or not; what you doe with the French salt you use not; what money you gave Miles at his goeing to the fishing or other provision; what slaughter you will make and what that voyage for Bristol will amount unto. I have writt to my uncle that you will send him the 100^l, as you write to me, from Bristol to London. But I ame informed that Dartmouth or Plymouth is better for sale of beefe, and for buying of traine of which consider well and enquir it out. Let me know if Mr Tomson will take the flannell or half of it or anie other cloths and stuffs. Hopps hear worth 7^l and 7^l 10^s per Cent. I thinck I must sell some of them if it be but for providing us some money for our p[ar]te of the corne. If you must needs have some of the hopps lett me know in haist and when you intend away, how and whither, what you carrie and your other purposes; soe in haist I rest,

Your loveing partner,
Chr. Lowther

[40] Tun?

Dublin $\frac{11}{9}$ 1632   meliora spero

To my uncle Robert Lowther,

1. Loveing uncle,

The last letter I wrote unto you was of the $\frac{5}{9}$ but yet the wind being easterly had no conveiance and because I send yt with this I make noe recital of yt. This day imediatly after dinner I received a letter from

2. Mr Edwards of Chester by Dick Baddelow which came inclosed to his maister with other letters.

3. Mr Edward's letter is as followeth:

"Chester $\frac{25}{8}$ 1632.   Mr Christopher Lowther, the inclosed received this day from your uncle. I pray advise me of this receeight and the former which I sent you per Mr Bartelet and hope is come to your hands, soe with comendations of my love, I rest yr. lo. frend, Wm. Edwards".

4. By which you may perceave he sent me letters from you, as I imagine, by Mr Bartelet whose bark, at the tyme when these letters was given me word, was, she was cast away in the Skerries, certaine ilands betwene Dublin and Tradath and there are the searchers gone downe this day to see the goods which were saved and the men wee hear are safe but I have noe letters from that barke. But those

5. letters which I now receive ar these, viz: one of the 6th October, with another in the same sheat of John Barton's writinge without date or your

6. name to yt, and one other of the 27th of October. The answer of which I procead in order and first to that of John Barton's writing, next to your $\frac{6}{8}$ and then to your $\frac{27}{8}$.

First I take notice that you received my letters from York and Kendal, etc, and that you hould my voyadge to Ireland not worth my jurney, which if it were or were not, it costeth you nothing. A good incoaragment for me to spend my money for our generall availe and yet I doe bear the charge and not merrit thancks! When you were in Munster you said it was a fyne country and the fynest part of Ireland which anyone may say but I say the contrarye for about Dublin is the finest parte, as Dublin, Kildare, East and West Measte[41] and parte of Louth; but I say yet farther, I noted the towens of trade as Carloughe, Cloanemell, Mallou[42], Cork, Bandon Bridge, the old head of Kinsaile, Kinsail, Hichlo[43], Wickloe and Bullock. I know a litle the manner of the pilchard fishinge, the herring fishing, what rates they bear this year; the pipe, hogshead and barrell staves, from Wexford, ther tun tymber and ther building of barques, etc, the cytuation of the cuntry, the harbours and what store of comodityes may be supposed each place

[41] Meath.
[42] Carlow, Clonmel, Mallow.
[43] Unidentified.

will vent, and this I thinck is as much worth as your travaile was hear. And further it is trew I writt from York [that] I sent you a particular of the prises of things which I then thought I had had but it was at Lowther. I have in a former letter acknowledged my error and sent you the same note I formerly spoke upp.

7. (2) The 2nd thinge you fynd falt with me in [is] for not writing you of the receight of your letters to which I answer I writt from Lowther of the 7th September of the recept of them, $\frac{24}{7}$, $\frac{7}{8}$, $\frac{20}{8}$, $\frac{29}{9}$, $\frac{5}{9}$ and now the $\frac{11}{9}$ and with the first passedg I send them still, and in my first letter I writt I would performe the commission. Now I must blame you. First I had not letters of creddit to take upp above 315^l. I never received any letters from Bristol nor anie from Chester before this day. You writ in your first letters of sending letters of creddit by Bristol and Chester. I yet see not any but these from Lowther, neither is ther any money under 6^d in the pound to be taken upp now, every one being of provideinge money for ther French, Spanish and Dutch voyadge the Dutchmen offer 6^d in the pound for it, nay ther haith bene given for it 3^l in the hundereth for it and more to take upp money for to passe for London by exch[ange], and I doubt I must give 5^d or 6^d in the pound if more plenty of money bee not in the towen being that I know of one who will provide as much for me at that rate as he haith if I need.

For your counsel which while it is for our good noe man shall be
8. (2) redier to imbrace it then myself by God's assistance.

9. (3) You write that I say that the Lord Deputy hats the Baddelow and Burr.[44] I take it that it was otherwise. I write indeed that I perceaved he had noe good affection to the duch and if it be soe I dow not know what prejudice yt might have given us, besides Barrie's house inconvenient for us if wee trade of lying upp coles or in any such comodityes of bulk, being then soe far forth from the ryver. Againe I thought to have bene with Baddelow indead and were at tearmes of agreement but first he had not but onely agreament to a lytle chamber for myself and man and not room then to put the very cloth and goods in that then I brought, soe that the straightnesse of his conveaniencie hindered me. Neither is the trade hear such a hidden mysterie but it is quickly
10. (4) learned. For to keepe house or servants more then Richard Wibergh I doe not, neither doe I bring, or will, any chardges save such as are proper to each severall parcells of goods, for noe one peny of my towne expence will I put in but for the house rent which I have taken, and is 20^l per year, which is for the trade, the stock, as a generall chardge, Richard Wibergh's dyet and allowance; and what I get again at anie tyme by reason of our house will both get and save us money more than anie house in Dublin could, which I wish you did but see.

---

[44] Or Barr, contraction for Barry or Barrie?

11. (5)   Fifthly you write you thinck the Lord Deputy will not come over. I am meerly otherwise perswaded, for his cotch and horses, his houshould furniture and servants some of them are come over, neither is ther anything done hear for want of him by the Lords Justics. But of things as you advize—well it is not good to rely neither will we, and slownesse with securitye is best.

12. (6)   My residence shal be solely in Dublin and that constantlye for anything I doe intend. My father saith he would write to you for the fellow, the salter, and as you had agreed with him he shall have.

If you doe come downe with him, as you write, to Whitehaven *Page 23* advise of things ther well, I pray you and yf you would come out to me hear that you and I might consider togeather viva voce, and then I to [go] back to Lowther with you and settle all things with the advise of my father. I would be very glad especially to have you hear but one week if it were, and I thinck it worth your jurney, which I pray you doe if your other busines will suffer you.

13. (7)   You say you understand I am at the Yellow Lyon etc. I never laid once their in my lyfe; but I keep at the house where formerly the King's Attorney, Sir William Reeve kept, near the Wood Key, over Sir Matthew Darencyes, the Dutchman. I took the house from Mr Jacob Newman who haith hithertowards alwais executed the office of the Rowells under the Maister of the Rowels, where I am dyeted and Richard. I know most of the merchants in towen and have fair correspondencie from them.

(8)   You say ther be that sell by wholesale but I know none yet who doth not retayell, but indeed some ther be who use to sell parte by wholesaile as anye one may, of which one Pluncket is one, but as I then ment, in cloth and stuffe, I know none. I spoke to some merchants as Champion and Standley and offered to serve them with all such comodityes as they dealeth withall which is about man's appa[ra]ll and offered it at 25 per cent which is 5ˢ in the pound above first peny and to pay at one month after delivery. They seamed not to denye it, or 2ˢ clear proffit in the pound, but they are perswaded that they will buy them at London themselves as well and therfore hould off, but if you were hear it may be wee might drive it to a head; but yet did not anieone bid us above 5 per cent clear proffit nor that neither could I get anie one to buy any quantitye. I cannot sell one Spanish cloth nor anie other thing but as I have written before, viz: 17 dozens, Spanish cloth, 8 peeces of stuff, 2 fryses, 3 bayes which were writ for into the north and sould by my partner the rate I know not; he haith yet for aniething I know unsould the rest, viz: 3 peeces of stuff, Spanish cloth 3 dozens, 2 fryses and 1 kersey. I have sould hear to Mr Bamber one phillip and cheney at 44ˢ 1 mohear 50ˢ; to Mr Roger Gernon 5ˡ 6ˢ 10ᵈ, one black serge with the guilt seale; to Arthur Cham-

pion, 2 fryzes of 83 yards at 7^l 16^s $6^{d(45)}$; Mr Steavens 1 kersey 23 yards 3^l; to Mr Weshton one dozen 4^l 7^s 6^d; to Richard Cokrone Yorkshire cloth black 16 yards at 5^l 9^s 6^d; to him one crowne rashe French greene at 4^l 8^s, in all amounteth to 35^l 2^s 4^d. The rest I have yett, viz: 1 stainell, 18 Spanish cloths, 15 crowen rashes, 6 moheaers, 5 phillip and chenies, 4 peropuses, 2 black pagons, 2 mixet carrols, 1 figaranay, 4 camelions, 2 carthages, 5 damoselloes, 6 colored and 2 black Dutch serges. I had not offered for any crowne rashes above 4^l; now for Clayes cloths one of them 10^l; for the 8 togeather, 9^l per peece; the rest nothing, Camelions out of wear, the peropusses course and will not sell, pagons not asked for nor damosellayes but they come in the worst season that could be for a fortnight before these came just about a fourthnight or 10 dayes after the merchants had sent over which hindreth them of buying aniething, but this tyme we must be content to sell for lesse proffit and provide in tyme against the next season to prevent them hearafter for divers of them, as Standley and others say, if the goods had bene hear before he sent over it may be he would have bought all. The Tearme begann hear last Munday and I hope this tearm tyme merchants will buy them. I see no hurte almost at all they got by cariedge neither by weat or otherwise in which you may rest satisfyed. You bid us sell them at first, second or third shewe: for soe it was for my partner knoweth as well as I and was hear, and if we should have soe done wee should have lost by them, neither could we then have them taken from us. I know not what tales you are tould from Rowland Jackson or others that you say, or els my presumption will prouv as it did with Rowland Jackson's dozens, which I will answer, I hope with noe disgrace to myself, and for you to use anie such upbrayding tearmes I scorne them, neither did ever aniething vexe me more when my care shal be turned to my scorne in them. I will stand to averre it either to Rowland's face or whosover it was, and yourself, for though I know not your meaning being a thing I never once dreamed of. Thus it was: Rowland haveing had experience that cloth would doe litle good at Dublin, and that he could never get abouve neither that viz: 5 per cent proffit, yet my father, he and I thincking it good to make a litle tryall by one pack, soe it was I sent for it to Whitehaven and then gott I it over for a third costome. I caryed it in a barke I had formerly fraighted for salt. I saved the costome of it at Dublin and then it being for sale I had noe reasonable proffit offered for it as much as came to 10^s in a cloth above the first peny; and 2^s a yard for bazzes, half money, half at Michaelmasse but being directed him not to take under 13^s 4^d I forboar till I spoke with him, and theruppon he brought a yong fellow to buy the cloths who more by chance then aniething els was content to buy them soe but all at tyme

---

[45] Marginal note: "Error: it cometh by to 7^l:13^s".

and 15th of October but is not yet paid that I hear of; his whole stock formerly present I thinck being not 60^l[?] by his owen confesson then; yet I thinck the fellow to be honest and noe doubt of it, and if I had not bene directed to the contrary I would have taken 10^s in a cloth above the first peny which had bene better for us, but that I remember your rule not in such cases to exceed dyrectiones. Therefore cast not me in the teeth in such cases before you hear me as well as others, and if I give noe sufficient answere then blame me, or if casually I doe anything wronge yet then seing it after I will be both sorry for it, endeavor to mend it and confesse my falt willingly, and if in this ther be any hidden mystery lett me knowe it for I cannot well imagine what you meane, and I will further satisfy you in it, for iff in soe smale a matter you doe so lightly waive my care, I cannot expecte but that you will fear to lett me have any greater matter in hand, but hearafter speak not soe obscurly. Lett me know wherein I am faulty and if it be in my power I will amend it.

16. (10)   Touching the ladeing of the shipp thus it is: 315^l was I onely to take up. I never yet received letters of creddit or bills of exchange to take upp any more yet in respect of your straight chardg for the prepareing the wheat and in expectation of the letters of creddit which by Bristol and Chester you say you sent and I still expected, but yet never see or heard of, I adventured to hould on to bye wheat and now 6 weeks agoe at least had I bargained for the wheat followinge, viz:

barrells ould wheat   *Page 25*

202	of Roger Gernon	136	7	0	new wheat	200	of R. Balle	
100	of Richd. Balle	67	18	4	kilne-		136^l	0	0
200	of Roger Gernon	140	0	0	dryed	56	in the market	
180	of John Gough	126	10	0			36^l	10	0
14	Richd Balle saith				unkiln-	249½	which some	
	he will have more				dried		beinge kilne-	
	14 barrels						dryed did	
—							hould out 50	
696							full.	

Wheat in all 945½

---

17. (11)   To bye more I hold of because noe money to be gotten under 2½ per cent and againe because I heard noe newes of the shipp or from you till this day. I want money to pay for parte of that I have bought and now the Tearme being come and tyme of payment is at hand, and I ame affraid I shall not gett money under 2½ per cent to pay for it. One

of my Lord Deputye's men Robert Adney had 160[¹] chardged uppon
Mr Baddelow, and he haith promised me the money and to accept bills
of exch[ange] for London for it but Baddelow shifteth him of[f], and he
can get noe money at all, so that you may know how scarce money is
hear and not onely with him but with all other men, for if I cannot
better it I must give money at this tyme to get money both to pay what
I owe for parte of that I have alreadie bought and to furnish the rest.
You advise me to lode 60 or 70 qtrs. more for our quarter parte to
bring her full ladeing of wines back, but money is at soe dear rates and
the cloths came in soe bad a season, being just after all merchants
had sent to London that now to sell them will make no proffitt, as
my partner while he was hear kneweth, and was as much troubled in it
as I, soe that noe moneys [at] present can be raised of them; that I have
thought of another way, that is Mr John Bamber, one whom if ever you
come over I doubt not but you will like well and desire rather a fellow-
shipp with him then anie other, he desireth to have in with us a coplement[46] of 10 tons and would send a man thither[47] purposlie to enquire
of that trade and what good might be done betweane Ireland and there
and the proceed of what he shall send to return it alonge for London
with us which may be I will rather do and wee with him at any other
tyme may have the like. He is a recusant but a very honest loveing
man, one whom my partner Rowland knoweth well, and I am most
beholden to of anieone in Dublin. But of this I will advise you further
in my next.

19. (12)   For the goodnesse of the graine when I bought the ould, it
was the best that aniewhere could be got for money neither was there a
better parcel in all Parchause[48] and Andrew Cherck's portion of 1,000
barrels which they shipped for Dunkirk, a better parcel than the worst
of mine is. 100 indeed haith a few blacks in it. I skreened it alle
but of the grosser blacks it would take none out but onely the musterd
seed and popples etc and some of the dead and smale corne; and the
tayles for the new it loketh very well.

20. (13)   You say if I had bene a merchant I would have writt you of the
receipt of your letters, and the letters of creddit, and that I would performe the commission. I see my writing is in vaine. Look in my letter
of the 7th September you will find I did, but I see you were soe busie
when you writt in finding fault that you forgott what you writt, yet
will I not say but in the very same letter you writt kyndly enough, but
uncle, let me entreat you that this austere predominent vain of writing
sease and if you see me faultie yet give me notice of it mildlye, rather
[than] in that forme as one should say I will speak my mynde and I care

---

[46] I.e. Consignment.
[47] I.e. To the Canary Isles.
[48] Parchauce? Badly smudged word.

for none. You know you have used it to my father and withall it is dis-
pleasing. I beseach you to take it not ill at my hands that I make thus
bould to tell you my mind for I know you are as loveing and kynd as
anieone lyveing, but that humour of carelesnesse is distastfull. You
know amongst all of us Lowthers—treat us fair you lead us where
you will but if we find ourselves disrespected, and that we be once
moved, unlesse a reconsiliation come, we carry ourselves as regard-
lesse on the other side. Therefore hearafter since a patheticall intirely
moveth us, and every good spirit, most to comply and labour the
effect of all honest desires, lett not you or I, the one to the other, use
any cynicall or biteinge speaches, or either of us to anie other, but lett
us with mildnesse still season all our entreaties. For my owne parte if
you turne your fraize, you shall not fynd me contrarie, but if you continue I ame affraid I shall not soe well brook it as maybe you suppose,
for it both dulls, kindleth coller, and will make me more carelesse then
they would otherwise bee.

21. (14)   For the getting a merchant to help me I was I thinck 20 tymes at
Baddelow but fair words I had and that was all and imediatlye after he
was above a month out of towne, and is comenly out, besides the
townesmen doe rather envye then love him becaus he is not a freeman
amongst them, and if he would I cannot perceave he could reasonably
be free, which my partner doth a litle know. But my way must be with
Mr Bamber, with whom if we will we may joyne in any voyage of his,
and if he doe soe with us it is noe great matter for it may doe us good.
All the Irish trade he will honestlie advise us as far as he knoweth and
helpe, aide and further us as himself he protesteth, and soe it is reason
we doe the like to him. If you thinck fitt to write to him comendations,
what your opinions and desires, I doubt not but he will give you satisfaction but I could wish you hear one week yourself and I hope wee
should consider for the best.

22. (15)   To the 15th clause of your letter I answere I must confesse that I   *Page 26*
doe not soe well know all the courses, orders and usuall formes as
yourself, but for advice on that better then my owne I shall ever thanck
you and be reddie to follow it.

23. (16)   To the 16th I shall send you the acc[oun]t of the corne as you
desire when it is cleer on shipboord and Mr Batties letters hearafter
or anie other man's inclosed in yours. Since I begune this I received the letters which Bartelet brought and in those the bills of
prizes[49] betwene which and the rates hear but litle difference, but this
observe, one can never hear of a sodaine vent anie quantity of any
goods at once for a litle cloyeth the towen. Copp[er] pannes about 60
pound weight a peece 5 qtrs. over, I could sell them at 18^d per pound,
but I can get none at Keswick, for the workes are failed. If we had anie

[49] I.e. prices.

such out from beyond sea, from the Low Cuntryes, I could sell them about 100^l worth. Latten[50] single and duble about 50^l at a time; maders about 30^l worth, steele hempe 50^l, indico 20^l but it is as cheap hear now as at London. Dales boordes 6^l per C longe, now none almost in towen; tarr of Westmoreland and Cumberland had bene a good comoditye this year worth ther 12^l per last,[51] the lardge band above.

25. (18) To the 18th and last clause of this letter of yours which by the same over againe I find to be dated the 27 September, I say it may be you suppose my letters are not according to your forme but that they want sence persuade me not for I would be sorrie to become sencelesse. For my cossen Wibergh and myself, I thinck you would not have taken the paines that wee doe about this busines and especially in getting up the 315^l which by the letters of creddit I was to receave, wanting yet 30^l of it from John Standley who haith on Saterday last suffered a great losse of his goods in the harbour hear with many others; the barke wherein they were by reason of a cable breaking by reason of a storme and runing herself ashore, most of the goodes soe wett with salt water and the bark almost quite lost, and from the like the Lord blesse us. Thus at lardge have I answered this letter as you desired; now to your letter of the 6th of October.

(1) Baddelow denieth he wrote to you or that he received anie letters in my

(2) absence, but I thinck he consealeth them, but I said nothing but took his

(3) answer, of which write to him if you please. I am sorrie of Captain Lee

(4) his death and take notice of others who haith taken his share. How things are in rediness you perceave before in this my letter and if I had had money I should have had all things lieinge by five, six weeks agoe, but, praysed be God, I doubt not if she were hear, but by taking upp money, for to put all things abord in a weak. Christian Burr[e] and some partners with him are in ladeing a shipp with kilne dryed corne for the Canaryes which came hither about 10 dayes since, imediately from the Canaryes, and brought with hir 60 pipes of sack, but not sould above 14^l or that per pipe. If your ship

(1) had been hear I could have sent her away at least a month agoe. The story you began with, my partner tould mee; for other things I have hearin

(2) answered them. I know your stock is all in and almost duble myne, viz: I gave my partner Rowland Jackson when he came to you for to buy cloth, hopps and traine [oil] 400^l; formerly I had in

---

[50] A brass alloy.
[51] A last of tar was usually 12 (sometimes 14) barrels, O.E.D.

acc[ount] betwene him and me in his barke 212^l 19^s 6^d. I brought over
to disburse uppon the goods as customer 50^l; coles uppon the hyll at
Whitehaven 24^l; in wares from you 92^l, in hooks 1^l 16^s; salt over when
I came 15^l 17^s 6^d; more in chardges as I can make appear laid out for
our generall use 10^l, is in all 813^l 0^s 6^d, besides money I have in Giles
handes and elsewhear which I reckon not, about 80^l; but all this while
my partner's full parte is not in that I know of. You writ that I must
pay for the wheat I haveing the stock. I haveing the least parte you
know not but that I might have sould them at tyme and may doe yet,
therefore what should I doe for money but charge it uppon you,
for our parte. I must doe it at present if I get not saile, though you
chardge it back againe on mee, and it may be then I on you till
moneys be in our hand. Now doubting not but that I have answered
all, I rest,

Your very loveing even as to himself,
Christ. Lowther

The bearer hereof Mr Strickson of Colchester, whom Humphray Rowland knoweth, and Mr Cudisworth and I thincke yourselve for he was a
commissioner about the shipp yow had goods loste in laste yeare. He is
the sole agent about the patent for serving Ireland with salte. I talked
with him about it of which he will acquaint you, but being juste upon
his goeing away I refer you to talk with him further, for it may concerne us at Whitehaven, and maybe wholey stoppe Rowland's comeing
downe of which likewise talke with Rowland what he knoweth in it,
in haste I rest.

[Below this in minuscule writing are added the following phrases:]

I gave a letter of advice to Mr Champion to send with the bills of
exch[ange] of the 100^l I received of him, for him to send to Mr Batty
with the bills, but I perceave now it is yet unsent, but the bills he sent,
which doth not a litle greave me, but if he did not send it but have it
yet, I will this day send it, more then that was I cannot. I cannot now
write to him of w[ha]t I would have writ to him, if it had bene but a
remembrance of my love, but now the taking in of the hopps my
partner bought at Sturbri[dge] which haith taken wett, hindredth mee.

Dublin $\frac{12}{9}$ [November] 1632   Page 27

To Robert Lowther, Merchant,

Kinde Uncle,

Soe it is: my partner Row[land] Jackson being at Belfast in makeing
of a slaughter for Bristol hath charged me to pay 100^l at 3 dayes sighte
and I could by noe meanes tell how to pay it; but as he writte to me which
is to charge it upon you, and he sayth he will send you the same from
Bristol upon sayle of the beefe he now maketh; and theirefore I have made

the meanes with much adoe to get the hundreth poundes of my Lord Mountnorris; and I doe give Mr Hull, my lord's steward, for mediating for it with
me to my lord 20ˢ, and glad for too, for at this tyme Mr Baddelow telleth
me, and moste in the towne know, the Dutch offer 3 per cent to take up
money by exchandge, and by noe meanes can get to fornesh theire turnes,
and if I had not got it here of my lorde I could not elsewhere have got it in
towne; and I thinck it was p[ar]tely upon my Lord Deputy's letter of recom-
mendation for me. I have given this day my bills of exchandge for it to my
lord, and have charged it upon yow at 8 dayes sighte, which I much
laboured for; and I pray yow have a speciall care the bills be payed, for if
yow be carefull to pay this money punctually I thinck we shall at other
tymes procure more of my lord, when it may be as it fell now [that] we
cannot elswhere be fitted. But if you fayle this tyme looke not that I can ever
take up any more of him. If you would but write to my Lord Mountnorris yourselfe that what money he will lett me have, if I charge it upon you
that you would as honestly pay it as any man, it may much avayle us and we
may have the returneinge of the moneys of the Custome House, which
hithertowards the Dutch have had, for he sayde to me himselfe if you write
to him that what I charge upon you you would pay it that I should as soone
as anyone have the returninge of the moneys of the Custome House when I
needed.

My letters of the 11th present showe you all things ells and thus not
haveinge further, expecting your answer, I reste,

Your loveing cousin,
Ch. Lowther

Copie of a bill of exchange
to my uncle Robert Lowther
Enclosure:

Laus deo adi[uvante] 12 november 1632 in Dublin 100ˡ. To Mr Robt.
Lowther, Merchant in London, first bill of exch. Att eight days after sight
hearof pay this my first bill of exchaunge, my second or third not being paid,
of one hundred pounds sterling unto Thomas Leak, Esquire, for the value
hearof recvd. of the Right Honorable the Lord Mountnorris, by me for the
use of ourselves and partnershipp.   Christopher Lowther.

Page 28   November 14th 1632 from Dublin
To Mr John Batty,
Worthy Sir,

I doe withall love, respecte and thankfulnesse remember myselfe unto
you, and doe not onely desire in this imployment to shew myselfe your
carefull and honest frend and servant, but assure yourselfe and rest soe
perswaded that not onely for yourselfe, but for anie frend of yours I wil
be a's diligint, careful and trustie as to my owne selfe, neither will I

desire anye welfare to my selfe longer than to you or any towards you. I have twice severally chardged you for money received which I forboar as longe as possibly I could, all because I would not to sodainlye chardge you with my last bills for the money I received of Champion. I writ you a letter of advice, but I hear now of late Mr Champion to whom I sent your letter by my man to be sent the same day I gave him my bills haith not yett sent, soe now I have taken care that it will come, for which I pray you blame not mee for, for that the fault was not in mee. For other things I referr you to my uncle Robert to whom I have writt at lardge. Your letters of creddit came not to my handes which I should have received from Bristol and Chester, soe I amm affraid I must take upp money at 2 and $2\frac{1}{2}$ per cent if I cannot better doe, for the payment of your parte, as all now doe and haith bene given 3 and above by Dutch, and yet is given, but that I know where to fynd a litle more cartosie, soe being by haist a litle interrupted I humbly take leave,

Your faithfull frend Chr. Lowther

Per Nathaniell Strickson, Saltmaster.

17th November 1632 from Dublin   Page 30

To my father,

Kynd Father,

1. I receaved your letters of the $\frac{19}{8}$ October and one other without date but I suppose it to be writt about the $\frac{25}{8}$, which I thus answer. You ar pleased to expresse your lykeinge of my letters which is noe smale comfort unto me; it is that which I shall ever desire, and that in all my wayes I may satisfie your expectation from mee. By God's assistance with all willingnesse and carefulnes I will ever labour, neither shall I wish anythinge more while I live or be more carefull in, neither will I attempt

2. that, when I may have your advice without it. I have not yet neither will I once take notice of any other agreement then our first unlesse uppon future advice you hould it fitt, but I shall hould on fairly with them; hearafter what I have and is due to be paid I shall better consider of for I suppose I perceave your meaneinge.

3. To gadge myself further for this wheat then for our owne share I meane it not.

4. I am glad of the Star Chamber attempts fallinge of, and shall ever praye that such malitious projects may in the budding be blasted.

5. I like well of my Lord President's[52] good conceipt of our salt works, and for the new corperacion in Ireland I refer you to the treatie of it hear inclosed.

6. I yet cannot know certainely what store of salt and cole is vented hear, but as soone as possibly I can I will write you word, for when my Lord Mount[norris] hear redd my Lord Deputy's letter and desired the

[52] I.e. Lord Wentworth.

sight of it, he shewed me some six lynes of the beginninge of it, but said the rest was not concearning me soe I had not the letter; he gave fair words but I perceave but a complement—yet my partner Rowland Jackson being in the north and haveing not money enough for his slaughter, haith taken upp 100^l and chardgeth it uppon me at 3 dayes sight; his bills were assigned over to my Lord Mountnorris, so I gave my bills of exchange to my lord, and chardged it uppon my uncle Robert as Rowland advized me, wherein he[53] did me a curtosie for otherwise I could not have had 100^l to have paid[54] under 3^l [per cent] himself at that tyme receaving soe, soe scarce was money then and is now. My partner writeth he will repay it to my uncle Robert from Bristol.

7.   I send you hear the lease of my cousin Wybergh's part enclosed which you wrote for.

8.   I am glad William Hodgson and the rest are served and amongst all William Burton was the stubbernest and best deserveth to suffer.

9.   For to advise you how my businesse goeth; first the ship from London is not yet come. I have received letters from my Uncle Robert of the 27 October, $\frac{6}{8}$ and $\frac{2}{8}$ and all at once by the way of Chester the 13th November instant, which imediatly at lardge I answered. The effect of his letter is that Captain Lee, one who had a share in the wheat, is dead and that the maister of the shipp haith taken his part with the others; that the shipp would sett forth about the middle of October; that litle John Barton is in her; that he[55] intendeth to come to Whitehaven with the salter; that he desireth to know what I have done of the which I shall shew you copies, and my answers as soon as I have leasure;

Page 31

I have bought ould wheat and new 1,005 barrels for which I have paid 342^l 16^s 4^d, the whole amounteth unto 683^l 12^s 8^d, soe the rest I have yet to pay for 340^l 16^s 4^d, which I ame to receave 30^l of Standley, which was chardged with the first letters of creddit. Cook and Champion and Weldon 24^l, Weston and Browen 7^l 7^s 6^d; in purse 3^l money, received by exchange 25^l. The rest I intende to take it upp per exchange uppon Mr Batty as my uncle biddeth me. Cloth selleth very badly hear. I cannot get 2^s in the pound clere proffit soe I cannot tell what is best to doe unlesse to sell for litle or nothing proffitt, though all yet that I have sould is uppon ten in the hundredth.

I hear from my partner, to whom Miles Bateman haith writt, that our barque in the north Ilands was 2 parts laden and that they hoped to load her out with herringes shortly, soe by God's grace I hope we shall doe good by them, for even herringes ar worth 27^s a smale barrell of 28 gallons. My partner by this tyme is readie for Bristol with his beefe.

[53] I.e. Lord Mountnorris.
[54] I.e. without having to pay.
[55] I.e. Robert Lowther.

The Master of the Roweles is not yet knowne. My cossen Gerard saith he thincketh it worth 1,000^l per annum with his fee which is 180^l per annum, his 2 sircuits and the perquisitts of his office. It were

10. a good place if you would look after it. My cossen Gerard tould me he had heard you should have it. Money, he saith, is 10^l per cent at interest and soe will and dailie doth the Chancerye allowe and sometymes more is given, but if it be knowne, he saith, the Chancery will not allowe it.

11. For joineinge with Mr Radcliffe and Mr Marris it may be you may otherwise consider of it, for if the pattantees hear have all salt prohibited but what is made by them for comeing in, we must rather thinck to joine with them to which end peruse the salt advice.

12. I had the copie of my Uncle Robert's letter you sent mee before by Rowland Jackson. Ther is none about me but Roger Wibergh[56] and I ame sure neither of us is idle. Him I fynd honest and willinge and I thinck to send him along with the wheat when it goeth.

13. The 400^l which Rowland Jackson had: 133^l odd money came the cloth to, hopps 96^l 14^s 11^d; lefte with Mr Maior of Bristol 80^l for earnesting of the traine [oil], in all 310^l. The rest he saith he bringst with him into Ireland and used some of it in setting forth the bark to the herring and towards his slaughter. My partner Ro[lland] Ja[ckson] saith it wil be the

14. latter end of Christmasse er he retorne from Bristol and then he will come to Lowther.

15. By God's assistance I shall in all things be as punctuall and undertak nothing without performance. What letters hearafter I send you by for my Uncle Robert I shall not forgett to endorse them.[57] I shall send you a seale the same with myne, as soone as I have gotten one made.

16. Salt hear is not customed by the way but by the barrell and the custom of a barrel is 3^d which is 2^s 6^d per way, 10 barrels which is 40 bushells to a wey, and soe much in answerr of your first letter.

17. To the 2nd letter, I perceave you received mine of the $\frac{22}{8}$, my last being of the first of November.

18. Till you speak of the stopping of the coles is answered, of which I am *Page 32*

19. very glad. I perceive the plates are come and since alsoe I perceive that ther is nothing but dales wanting, but soe it is hear. [There] is none hear but those that are not worth anythinge almost and if one cull out the best then ar they worth 16^d per peece, and if they wer but 12^d per peece yet is much oak boarde better, and if they be at 36^s per rood yet are they cheap than dales at 12^d besides being duble better than dales; soe I thinck it better to get such boardes sawen at Irton or tymber brought from thence to Whitehaven and sawe them there.

---

[56] Error for Richard?

[57] Last seven words repeated in error.

20.   For my likeing of buying and selling of Rowland or my uncle I cannot well tell what to thinck, but this I can say: ther be divers merchants, of the greatest dealers in the towen, that willingly, they say, would give me 2^s in the pound clear profitt to be served readdie money and be wholey served from London but they say againe, when they see our goods and that I would be content with 2^s in the pound readdie money, that either my partners buy not well or els not honestlie, but they say they buy cheapp!

21.   Soe haveing answered your letters as I suppose I humbly take leav praying that God in all things may abundantly bless you and preserve you out of the hands of our enemyes, with my mother, brothers and sisters and all [who] wish well unto us, I rest,

Your loveing sonne,
Christopher Lowther

Sent with it a letter of atturney [to?] my father with an advice of salt, per *My Ladie C.?.ent*[58] bark.

23 November 1632 Dublin

To Robert Lowther,

Kynde Uncle,

    My laste was of the 11th instante and 12, in answer of yours of the $\frac{27}{8}$ and your others of the $\frac{27}{8}$ and your others of former date, and concerning also one hundred poundes which I charged you withall, and I doubte not but yow will see it discharged, and soe it is now that by meanes of a frend haveing procured 25^l I have chardged it uppon you to pay at ten days sight, for soe scarce is money yet it will not be gotten under 6^d per pound though I shall pay nothing for this, and may be I shall have more of of him. And what money els I can get soe as far as I have not to pay for our part, I will chardge it uppon you; for all the monies that I have received for anye goods sould will not amount unto full 100^l, and our part of the wheat you know will amount to above 200^l. But if I can sell any goods to get in money I will not further chardge you, but for money to supply Mr Batty and the rest shares of the wheat, etc, I ame much affraid I shall not get under 6^d in the pound, for I have hithertowards held of[f] to take upp anye by exchange, expecting money to have bene more plentifull but yet I fynd it not; nay, I cannot yet gett in Standley's 50^l out, for of it I have but yet 20^l and the rest every day doe I ask for but cannot yet get it. The hopps my partner bought at Storbridge one of the baggs was soe broken soiled and 22 lbs weight I thinck verilie stolen in England, soe I was gladd to sell it of[f] at 7^l 5^s per cent for further cariedge it would not endure; the other six baggs I send tomorrow to Belfast be a Scotch bark by sea whither my partner writt for them. One of them had all the

---

[58] Illegible.

canvas almost quit rotten away, and about 10 lb or 12 lb rotten with wett which we cast out. More harme I see not. I heard yesterday that about Belfast and Knockfergus hopps ar worth 10^l per cent, and if it be soe I hope we shall get something by them. I bought this day 50 barrels of wheat at 12^s per barrel of one Lanygon to whom formerly I was glad to give 13^s per barrel, soe the houlding back hath done us noe harm.

I pray you talk with Mr Strickson of the salt pattent and see it if you can and the articles, and know certainely what wil be the event of it. Alderman Parkes I hear is one of the patenties; and write to my father what you thinck of it, for if it goe forward Mr Strickson haith offered that I may come in to the pattent and sett the works upp at Whitehaven, but if you see noe hinderance that they can doe us, then may we the bouldlier hould on.

The ship you ar to send I yet hear not of hir. Quoyman's ship that came from the Canaryes is now loadeing wheat for there againe. Noe news hear, but I pray you remember me kyndly to our good frend Mr Batty, soe committing you to God's protection I rest,
Sente with this letter a bill of exch. for 25^l underwritten.
Post script, I perceave Kentish cloths are altogeather for this towene and not Spanish. The reason is they desire altogeather a broad cloth, but those narrow cloths they care not for, neither will any stuffs be once loked uppon this season. Black the onely stuffe asked for.
Per Mr Pawlets . ? . este[59] to be conveyed with the bills.

Your loveing nephew and partner,
Christopher Lowther

[Enclosed a bill of exchange drawn in favour of Sarah Paulet for £25 received of John Paulet in Dublin, drawn on Robert Lowther and dated Dublin 23 November by C. Lowther.]

23 November Dublin

To my partner Rowland Jackson,
Loveing Partner, or in your absence Mr Foster,
My love and best respects to you, Mr Tompson and the rest of our frends with you remembered. I have received your last of the 12th and 13th of this instant. My first to you being of the 1st of October and my last by Thomas Jackson. Since which I hear nothing out of England from any.

One bagg of hopps I have sould to Mr Bamber which came hither all broken and would not carry further, those hopps it seeme being abused in cariedge, and wanted of weight 22 lbs soe I thought best to quit it off[f]. Those I now send ayle nothing since onely the poorer bagg which to the quantity of about 20 lbs weight was a litle wett by reason of the breach of the canvas and this wee pickt out; soe now I know noe fault with them. At London[60] worth 8^l and lickly to rise to ten, for my uncle writes at Chester 9^l

[59] Illegible.
[60] The word "pipestaves" probably omitted in error.

per cwt for pipestaves. I heare nothing. The shipp is uncome. Yf cloth, stuffes or stainell will sell write I pray you for hear att present all are provided. Write I pray you how your business goeth. I have noe more corne then one thousand barrels yet provided, by reason I cane gett noe moneys uppon exchange under 6^d per pound which I ame verie loth to doe, neither can I sell anything yet to gett any more in. I wrote to my uncle that you will retorne him the 100^l from Bristol which I discharged hear according as you wrote. Soe not haveing not more I rest,

Your loveing partner,
Christopher Lowther

Post script.   I thought to have sent these hopps by Geo. Melling, but he would not warrant them from wetting soe I would not but by Mr Bashford's bark, God willing, I will send them.
Per G. Melling, a Dannowhadee Man?[61]

24/9 Dublin

Page 32

To my partner Rowland Jackson,
Loveing partner,
   I yesterday writ unto you in the fornoone in answer of yours of the $\frac{23}{9}$ and thought to have sent the hopps by a Dannowhade[62] man, and agreed for fraight and when all was done the owner would not warrent them from wett and soe I would not madly and to hastelie send them on such tearmes. I ame glad of your newes from Myles of ther herring fishing. Herring hear worth 27^l the skore, so whether you will have him to make sale hear of them or lett him hould on for France, because of retornes of wines, vinegar etc, what els you advise of best, I refer it unto you. My father writeth mee that he haith now some moneys to lend you to augment your part, if that you were but with him to speak with him yourself. I can sell nothing soe thinck I shall not have of a sodain [money] either to buy tallow which you writte of   to pay for our quarter parte of the corne,

Your loveing partner,
Christopher Lowther

Sent per Richard Butcher $\frac{26}{9}$.

$\frac{25}{9}$ber Dublin 1632

To Rowland Jackson,
Loveing Partner,
   I received your letter of the 21th instant wherein you expresse not receipt of anie letters from mee but of my first of October, but if Thomas Jackson had not had the measels he had bene with you 4 dayes soner than he was, who I perceave per this bearer was come the same night (but after) you writt this your letter, which I now answer:

[61] Probably Donaghadie, Co. Down.
[62] See footnote 61, ibid.

1,005 barrels of corne hav I bought now for which I have paid 326^l 16^s 4^d and yet for the same corne remaineth to pay 321[^{l}] or thereabouts, of which I have not above 60^l in debts to take upp to pay it with, or any other waies, and of that 25^l have I received per exchang and chardged it uppon my uncle so that for the rest as I writt formerley I know not whear to have it, unlesse I give 6^d in the pound for it, and that maks mee alsoe to forbear buying anie more corne or the candles till the shipp come or that moneys be gott. All that is sould is thus:

Page 33

Mr Bamber one phillip and cheyney 44^s, one mohear 50^s; Roger Gernon for the Dutch serge 5^l 6^s 10^d, two fryzes to Champion 7^l 13^s more; 1 grey dozen 4^l; Richard Cook, black 16 yards 5^l 9^s 6^d; one greene crown rash 4^l 8^s; hopps Mr Bamber 2 c[wt] 26½ lbs at 7^l 5^s per cent, 16^l 4^s. Mr Weldone, if he take a Spanish cloth, the rate agreed 11^l; Mr Weshton, one kersie 3^l; i dozen 4^l 7^s 6^d; in toto 66^l 5^s 10^d. Soe you see 66^l 5^s 10^d is all I have toward our 205[^{l}], a quarter of the wheat, etc, and the 25^l I chardged uppon my uncle which is in all but 91^l 5^s 10^d. I perceave by Mr Bamber that some are come hither with Ireland herring and are but offered 20^s per barrel; whether the reason is in the fish or the making I know not soe for France if you lyke to directe our bark when she cometh or otherwise as you please. The 6 baggs of hopps with the first conveiance I shall send.

Your loveing partner and kinsman,
Christopher Lowther

per Richard Butcher $\frac{26}{9}$

Dublin the $\frac{29}{9}$ber 1632

To my partner Rowland Jackson at Belfast

Partner,

Litle have I now to write more then I have formerly said, but that yet the ship is uncome. I have now bought more of Ball's 200 barrels of wheat for which I am to pay 69^l per hundereth barr[ells]. God send me yet money to pay for it for I see noe other then that I must give 50^s per 100^l for to have it per exchange for London. Burre, Quoyman and Foukes [?] send a shipp for the Canaryes with wheat which next Saterday wil be loaden out. Mr Weldon taketh the cloth of 11^l which I wrote of. Since this day I have sould 2 paragons black at 7^l and could not have one penny more, from which we shall not gett one peny proffit for all we saved in the costomes, for 6^l 16^s [was] the cost first peny. Yet money must be had and I thinck when all is done we must be glad to send them along to the Canaryes. I would have sent the hopps since by a Frenchman with Mr Tompson's salt but neither would he take in any, and yf he had rome yet not under 10^s per bag, soe with the first we can wee will send them. Soe with my love remembered to you and George, I rest,

Your loveing partner,
Chr. Lowther

Sent per Bryan Robinson the $\frac{29}{9}$

Dublin $\frac{30}{9}$ 1632

To my partner Rowland Jackson, at Belfast

1. Mr Jackson, this day received I a letter from your sonne George. I perceave you are to take upp 100^l. Tis well for scarce hear.

2. but to buy[63] herringes where I know not, but wheresoever it be I advise you not bring them hither, for of the north Iles herrings hear haith bene alreadie sould of them but for 18^s a barrel. The reason is the Scotch makeing is not hear lyked of, soe that [they] will doe noe good unlesse for some other place, as for Bristol, but neither know I the rate ther. Neither hould I in either case for rize or for wheat,[64] becaus I know my uncle will thinck very much to have 100^l chardged now of him ther being alreadie chardged on him 125^l and I know I must chardg 100^l more on him to fitt up moneyes for dischardging our quarter part; and besides I bought 50 barrells of wheat hear and soe could have had more for 12^s and I thinck better then the corne with you.

3. For if you come to Dublin shortly, and have not disposed of the 100^l you thinck to have rather bring it with you to serve our necessityes hear.

4. I ame sorry for Tom's sicknesse with all my heart trewly.

5. I shall send the hopps with Mr Masser's barque if he send.

Noe news more then what I writt yesterday so with my love to Mr Foster and Mr Thompson and the rest of our frends, I rest,

Your loving partner,
Ch. Lowther.

Sent per Mr David Masser.
the $\frac{30}{9}$

4th December 1632 Dublin

To my uncle Robert Lowther,
Loveing Uncle,

My last unto you was of the $\frac{23}{9}$ with which I sent unto you a bill of
1. exchange of 25^l which I had from Mr John Pawlet [65] and I suppose er this you have receaved it and discharged the bill; since all things which I can

2. informe you of ar thus: first, I have not received Standley's 50^l fourth yet by 5^l. By exchaing I have received 50^l of Mr Robert Adney, my Lord Deputy his man, for which I must confesse I am very beholden unto him. I chardge it on you, as formerly I advised you, for to supply our quarter part, which I

---

[63] Error for "sell"?

[64] Means he does not approve drawing on London £100 to buy rice or wheat.

[65] Originally there followed "I wrote unto you advise", "wrote" was then altered to "sent", and then the whole phrase was crossed out.

3. hope will near serve with that I have of our owne, for by a breefe note on the other side you may see what the goods I have sould come unto, as likewise of our wheat affaires.

4.   Burr Quoyman and Skot's shipp are readie for the Canaryes loden with kilne dryed wheat, about 1,000 barrels and pease and beanes about 100 barrels; salted barreld pork about 50 barrels, neat's tongues barreld about 10 barrels, with candles. And if our shipp had bene hear before them she had bene gone afor this came, but now they have the first of the market, before us, in which I ame sure I ame not faulty.

5.   Yet doe I hear nothing of the shipp you are to send, God send her hither safe.

6.   I heard from my partner Rowland Jackson at Belfast the 23 November that wheat is but worth ther 11^s per barrell and hear at that tyme 12^s but now it is risen to 13^s againe since.

7.   And I heard further that he was about to tak upp 100^l and chardge it on you for to buy wheat there with, but I have writt to him not to doe soe because I imagine that the 100^l he did alreadie take upp which I first chardged uppon you, and the 25^l of Pawlet's and this 50^l I now charge you with you will thinck too much but for my part I ame sorrie that things fell noe better and that I chardge you with any at all, but otherwise I could not helpe it.   *Page 35*

8.   I hope good by our North Iles fisheinge and hope with these north west winds they ar in comeing home, for I heard for certain that they[66] came in faster then they could mak them.

9.   I have this long kept my wheat masters of[f] with love and a fair cariedge that now Champion who formerlie would not take under 2$\frac{1}{2}$ per cent to fit me uppon exchange will now take one and a half which for Mr Batty's love and the rest's good I have hithertowards labored for, and now must I give soe much, being not able to put them of[f] anye longer, and for my cariedge in this business, all things considered and my reasons (if they were given) I fear not anie loiell sensor.

10.   I hear of no alteration in the rate of comodityes hear since I last sent you a bill of prises.

11.   I had not yet a conveience by my shippinge for to send 5 bags of hops to Belfast to my partner Ro[wland] Ja[ckson] but a Scott who had an open boat and would not warrant them from wett; but now ame to send them by another with the first wind, nothing els can I now inform you of but shall ever rest.

             Your honest by God's assistance careful and
                       loveing cossin, Christ. Lowther.

Sent per Mr Potter by way of Bristol
     I wrote in my last letter of the $\frac{11}{9}$, 7^l 16^s 6^d but I miscounted itt.

[66] I.e. herring.

[Account, presumably enclosed in the letter:]

		l	s	d
1	phillip and cheiney	2	4	0
1	Mohayre	2	10	0
1	Dutch serge	5	6	10
2	fryzes	7	13	0
1	Gray dozen	4	0	0
1	Black 16 yds	5	9	6
1	greene crowne rash	4	8	0
1	kersie	3	0	0
1	dozen	4	7	6
1	Rogers Spanish 20½ yds	11	0	0
1	hitchcock 23½	17	0	0
1	phillip and cheney	2	5	0
2	paragons black	7	0	0
1	crowen rash skarlet	4	8	0
1	crowen rash black	4	4	0
1	Dutch serg ordinary	4	5	0
1	damosella flored	2	10	0

—it was returned again for 18 peeces amounts but unto 87^l 6^s 10^d.

		l	s	d
19	peeces Reddie money	91	10	10
		46	15	0

salt, hopps & coles:

	l	s	d
56½ barr. salt	24	0	0
2 ct 26½ lb hopps	16	4	0
9 ton ½ coles	6	11	0
	46	15	0

	l	s	d
Reddie money in all	138	5	10
3 Yorkshire dozens	12	10	0
2 cwt 1 qrter of hopps	(blank)		

to pay at Candlemasse per bill, an honest reputed man. I shall

sell this day about 7^l 10^s I thinck.

Bought 1,245 barrels of corne amounteth unto about 850^l first peny. 452^l 6^s 4^d I have alreadie paid, remaining 379 13 8 unpaid, but to pay the same I have and shall have for us 63^l and the bag of hopps I sell now, about 17 pounds and 350 I shall get of Champion and others at 1½ per cent which let Mr Batty prepare himself for, for I shall but have a short tyme upon the bills. More I entend not to chardg you withall for the wheat unless one 40^l and yet I shall not very much need it. This 50^l and the former 25^l I get for nothing but the bestoweing 6^s 3^d in a pair of gloves or some such thing, and therefore chardged it uppon you lest I should not prevaile for the like curtusy of anie other in tyme but to supply Mr Batty, etc's parts in

good faith I can not labour to get it under 30^s per cent, which accquaint him.
[Enclosure: a bill at three days sight on Robert Lowther for 60^l payable
to Henry Dawson, in return for the same paid to Christopher Lowther by
Robert Adney, dated 4 December 1632.]

The 4th December 1632 in Dublin   Page 36

To Mr John Batty merchant in London
Worthie Sir,

My love and best service to yourself and anye towards you ever remembred. Yt may please you to take notice (my last to you being of the $\frac{14}{9}$) that
since I have noe news or alteracion hear to accquaint you withall, but that
I have had the wheat provided this good while and have now bought 1,245
barrels of wheat of kilne dryed and other amount that will be above 1,200
barrels kilne dryed and ould and it amounteth unto about 850^l first peny
soe that for the $\frac{3}{4}$ parts I must yet chardge you with above the 265^l I have
alreadie chardged on you about 400^l, and in truth I have purposlie forborne
hithertowards to chardge any moneys uppon you at 2$\frac{1}{2}$ per cent, because it
was not till now under 50^s in the hundereth and now none can I gett under
1$\frac{1}{2}$ now soe I must give, for longer cannot I persuade the corne maisters to
forbear. Soe I thought fitt to give you notice before hand for 300^l, if not
four, I shall have within this fortnight, and I chardge it uppon you. The
shipp is not yet come unto mee, and the corne you knowe will every day
waste with the ratts and drying in. I marveile much I never yet heard from
you one word in this busines. For other things I referr you to my Uncle
Robert his letter of the same date. Soe haveing not els I humbly take leave
and rest to you as to myself in all things faithfull and carefull.

Your loveing frend,
Chr. Lowther

per Mr Potter by the way of Bristol

4 December 1632 Dublin

To Mr Hobson, Maior of Bristol,
Worthye Sir,

After my harty thancks unto you for my kynd entertainement, at my
being with you at Easter last, I humbly desire you to be pleased to send
these letters as directed, by some conveience as you shall thinck best,
and for the same my partner Rowland Jackson and I will ever rest as we
are your ever well wishers and frends,

Yours in any curtosie to be comanded,
Chr. Lowther

Sent per Mr Potter by Bristol.

From Dublin the $\frac{10}{10}$ ber 1632

To my uncle Robert Lowther, merchant in London

Uncle,

My last unto you was the 4th December instant by the way of Bristol amd since I have received uppon the 8th instant one of yours bearing date $\frac{2}{9}$ ber by the way of Chester, which to answer I proceed:

I take notice of your fault fyndeing with me for my brevity to Mr John Batty and thanck you for it, but knowe it was not through either lasines or

1. carelesnes, but at that tyme beinge importund by haist by Mr Barry, and since I have writ severall tymes unto him, most inclosed to you and unsealed, of which I pray you advice mee and in all things els of my errors as in this. To you I have formerly writ at lardg of all things I am sure, and with reference comenlye of Mr Batty's letters to yours which I thinck sufficient.

Page 37

I take notice likewise of your takeing of money uppon my brother to pay our fourth of the waxe and rice, and of your 70^l 0^s 6^d in above, your

2. 250^l in which I take it you suffer noe wronge, for I have likewise above 500^l at least 300^l, which will above answer your propotion and doubt not but that for your 70^l 0^s 6^d you shall have it accounted to you as well as the rest, and soe lykewise yf it were more.

3. To the 3rd part of your letter I say I ame rather gladd you sent not the goods my partner Rowland Jackson spoke of, since that things sell soe'ill as they doe, for I perceave the merchants hear ar so tyed to ther costomers at London that alwaise being indebted to them they know not now how to leave them.

4. I have writt I know it both at lardg and as oft as you have—if they come not it is not my falt and therein I have writt you how the stock I put in was bestowed, of all sales and towards this voyage of the wheat.

5.· To send Jack to mee I wonder much you knoweing the conceat I had alwase of him, and to send him along the Canaryes I know not to what end, and for me to trust or imploy whom you dare not or willingly will not, for my parte you myght thinck me a foole to doe it, neither will I venture of it myself without my father's privity.

6. I hear this day the shipp is at Waterford and I hope the first sotherly wind will bring her hither.

7. Our bark the *George* is not yet retorned from the north Iles fishing, but now we expect her every day. Myles Bateman writteth the 12th November that they were half loaden then and by fishermen that be come from thence after the tyme that he writt, we hear that he had one morning five last come in, soe I hope wee shall have some good of them,

8. and wee intend them for France, soe that it cannot now be possible as you advice to send her for Hamborrow [Hamburg] unlesse we should sell our herring hear and soe load her thither, but butter being now 3$\frac{1}{2}^d$ per pound it is not fitt I thinck.

9. The weights and measures are thus: corne either by the peck or barrell, the peck upheaped, 24 gallons; barrell strokte[67] 32 gallons; in the cytye soe [are] wheat, rye, pease, beanes. In the cuntry the measures, in all things almost, differ. Herrings is comenly made up in caskes of 28 gallons. Salt, French and Spanish, is sould per water measure, viz: 40 gallons, 80 gallons the hogshead, now worth about 20^s and scarce that; salt, English, by the Bristol band of 32 gallons with 2 or three shakes or els packed in caske. If it come in caske now worth 9^s per barrell. The stone hear consisteth of 15 l[bs] unlesse one otherwise provide it by ther bargaine, as in wool where the buyer haith gotten it within this year or two to 16, but otherwise it holdeth in other things 15 pounds comenly and sometymes in woole itself, the best now being worth 11^s or dearer a litle, 16 lbs to the stone. In cloth hear by the English yard and ell except that by the first as in England they doe Kentish, they sell in Kentish cloth, but all by inch, if by wholesale they buy any they will have the fist. In the cuntry ther yards and bandolls[68] differ everywhere. Butter by the wine quart or pound, for which in the cuntry, if they will in the spring tyme give money, before hand they may bye it at 2^d ob a pound and in the citye till about Michaelmase at 3^d as it cometh in, til Christmasse 3^d ob; til Easter 4^d and dearer. In coles 40 gallons now but before 36 gallons and not long before that 32 gallons, the measure at Whitehaven of coles Chester band, viz 30 gallons but come ther it is not soe good as 30 for the horses that bring them are poore and weak and they never measure but *Page 38* fills the sack which houldeth but 28, I thinck, soe hear 16 would not yeald 10, but behould the supposition which I know to be as near as anieone can doe it. At Whitehaven 300 bushels of salt there being about 16 gallons to the bushel either packed or lightly measured with a shovell and two shakes will make one Bristol band barrell there.

	l	s	d
300 bushels at Whitehaven at 2^s per bushel ys	30	0	0
Shipping at 4^d per skore		5	0
Two mesurers		2	6
1 loader of the bearers		1	3
Ale comenly to them		1	0
Costome at 1^s 4^d p[ai]d per waye is		13	4
fees in all almost		10	0
Fraight at 1^d per bush. or 1^s per barrel	5	0	0
Fees at Dublin		6	8
Gabaredg[69] upp to the key		10	0

[67] I.e. levelled off.
[68] Bandle, an Irish measure, 2 feet in length.
[69] I.e. lighterage.

Primedge to the mariners about		2	6
Water baliffs fees		10	0
Maister porters for mesuring and others to help		5	0

300 bushells of white salt makeing upp at Dublin			
100 barrells	38	7	3

100 barrels at 2 shakes to a barrell at 8^l 10^s per skore	42	10	0
ys but if none of the salt be under one month ould before			
it be shipped it will yeald 5 barrels yf not more	2	10	0
Yf 2 monthes ould it will yeald 5 barrels more alsoe	2	10	0
	47	10	0

Yf salt can be made cheapp then more proffitt; yf dearer, lesse, or if yt would not wast soe much for I accounpt 48 gallons at Whitehaven but to hould out 32 gallons.

Whitehaven

	l	s	d				
100 Ton of coles put abord at							
2^s 4^d per ton	11	13	4				
Costome of the third entred at				42^l 14^s 0^d	they stand		
4^d per ton		11	0		unto		
Fees		6	8	sould for	49^l	0	0
Fraight at 5^s per tonn	28	0	0	profit	6	6	0
Costome and fees at Dublin		18	0				
Cabaredge at 6^d at Dublin ton,							
make out 70 ton	1	15	0				
Water baliffs and porter fees	2	10	0				
Sould 70 ton at 14^s per ton							
amounteth unto	49	0	0				

10.   My partner Rowland Jackson took upp in the north 100^l and chardged it by bill of exchange uppon you. He brought it hither and gave it me and I shall use it for Mr Batty's and the rest $\frac{3}{4}$ and therefore I have writt to Mr Batty to pay it if you have not, or if you have to repay it unto you, which speak to him of it.

11.   I sent him a particular of the wheat which you may see with him.

12.   I hear this daye our shipp is at Waterford.

13.   My partner Rowland is hear and with the first wind will goe for Bristol, whence he will retorne the first 100^l which I chardged on you at London.

14.   His sonne George is abord the slaughter barke which meteth him at
        Bristol if she cannot conveniently call of him hear before he be gone.
15.   The bagg of hopps I spoke of Bamber took at 7^l 10^s per cent.
16.   I have sould nothing more since I last wrote unto you and therefore
        expecte not a retorne of any money from me till I sell some cloth for
        what my partner sould is all at days, viz May next and March next.
        Nothing els is there which I can now advice you soe I rest,   *Page 39*

Your loveing cossen,
Chr. Lowther

Sent per the conveiance of Mr Batty his letter of advice.

In Dublin $\frac{11}{10}$ December 1632

To Mr John Batty, merchant in London
Worthye Sir,
    My last unto you was of the 4th instant by the way of Bristol inclosed
in one to my uncle Robert, wherein I gave you notice that I should shortly
chardge you with some money, which I now doe and it is 200^l for 200^l I
received hear of Mr Arthur Champion, for in truth under one and half per
cent I could procure none and soe I allowe him in the receipt of this, and
longer could not put of[f] the corne maisters. At lesser rates I have not
heard anye money in towene procured but duble, I ame sure, haith bene by
dyvers given, for the like scarsity of money haith not bene hear by report
this seaven yeares. My partner casually in the north haith taken upp 100^l
by exchainge uppon my uncle and haith given his bills for it, and if the
bills be unpaid by my uncle or these come, I desire you that you will pay
that 100^l, and if he have paid it that you will repay it him, for it cost
nothing the procuring it. And I have hear received it of my partner and
intend it shall serve in payment towards your $\frac{3}{4}$ parts which I praye you lett
me knowe of for hithertowards indeed I never see one word from you but
what onely my uncle Robert writeth himself. I send you a particuler of the
wheat I have bought. I hear the shipp is at Waterford, and with the next
sotherly wind I expecte her. I have not yet received forth Mr Standley his
money (the 50^l) soe I yet chardg it not on you. For all other things I
referr you to my uncle to whom I alwais write at lardg. I perceave by my
uncle you thought my first was something breefe but in truth I was
sodainlye taken then that I could not mend it. In aniething hear wherein
you would desire to be advised from tyme to tyme let me know it and I will
willingly doe it, and ever rest as I ame, for the trust and confidence you
repose in me,

Your thanckfull and bounden frend and servant,
Chr. Lowther

Laus deo adj[uvante] 11th December 1632 in Dublin

[Enclosure:]

To Mr John Batty merchant

Att seaven dayes after sight heareof paye this my first bill of exchange, my second or third not being paid, unto Mr Jeames Angell the some of Two Hundereth pounds sterling and is for soe much received hear of Mr Arthur Champion at one and a half per cent at the daye make good payment and put it to accoumpte as per advice.

Post script added to Mr Batty his letter

This day since I writt the former one Mr Cullom ys pleased to lett me have 110*l* at 15 dayes sight for which I shall pay nothinge for exchange. I thought good to give you notice of yt.

[Enclosed accounts:]

11th December 1632

A particuler of wheat bought as it cost the first penny betwene Michaelmasse last and the 11th instant, sent enclosed to Mr Batty in his letter of advice next before:

	l	*s*	*d*
Ould wheat			
402 barrels of Roger Gernon	276	7	0
110 barrels of Richard Balle	74	14	2
180 barrels of John Goughe	126	10	0
692 barrells of ould wheat first penny	477	11	2
New wheat unkilnedryed			
In the market: 63 : barrells	40	17	6
Of Mr Danyell Lynegan : 50 barrells	30	0	0
113 barrells	70	17	6
New wheat kilne dryed			
100 barrells of kilne dryed wheat was the 113 barrels above written unkilnedryed	000	00	00
440 barrels of Richard Balle kilne dryed by him and soe barganed	304	0	0
540 kilne dryed			
1,232 barrells ould and new amounteth unto in all	852	8	8

Besides garnering, porteredge and other petty chardges.

· The candles I have not bought yet but in one weeke I can have them all.

Sent enclosed in Mr Batty his letter of advise as on the other side.

In Dublin 11th December 1632

To Mr John Batty, merchant in London

Worthye Sir,   *Page 41*

This day I have formerlye writt unto you, and my Uncle Robert, to be sent with bills of exchange unto you by Mr Arthur Champion of 200 ^{l} I received of him for which I gave him one and a half per cent; more then in my former and what I write unto my Uncle Robert I have not now to write unto you saveing of the 110 ^{l} I since received of Mr Phillip Culum which I thought good not to lett passe. I have given him my bills of exchange for yt and chardged it on you. I send you lykewise a breefe of all the money I have and shall have to be chardged uppon you for the $\frac{3}{4}$ts, makeinge in all 725 ^{l} as per the note inclosed. Yf I need more I shall take care of it. Thus feareing further to troble you I rest as you shall alwaise fynd mee as carefull for you as for myself.

Christ. Lowther

[Enclosure: a bill on Batty in favour of Richard Darley or Tempest Milner for £110 for the same received of Phillip Culme by Christopher Lowther, to be paid at 15 days sight.]

[Enclosure 2:]

A note of what moneys I have chardged on you Mr Batty untill the 11th of December 1632.

165 pounds I had of Mr Edward Barry
100 pounds of Mr Arthur Champion
200 [pounds] more of him.
110 pounds of Mr Phillip Culme now
———
575 already charged
 50 pounds of Mr John Standley yet to chardg.
100 pounds chardged on my Uncle Robert Lowther by my partner Row. Jackson which I expecte you will likewise pay.
———
725 pounds in all for Mr John Batty and his partners of the $\frac{3}{4}$s to pay.

In Dublin the 17th December 1632   *Page 42*

To Mr John Batty, merchant in London

Mr Batty,

My last unto you was of $\frac{11}{10}$ since which the *Lemon* is arived and thancks be to God in savety upon the 13th instant; the ship I formerlie gave you notice of which then was in goeing for the Canaryes, the winds being contrary, ys not yet gone. I was abord them and Ir see they all lade in baggs; then baggs noe way found better, first in that the canvas will be good money there, after it haith bene used it will for the same occasions fitt againe, and therefore I have thought fitt to gett what baggs I can possible; they will stand to 1^s 6^d and 1^s 8^d per bag or thereabouts, which will require some money, therefore at this tyme being entreated for the exchainging of 73^l 7^s 4^d over by Robert Adney, my Lord Deputy's man, I thought it not fitt to suffer slipp any opportunitye but to take it, soe that at 8 daies sight I have chardged it uppon you. The fraight that was taken in at London of other men's goods haith and doth yet hinder us from putting anything abord soe that till Thursday or Fryday next we shall not be able to get her loadeing and Christmas hollidayes will stay us the longer for otherwise now in 6 dayes I knowe I should have laden all for the wheat and 50^l worth in candles is reddie for her, soe haveing not els and being sodainlie hastened by Robert Adney, I rest, and in my next which God willing shall be tomorrow, I will write further unto you.

Your loveing frend,
Chr. Lowther

Per Robert Adney, his conveyance.

[Enclosure: a bill on Batty for 73 7^s 4^d in favour of Henry Dawson for the like value received of Robert Adney by C. Lowther on 17th December 1632, payable at eight days sight.]

December the $\frac{18th}{10}$ in Dublin 1632

To my Uncle Robert Lowther

1. Uncle, my last unto you was of the 10th December instant of which I send you a copie hear inclosed, since which:

2. I have received yours by the *Lemon* from Waterford, the shipp then beinge there, with a certificat and a letter to Mr William Hall[70], of which I send you a copie inclosed, the factorye alsoe and bill of ladeinge, and one other letter to Mr Hall sealed upp.

3. I cannot stand to touch the particulers of your letters at this tyme, but onelye that I shall endeavour to followe what you directe, and nowe breefe unto you how things are hear.

4. My partner Rowland is not yet fitted with a passedge for Bristol, the wind not yet servinge, and by reason thereof we doe not expecte for [the] *George* from our fishinge, [or] the *Rainbowe* from Knockfergus, [n]or doth [the] *Consull* of London which goeth for Burre and Scoote [Scott?] for the Canaries being reddie now yet set forthe...[71]

5. The *Lemon* arived hear thancks be to God in savety the 13 instant but yet is not clear of the fraighte she tooke in at London, the weather being tempestuous that the gabers[72] cannot unload her and the hollidayes now being at hand it will hinder us very much; otherwise in six dayes I know wee should have loaden hir.

Page 43

[70] Merchant in the Canary Islands.
[71] Paragraph unfinished and muddled.
[72] Lighters.

6.   I ame advised to kilne dry even our ould and soe doe I most of yt, and to load all in baggs, but being not hear soe many possibly to be gott on a sodaine, I cannot load it all in the forme, but what I can gett baggs for I will, for now all strive to load that way, and the other shipp now given that it is to goe, is soe loaden which I purposly went to see.

7.   The baggs will require some money soe I have chardged $73^l 7^s 4^d$ on Mr Batty which I received of Robert Adney at 8 dayes sight, which if this letter come unto you before his bills accquaint him.

8.   My partner is reddie for Bristol the first wind.

9.   Since I have sould the stainell at 12^s per yard but you writt it cont. 36 yards and my partner see it measured and it held but out 32 yards $\frac{1}{2}$, neither was it marked uppon the seale more.

10.   Hill retorned a black crowne rash because of the deceaptefulnes of it proving not anything near like the showes.

11.   As I formerlie writt unto you concerning Mr Bamber's comeing in unto us I yet hould the same best, and instead of putting in the surplus of 70 quarters for ourselves, because I thinck we have alreadie in enough and that monyes yet riseth not, for that cloth and stuffes, that we suffer him to put in 10 tons or something under fraight; he will pay as wee doe and retorne it in wines as wee. And he is content to artikle with me that he with me and I with him in all voyages wee please to share in what parte wee please; and in my absence he, and in his, I, to be factors for each of other at one half per cent, and in all things to advice togeather, and assist each other.

12.   And what Mr Bamber now ladeth shall not be of anything that wee lade, but in sundry other comodityes, a litle of each to see the trade, to which wee shall be privie and I doubt not but it will give us a great light into the trade for those parts.

13.   50 pounds worth of candles I have reddie, besides the wheat, and if you had given the shipp directions [that] yf they had touched at Waterford or Wexford to have taken in some pipe staves it had not bene amisse for as at this tyme it fell out they might well have done it, and comenly all shipping from London touch there, soe against another tyme take notice of yt.

14.   For John Barton I dar not adventure to take him without my father's privity, besides I perceave noe affable nature in him, but I verilye thinck as you were so should I be ever trobled with him.

15.   Your last letters you write soe loveinglye as I take them very kindly, in which straine if you hould you shall never hear but as loveingly from mee and ever bynd mee as I desire to bee,

Your loveing and truely Reyall cossen,

Ch. Lowther

Per Mr Rowland Jackson

In Dublin the $\frac{18}{10}$ 1632

To my loveing father,
Kynd Father,

1. My last unto you was of the $\frac{17}{9}$ Nov[ber] by the way of Whitehaven since which my partner Row. Jackson is come hither unto mee and haith bene hear this 10 dayes, the wind contrarying him, but ther is shipping reddie for Bristol in which he intendeth to goe in tomorrow if the wind hould.

2. He and I have bene talkinge togeather concerning his sonne who is with a shipp that carrieth our nor[thern] slaughter for Bristol, and will meet his father there. The boy his nature I like well of, and had rather entertaine him then Mr Marris his cossen, for I ame affraid least Mr Marris should be curious to please the disposinge of his cossen; and his cossen may be thinck much to be comanded as an apprentice ought, and especially in this callinge—unlesse his nature be wholye bent that way which whether it be soe or noe I know not. And I would be sorry to incur any blow especially by great ones. Whereas if I have Geo. Jackson I know—if I be not deceaved, as I thinck I ame not—will be comanded and willinglye apply himself as he ought unto this callinge, and I hope will activelye stir himself therein, and my partnr is willing that he be with me, which nonetheless till I knowe your mind I will not meddle in, but as you are pleased concerning the same I ame and shal be ever willinge unto.

3. As concerning the salt and cole I perceave both my partners are willing to be sharers in it, but I see not what certaine end can be therein till the pattent either proceed or faile, and that the end of it be known if it doe fall of[f], or that it be noe hindrance any way unto us, and that onely of ourselves wee proceed. Yet this partnership with Mr Marris wil be troblesome unto the partnership with Ro. Jackson and me and my uncle, for I being hear shall not be able to manage all the accompts in the same and that busines there; but as you agree with my uncle and partner Rowland Jackson, I ame pleased, and I thinck either must wee three take all the salt that is made at a certaine rate and the cole wee shipp, or wee three must be one half and Mr Marris and Mr Radcliffe the other half, or that in all things some new agreement be studied, for it is not thought fitt that Mr Marris and Mr Radcliffe shall put in a great stock, and they onely controwell the accoumpts and expecte and receave all the proffitts, when it falleth, and wee to bee ther factors and have noe allowance; and if for what stock they putt in they allow us a competent factoredge it will not seeme so disconsonant altogeather to reason.

4. The ship from London, the *Lemon*, aryved in savety the 13th of this instant; some fraight of the Lord Deputy's and other merchants hear she took in at London which yet she haith not unloaden by reason of

the tempesteous winds that they cannot be brought upp. This shipp is of a burthen 140 tons maned with a master, 19 men and a boye, ten pees of ordenanse and four murtherars; bound Oratava in Teneriffe, one of the Canary Iles. Her fraight to and againe for London 4^l 10^s per ton. *Page 45* To stay hear 30 dayes—if not loden soner—after hir anchoredge hear, and in the Canaryes 50 dayes. Yf longer at either place then to pay 3^l per day. demoradge; in accounte of ⅜ths viz: James Man ⅛, Robert Holmes ⅜ths, Chr. Lowther ⅜, Francis Sherington ⅛ and Edmond Bostock ⅜ths; the whole gargaston[73] consigned to Mr Wm. Hall at Oratava in Tenneriffe, from London, 11 roules of beeswaxe weiing net 56 cwt 0 qtrs 20 lbs, cost 7^l per cwt, more from London put there abord alsoe for the Canaryes rice weying nett 15 cwt 1 qtr 20 lbs at 30^s per cwt in toto, the wax and rice first peny 620 pounds; wheat there wil be 1,200 barrels at 14^s per barrel one with another, 840 pounds; candles 50^l worth at 3^s 6^d per dozen, cotton weeck, first peny; her gargason about 1,500^l, with costomes, baggs, and other chardges about 150^l which maketh up 1,650^l pounds which is as neer as I can compute for.

5.   For the dischardge of the which: at London paid for the waxe and rice 620^l; that I have received by exchainge on Mr Batty towards ¾ths of the wheat 798^l 7^s 4^d; chardged uppon my Uncle Robert towards our ¼ part hear 75^l; that I have disbursed for our prop[ortion] and have reddie 194^l 8^s 0^d, in toto 1,687^l 15^s 4^d, soe I hope I shall have money oweing to dischardge all and clear away this gargason.

6.   My partner Rowland Jackson haith taken upp all the debts wee made in summer. He killed for Bristol the beefe which weyed net 66 cwt 3 qtrs 20 lbs; hydes weyed 59 c[wt] 1 qtr 23 lbs; tallowe weyed net 55 c[wt] 1 qtr 1 lb which at 1^d per pound—1^s abeyted in a beast—amounted unto 216^l 15^s 10^d, more in rended tallow 8^l 12^s 9^d; hydes more 5^s 6^d; 300 barrell staves 10^s 1^d; rendering of tallow 1^l 11^s 4^d; custom 14^l 0^s 8^d; salting and packing 2^l; loadeing, selleredge, etc, with fraight 17^l 2^s 2^d; salt 28^l 8^s; in toto amounteth unto 289^l 6^s 4^d.

7.   All the Yorkshire goods by my partner in the north and me hear ar sould of[f]. I have sould hear likewise 3 bags of hopps and in all sould by mee of the Yorkshire cloth, coles, salt, hopps and London wares about 200^l pounds worth of which all reddie money but 12^l per bill at Candlemasse of one very sufficient man; my partner haith sould to a day, viz: 20th March next and 1st May 160^l seaven shillings and reddie money besides 4^l 16^s 6^d, in toto sould in all about 365^l 3^s 6^d.

Your loveing sonne,
Ch. Lowther

---

[73] [*Sic*] gargazon or cargo.

                                          Tenth of January 1632/3, Dublin
To Mr William Hall, merchant in the Canaryes,
Worthy Sir,

   Though unacquainted yet by this present imployment and my owne interest therein I am invited to give you knowledge how I have accomplished that which, by my hearein interested parties, as by this ther inclosed letter you may perceave, was reposed unto me, which I have accordeinge to their desires shipped in the *Lemon* hear of London 600 quarters of the best wheat this kingdome affords and 31 c[wt] 3 qtrs 3 st. ½ weyght net of candles which the invoice will shew unto you. There is alsoe 11 roules of English waxe and 40 baggs of rice aboard as by an invoice inclosed from London you see. For the wheat I provided hear there is of it 358 baggs of the growth of the year 1631 which I had 3 months garnered before shipped. It is fuller of pease then the new wheat of this year but our bakers hear fynd it doe make whiter bread and will not be heavie as kilne dryed wheat wil be in bread; it cost as deare undryed as new wheat kilne-dryed did; if it prove ther as hear it was shipped swete and sound though the blacks may seeme to hinder it yet I doubt not but beinge once tryed it will be the best vent of all. The rest of the corne is new excepte some litle, but it is all kilne dryed and of yt is bagged up 100 baggs, which I did purposely to see the difference of the bagged and bulke corne. I ame advised besides that the baggs will yeald some proffitt besides that they cost hear, wherefore I desire you to make present sale of them as well as of any other goods, and for the sale of all, both of the wax, wheat, rice and candles, wee desire alsoe may bee with what convenient haist that may be. For her reladeing I referr you to my partner's letter inclosed and for what els concerning this gargason. Yet I ame further to desire you to tak notice of 20 quarters of especiall choise wheat more, which is bagged upp in 45 baggs under the mark in the margent,[74] and the proceeds to invest, as the wheat is of the best, soe in the best wine, or suger, if to be had, and that you hould it better, and to let the proceed of it be under this same mark in the margent. I send you hearwith 2 certificatts the one from London, the other [from] hence, 3 bills of ladeing, 3 invoyses and 2 letters from London and withall I desire your especiall care in this consigment as I doubt not of it, hearinge of each soe good a report of you, and if I may obtaine that curtesie from you as to lett me know which of our Irish comodityes and in what season they bear the best rate and ar requested, and what is ther comon rate: as pipe staves, wheat, and other grain, butter, cheese, beefe tonge, hids, porke, bacon, tallow, herrings, pilchards, salmon, Yorkshire dozens, stuffes or anything els, and I shall not onlye esteme of it a speciall kyndnesse but yf I perceave that good may be done by a continuall trade here unto you I shall be very glade to give you dayly[75] further imployment. I am furthermore to desire

---

[74] A monogram of C.L.
[75] Copying error for "duly"?

you in the behalf of a youth which cometh alonge in the *Lemon* called John Barton, servant formerly to my uncle Robert Lowther in London, Hamburg merchant, for to place him with some merchant there, if anyone ther have occasion of imployment for him in his service. His abilityes may yourself examine. He haith bene bred up a litle with my uncle and the boyes desire is to travail abroad for his information which my uncle was pleased to allowe him his desire but yf with conveniency you cannot place him then may he retorne againe for London. Thus questioning noe want of care to further these affaires I comitt you to the all pourful keep of us all and rest as I desire to be,

Your faithful frend,
Chr. Lowther

Sent per the *Lemon* of London, Mr John Tanner.

In Dublin the 12th January 1632/3

To William Hall, merchant in the Canaryes
Mr William Hall,

Besides what this day I have formerly writt you may be pleased to take notice that being advised from London to put in hear besids 600 quarters of wheat and the candles aboard the *Lemon* to load 70 quarters of wheat more yet as per my other letter you may perceave, I have but in lewe of 70 put onely abord 20 quarters and instead of the rest I ame willing at the request of my especiall frend Mr John Bamber to allow unto him a coplement of eight tonnes hear in this ship, which with his man goeth alonge, whom I desire you to direct and assist in the sale, and in what els you may thinck convenient for him concerning his master's good. And your factoredge with many thancks he will willingly allowe you; and I ame further to give you notice that as he haith hear a coplement of 8 tons aboard soe ame I agreed with him that he shall have six tons at least in her retorne back for London, and yf with convenience yt may bee that he may have in the shipp fraight for the whole proceed of what he haith hence shipped; and for fraight he payeth as owed by charter party at London. I pray you further to receive three pounds fivetene shillings sterlinge of Mr Bennet for fraight of 15 barrels from hence and put yt to accoumpte. Soe haveing not els I rest, to troble you further, and remaine,

Your loveing frend,
Christopher Lowther

Per the *Lemon* of London.

Dublin the 28th January 1632/3

To my uncle Robert Lowther, merchant in London   *Page 49*
Loveing Uncle,

My last unto you was of the $\frac{18}{10}$ per my partner Rowland Jackson, since which I have received yours of the 7th December, from Mr Radcliffe enclosed in one of my father's from York, whereby I perceave you have received dyvers of my letters and with some of them seame to be displeased for which end I never writt them, neither will I ever voluntarily and knoweingly give you anye occasion of offence but sure I ame I have hithertowards rather labored both to please you and all men els but to answer your letter I first saye it is trew that Champion, Standley and Barry, when I first delivered unto them the letters of creddit, they did not onely say that they would pay mee that money which they were required to doe, but yf I should need more, and that they had yt, that I should comand yt as sone as anyeone; and for Champion he lett me have 200^l at one and half per cent uppon exch[ange], when not long before he had of others 2$\frac{1}{2}$ per cent paid him; but for Barry more then the 165^l which I first had of him, he had it not to help mee with, his debts comeing not in as he expected—otherwise he would. For Standley money was soe scarce with him that of the 50^l I should have had of him I gott but att many several payments but to 45^l, and in the end when I could not gett the 50^l out in tyme, haveing finished the gargason I have paid him the 45^l I had of him, soe of him I have taken up nothing, as by the account you may perceave. For the letter of creddit you last sent to Mr Culme I made noe use of yet, being fitted before. Next whereas you write I both abuse you and myself, with other matters of discontent, I ame sorry for yt, neither will I stand to argue the matter at this tyme; and for that you entreat to part with us (though I knowe of noe occasion) yet for my owne part if my father soe please I am content, soe wee may end as wee beganne in love. And if you dislike partnershipp wee wil be onely as factors when occasion is, the one to the other; for any money I chardged uppon you yt could not otherwise be avoyded, for the goods you sent would yeald noe money unlesse yt had bene to losse, which I thought would have soulde in Michaelmasse tearme. Yf that you had writt how you would have had the goods you sent divided I should have delivered 250^l worth to Baddelow of them, but if I had delivered to Baddelow your 250^l worth I ame persuaded you would have repented yt for he deals very strainge with Robert Adney, and he denyed the receipt of my letters you

Page 50

wrote unto mee which you writt that he writt unto you the 10 September of the receipt of them in my absence; and yf I should but particulate onelye that miserye which Robert Adney suffered of him I ame sure you would not trust your goods with such a one. I have received the account of the waxe and rice, and the letters to Mr Hall and the maister yesterday from Mr Radcliffe which I have sent aboord to Mr Tanner and have seconded that letter to Mr Hall.

Enclosed I send you the account of the wheat and candles which to the best of my knowlege is just, but yf ther be anything wherein you thinck yt not right I pray you to rectify yt and to that end I send you a blanck sheete signed by mee wherein you may doe it, for whether the forme be to your mynd or noe I know not. By the account you perceave what money I receave for ther $\frac{1}{4}$ and that I have uppon the account chardged them to pay you (more then I chardged anyway) 29^l 5^s 7$\frac{1}{4}^d$, which I disbursed as per the account apeareth. Of our money the factoredg I have put in and garneredg at my house, which I will answer in our owne accoumpts. I send you alsoe the factory's bills of ladeing and copie of a bond of John Bamber taken for fraight which he or his servant which cometh from the Canaryes will dis-chardge. He haith laden in the *Lemon* 8 tons of lynnen cloth, beefe, pork, neets' tonges, barreled mutton, salted, and redd herrings, and sent his man along in the shipp. His goods are of valew about 200^l. I purposly enter-tained him because the proceed of them will prevent dead fraight back; and one Mr Bennett goeth in her passenger who caried my brother Will for Hamburg and carieth 15 barrells of pork, beef, bacon, etc, and is to pay for fraight thereof thither 3^l 15^s, and I took him in because the master and his mate have dyvers tymes falne out since they came from London and the master's mate would needs leave the shipp hear, which if he had done Bennett would have supplyed his place. John Barton is gone along in the shipp; yt may doe him good and I wrote with him as you desired. I have paid Mr Tanner four pounds for his dyet for four months past and to come and tenn pounds I lent the master to furnish the shipp with victuall which els had bene unprovided and I wonder the owners would lett him be soe ill furnished with money. I have taken his bills of exchange for the 10^l chardged uppon the owners of the shipp payable to you dew per the accoumpte maketh in all 43^l 5^s 7$\frac{1}{4}^d$ with 10^l, and 4^l for John Barton's dyet and 29^l 5^s 7$\frac{1}{4}^d$. The rest of the 75^l, which I chardged at 2 several tymes, are uppon you towards the furnishinge of our quarter part hear. I shall send you per exchange as soone as money cometh in, which I hope wil be shortly, for the 100^l which I chardged uppon you taken upp by my partner Jackson. I doubt not but it is, or shortly wil be at least, paid you by my partner at Bristol or from thence, and for the 149^l 3^s 6^d for our part of the waxe and the rice either shall my partner Rowland or I studdie to get it you with all possible haist that may be, though I thought you would have made your 250^l—500^l and soe Rowland his 250^l 500^l, for otherwise *Page 51* I shall have 1,000^l to your 500^l betwene you. Besids 1,200 barrels of wheat and 50 chests of candles in account of $\frac{8}{8}$ I have shipped 40 barrells of wheat for our owne account which you see is underwritten. I wonder uncle that my bills should anyof them be doubted of, though noe letter of advice had bene sent, you knoweing my hand well enough, and writing to me that all should be currantly paid, though uppon my salvation, as my man Richard Wibergh knoweth, I sent not any bill but I gave them alsoe a letter of advice with it, and yf be not[t] delivered or miscaried it is not my fault; and for my slowe-nesse in advice, I have writt as much to you, I thinck, as you to me. For other things I refer you to the Compainyes letter which you may seale and deliver yf you thinck fitt soe haveing not els, but onely desiring that noe crossing but love and frendshipp may continue amongst us as for my part it shall ever be by me, I rest.

Account in $\frac{3}{4}$ barrells of wheat shipped aboard the *Lemon* of London, viz: Robert Lowther $\frac{1}{4}$, Christopher Lowther $\frac{2}{4}$ and Rowland Jackson $\frac{1}{4}$ consigned to Mr William Hall in the Canaryes.

Brrlls. 44 bought of Danyell Lynegan at 12^s brrll. first peny

which dryed in unto 40 brlls amounteth first penny	26	8	0
For kilne drying at 4$\frac{1}{2}^d$ per barrell		15	0
Portadge to the Gaber at 1$\frac{1}{2}^d$ per barrell		5	0
Gabaredg to above		4	0
45 baggs at 19^d per bagg	3	11	3
Garnerege one month		5	0
	31	8	3

Your loveing nephew to his power,
Christo. Lowther

[Enclosed a bill of exchange for £10 in favour of Robert Lowther drawn by Capt. John Tanner of the *Lemon* for £10 paid him by C. L. in Dublin, addressed to Mr James Manne "and the rest of the owners of the ship *Lemon* of London". There follows:]

Enclosed hearin a copy of Mr Bamber's bond, 2 bills of ladeing, Mr Tanner's bill of exchange, a copie of the fraight received by Mr Tanner of goods brought from London, the companye's letter, and Mr John Batty's letter, the account and facto[re]ge of wheat and candles and Mr Tanner's letter of advice.

Sent per William Rodney to Whitehaven and so by the way of Lowther.

Page 47   In Dublin the 29th January 1632/3
To Mr Manne and Company,
Worthye Sirs,

I have received dyvers letters from my uncle Robert Lowther for the furnishinge forth of the ship *Lemon* with 600 quarters of wheat and some candles which I hope to all your contents I have done. For the proceeding hence you may be pleased to tak notice thereof as follows: upon the 13th of December last the shipp ancored in the Bay of Dublin, and the wether being then very tempestious she was not dischardged of the fraight of others which at London she tooke in, soe that the maister could not take in anye goods before Christmasse, though I at her first comeing was reddy for her loading. Yet did I not neglect anye tyme, as the maister and company can testifie, for althoughe both the holidayes and extreamity of weather hindered us yet within the tyme of her appointed staye hear I gott hir loaden, not being within the compasse of demurage, and yf they had but had their provisions of vicktualling reddie when they were loaden they might have gone with the ship *Consull* of London, which by reason of contrary winds staid loaden in the harbour with wheat some two months, and went but from hence but the 15th of January; but our baker was soe slow yt could not *Page 48* possibly. Yet uppon the same day sennet beinge the 22nd of January the *Lemon* departed the harbour, since which I hear she was put into Milford Haven on Thursday last and departed thence as I hear on Saterdaye with a fair wynd, which continued that day and Sundaye, soe I hope they are nowe in the Mayne. I put abord her for our accoumpt in $\frac{8}{8}$ 1,200 barrels of wheat old and new which was the best that could be gott for me, neither haith there [been] better or better ordered corne shipped hear as all that saw it will say. I shipped also 50 chists of candles for our said accoumpt in $\frac{8}{8}$ths, and I have taken in 8 tons fraight in her besides of one John Bamber, merchant hear; the copies of whose bonds, which I send you hearwith, will shew you the conditions whereuppon I took yt in. And there is alsoe 15 barrells of beefe, porke, etc, of one Mr Bennet, a passinger, for which he is to pay 3 pounds 15^s sterling fraight to the Canaryes which I have appointed to be paid to Mr William Hall. The accounts of all and factoredges, bills of ladeing and what els concernes her loadeing I send hearwith. The money imployed for your $\frac{3}{4}$ths of the loadeing I chardged uppon Mr John Batty as per comission from my uncle, Robert Lowther, saveinge 29^l 5^s $7\frac{1}{4}^d$ which I have disbursed of my own as per accounte, which I desire may be paid unto Mr Robert Lowther, my uncle. I have alsoe furnished Mr Tanner our maister with 10^l, which he wanted for provisions of the shipp, for which I have taken his bills of exchange payable by Mr James Manne and part-oweners of the ship *Lemon* unto Robert Lowther. I have sent Mr William Hall the letter you first writt unto him, the bill of ladeing and factorege of wax and rice, the certificat you sent and a latter sealed upp which came therewith unto me. I sent him also a factorage of the wheat and candles, a bill of ladeinge of them; a certificat from hear, and writt therewith myself unto him, and afterwards uppon the 20th of January I received another letter from you to Mr Hall contrary unto the order in your former letter which I seconded and have sent the same by Mr Tanner. And if in the furnishing of this gargazon I have answered your expectation to content-ment I shal be glade and it shall further encorage mee to doe unto you the like or any other service when your occasions shall call mee but yf other-wise I ame sorrye I have taken this paines and not to please being yf that I had bene soolye interested hearin I could not have done more. For what els you desire to know I referr you to my uncle's letter and Mr Batty's, to whom I alsoe writt. The same I have written by Chester, soe haveing not els I comit you to the protection of the Almighty and rest,

Your loveing frend,
Ch. Lowther

per the way of Whitehaven

Dublin 29th Jan 1632/3

To Mr Batty,

    Mr Batty, my last.unto you was the 11th December and 17 December, and in that of the 11th I sent you a particull[ar] of all the wheat I then had bargained but when the ship came and that I went to measure what with everyone I had bargained some fell short of there proportion I was to have, and I was glad to come to other tearmes with them as especially Gough and Gernon but now I thank God I have finished all and what wheat was bought, of whom, how ordered and the chardges, the candles bought and there chardges, what money I chardged on you and all things els, cleerly you may see by my account and factoryes sent to my uncle Robert. Standley's money I have not got neither will I chardg it uppon you, for when I could not gett the whole 50^l I rep[ai]d him that which I had received. My uncle writeth me that you had like to have protested my bills for want of letters of advice with them, which in truth was noe fault in mee for I sent letters with all my bills. Soe desiring your welfare in all your affaires, I rest

Your loveing frend,

Chr. Lowther

per Robert Lawrence

To my father:
1. That her peruse the former letters and sende them.
2.
[No further written and half the page left blank.]

Dublin the 14th Feb. 1631/2[76]

To William Atkinson,

    I received thy letters by Robert Lawrence and my father's. And I perceave you have gotten upp the one panne to make salt which ys hear now worth ten shillings per barrell. Therefore prepair a barke load against I come over or before yf thou canst and send yt. I have hear sent the 100 fetherslitt dales[77] for your covering the other panne, 1,000 ten peny nailes which cost 6^s 4^d and 1,000 six peny nailes which cost 4^s. The dales cost 7^l the 120 and 30^s slittinge. Other dales for to give my Ladie I cannot gett till about May that they come in.

    Take the coles of Tubman and sell them to the barks as thou writest. I cannot yet gett a panniple[78] for the salt panne, but yf I can gett one I will send yt or bringe yt over with me. Hear is noe such wood to be gotten as thou writest till it come from Wexford, therefore strive to gett some with you least none come in hear in tyme.

    The 40^s I have not yet imployed but I will in one thing or other send it

---

[76] From the context this date might be an error for 1632/3.
[77] I.e. timber split or slit into thin planks for roofing the salt pan.
[78] [*Sic*] meaning "panoply", i.e. covering?

thee by Lawrence Herbert or bring it in something with myself, for I entend if I can with Lawrence Herbert to come over but I cannot at present because of the *George* our barke is now with mee laden with herrings from the Iles of Scotland. I sent the London shipp away the 22nd of January last and I hope she is err this tyme neer the Canaryes. Writte me what herrings or any other comodity is worth with you, soe I rest they loveing master,

Chr. Lowther

Thou must pay for fraight of these dales 13^s 4^d.
Sent per Tubman's bark.

In Dublin the 20th Feb. 1632/3

To Sir John Lowther of Lowther
Kynd Father,

Since I last wrote unto you which was by Robert Lawrence his bark I have nothing hear to give you further intelligence of, for of the *Lemon*, the London shipp I hear not aniething but hopes she is safe on her way or at the Canaryes. The *George*, our owne bark, with some 7 or 8 saile of shipps bound for France, by contrary winds are staid in this harbour. This cytye expecting sale by some of them of ther herrings, the price of them are hear fallen from 27^s to 21^s per barrell and I fear will skace yeald that, soe wee have not yet sould anye, neither will yf the wind turne fair to carrie us for the south of England, for my partner Jackson advized us in January last that at Bristol they were worth 34^s per barrel. I fear a better market at Southampton but yf the wind hould any while contrarye we will sell hear, and yf soe I intend for Whitehaven, and fetch salt, which will make us I thinck best proffitt, and till I see what end wee are likly to take concerning our herrings, being about 220 odd barrells, I cannot well come home for England. For France we doe not intend, ther Lent beinge almost ended and if we sell hear there is noe comodity to carry from hence to gaine by. Soe Fr[ench] wines we are not lickly to bring anye this year. Soe haveing not els at this tyme but desiring your blessing and comitting you to God, I rest,

Your obedient sonne,
Christopher Lowther

Tubman's bark per Lancelot Herbert.

Dublin the 20 Feb. 1632/3   *Page 54*

To William Atkinson,
Wm. Atkinson,

I received a letter from Tubman wherein he complayneth against Lancelot Wilkinson for not supplying the number of the tonnes of coles he ought and thou knowest that the lyke complaint being before, I left yt to his discretion to keepe him in or out him at his pleasure, and though I wished Lancelot well yet neither was or ys it my mynd that either Wm. Tubman or I suffer by him, but yf we cannot mend yt by haveing him then as well Tubman promised to get us another to supplye his place. I especte, as thou formerlye writt, to have the colles from Tubman and pay him 2^d per ton lesse and thou to make sale of them to the bark. I am soe busied hear that I cannot yet come over but when I have determined of some course for our bark, the *George*, to take I will come over to you. The barkmen tould me of peas for thee but neither they nor I knew what thou ment. Wood of the size thou writt for ther is none of yt yet hear, nor dailes for my ladie. Provide or send some salt hither for yt ys now worth 9^s per barrell. Yf thou canst bargain with any bark for a year or two or lesse to bringe mee coles for Dublin at 6^s per tonn, Dublin measure, fraight or 5^s per ton, our ton measure, fraight, or tenn shillings Dublin measur per ton delivered me betwene [? omitted] and the bridge of Dublin for the cofes[79] and I to be at noe further chardg, but they themselves to pay for the coles at Whitehaven and bring and deliver me them hear at Dublin. Bargaine thou with them, for hear, unless the owners of the barkes themselves come, I cannot bargaine with them. Yf my father bee at Whitehaven advise thou with him of yt for hear coles are worth Oct., Nov., Dec., and Jan. 14^s per ton this measure at least, ordinary 16^s and often 20^s, soe haveing not els I rest,

Thyne as thou deservest,
Chr. Lowther

per Lancelot Herbert

In Dublin the 6th March 1632/3

To my father,
Kynd Father,
    My duty remembred, it may please you to tak notice that since my last of the 20th Feby. per Lancelot Herbert I received a letter from George Jackson from Milford of the 18th February. His father Rowland and he then being ther on ther way homeward. I perceave they have sould ther beefe, hide and tallow reasonable well but to noe extraordinary profit; ther beefe 26^s, 25^s, 24^s and some 23^s per barrell; hydes 7^l per skin; tallow at 33^s 6^d per hunde [cwt]; and that they have reloaden 12 tons of traine oyle at 17^l and 17^l 10^s per tonne; 40 barrells of beer at 10^s per barrell, 2 butts of sack at 12^l 10^s per but, one ton of St Christopher's salt and one ton of Spanish salt for us at Whitehaven to try at our salt pans, and some other small goods, what they are I know not. I ame resolved to sell our herringe hear. I have sould alreadie 95 barrels but I can gett but 20^s per barrell saveing three barrels which I got 21^s per barrel. I doubt I shall not soe sell them all but I doubt not er ten dayes be past I shall sell them all and then will I come for Whitehaven in our owne bark. I have yet 250^l worth of cloth unsould neither will it goe in haist. I have bargained with one man hear to tak of me 300 barrells of salt betweene [omitted] and October,

Page 55

79 [*Sic*] "corves" meant?

100 barrells at a tyme. I thinck for more with other men. Mr Radcliffe haith bene in the cuntry, and is but now come to towen. And this week I thinck to speak with him about the peer[80] and all things els. My great uncle Sir Lancelot and Sir Gerrard have both lately buried ther wifes, and all ther children, and soe remaine both sanse issue. I hear ther is a pirat in the channell and haith taken 3 barks of Wexford and Minyott. Soe haveing not els I rest desiring your blessinge, and rest with my prayers to God for you and us all,

Your obedient sonne,
Chr. Lowther

Sent per John Fletcher

In Dublin the 12th of November 1633   Page 77[81]

Mr George Lane [of Bristol]

My love and best respects salute you. You may pleas to remember that at Easter last gone a twelve month I beinge recomended to your acqaintance by Mr John Batty, merchant in London, I then desired yee to be my factor in your towne, for what trading I should have there, which my request at that tyme you intertained. In regard whereof at this tyme I make bould to consign unto you these severall smalle quantityes of goods as the invoice inclosed sheweth, for a tryall, which yf they doe well I intend to make further adventures of more valewe, and to drive a constant trade to your port and to troble you the oftner.

The last Christmas wee had a litle adventure of beefe, hids and tallow to your towen, and but onely that my partner Rowland Jackson was with yt himself, I had consigned yt to you. And I ame sorry he did not then acquant himself with you. Of these goods I pray you to make present sale to our best advantedge, as I doubt not of your care therein; and imploy the proceeds of them in plate iron for salt panns, about fyve tons, yf under fourteene pounds per tonn. It was offered me when I was with you for 13^l per tonn. Lett them be good tough iron without cracks; they are about a yard longe, half an inch thick and nyne inches broad, but they are better to be ⅓ of an inch thick and not thicker for my purpose, and about 10 or 11 inch broad, such as are used at Newcastle salt works. And lett the rest of the proceed be imployed in a tonn or tow of tarr yf under 18^s per barrell lardge band, in a tonn or two of hammers, hyrsts and andvills for iron forges, yf about ten pound per ton, but lett them be good ones though 20^s in a ton dearer; two batts of sheres sack if about 10^l per batt;[82] 2 cwt of lose suger yf about 17^d per lb and the rest in 10^s beer, currants, pruns, raisins and hops, which

---

[80] I.e. the Whitehaven pier built by the Lowthers in association with Sir George Radcliffe about this time.

[81] Remainder of the page is blank as is the following page. The next letter (almost certainly in Christopher Lowther's handwriting) begins on p. 57 and is dated 12 June 1639. I have re-arranged the letters chronologically.

[82] [Sic] butts?

you thinck will make best proffitt, or in anye of the former comodityes which are cheapest.

And retorne the same by port cocket for Whitehaven, Workington or Parton in Cumberland, Milnethorpe in Westmoreland by some Scotchmen as they goe home for Scotland or Wyer watermen, but yf you cannot conveniently light of fraight for those parts, then for Douglas in the Ile of Man, or Dublin hear. But yf you shipp it to anie other of the places aforesaid then Whitehaven yet must I afterwards carry yt thyther, soe you may enter yt by permitt or port cocket, for at Whitehaven I wil be myself to receave yt. With the first wind I goe yet leave my servants hear at Dublin. Yet yf yt come to Dublin my servants wil be there alwaise to receive yt, and what way soever you shipp yt give notice of it I pray you to Dublin to my servants there at my house uppon the Wood Key as lykewise to Kendal in Westmoreland in England to be left at Mr Rowland Dawson's to be conveied to Lowther. For your factoredg I pray you satisfie yourself.

Page 78

I have another gargason of beefe tallow which I intend to send unto you from Knockfergus which yf yt come before you returne the proceeds of these goods, you may returne yt in the ship that I hope shall bring you the other gargason. Write me I pray you how comodityes rule with you, especially our Irish, and their season, and how you thinck herring will sell with you this year. I have thre barks fourth at the Ilands fishing, and yt may be will send one to you, soe rests.

Your loveing frend in the like to be comanded,

Chr. Lowther

Corne hear is prohibited to be exported for fear of dearth, yet ther ys noe cause being but about 12^s per barrell.

Page 92

Whitehaven the 11th August 1634

Right Honorable,[83]

I received your lordship's letter of the 24th July to my father and since I received it I have nott spoake with my father, yett I thought good to lett you know thatt heere is none that will by anie meanes meddle with the taking of your saltpanns save my cosen Wibergh who telleth mee hee would give you 40^l per annum, all rents discharged, for 7 years for your lease & Will Hunter saith hee offred 60^l per annum for 7 yeares. I know nott who will bee his securitie he ofred two & I heare say they refused and Tho. Hambletoun hee offred 20^l per annum during your lease, as Will Hunter telleth mee, and these are all; my cozin Wibergh hath beene infinittly displeased and is, thatt I did nott suffer him to enter to the pannes as forfitted for non-payment of rent as they had beene if I had nott concluded

---

[83] Probably Thomas Roper, Viscount Baltinglasse, obit 1637, member of the Irish Privy Council. The letter is not in Lowther's handwriting, and some confused passages may be due to copying errors.

with Will Hunter when I did; for the overplus of the coales I reserve them for to serve my owne panns, etc, haveing soe settled my business and for the 8^l I give you for them per annum for which this yeere I shall abaite your lordship soe much in the rents arreare to us by you, and indeede I wonder much, my lord, that the three rents arreare, before this quarter that Will. Hunter came and thatt I wrought the pans for your lordshipp, thatt you did neither send over to us nor pay it to my man at Dublin which I desire you will now bee pleased to doe ore els my cozen Wibergh will outt your lordship for non payment, and for this quarter thatt I had them the sault thatt they have made I have freighted over to my man Mr Richard Wibergh at Dublin to sell; and when itt is sould whatt is made cleare of itt, if more then this quarter's rent, I shall bee answerable to your lordship for itt, and if your lordship will send anie of your servants to assist him in the saile of the sault hee may take notis how itt is sould butt the monie my man must receive. And to lie outt soe much monie for your lordship's businesse and to take the care thatt I have donne, none would doe itt and I assure your lordshipp I am wearie of itt and I cannott afford outt of my stock to doe itt, wherefore I desire thatt you will bee pleased to take some other course with them.

And for my assistance you shall ever command but to have the soale care itt diverteth mee from my owne businesse, and give mee leave to tell your lordship thatt Mr Williamsonn that had the hole coalmine and sault-panns and sould sault att 2^s 6^d per bushell would nott have p[ar]ted with them for the 100^l thatt hee gave Osburne for them if there had beene proffitt in them, he being an understanding, provident and careful man, neither wee to your lordship, yet would nott you beeleve mee att the first, and in good faith, since the last of August till the 24th of June last when I cast up my accompt I was a great deale loser by my owne panns in soe much as I would gladly lett my panns att reasoneable rents but I cannot, soe having nott els I rest,

Your lordship's humble servant,
Christopher Lowther

In Whitehaven the 20th of Januarie 1634/5   *Page 81*

Worthy Sir,[84]

My last to you was by our own barque in December wherein I write unto you the sume of the herring amongst us which as it was true according to my partener's accoumptes, then left with me, which I had drawne up in order, yet then he came to Whitehaven afterwards he had ought[85] in his charges at the returne of the shippes from the fishing and in his Swethish voyage with some other thinges as in his accoumpte appeareth, which being added the accompte standeth thus, viz:

---

[84] Sir George Radcliffe.
[85] Ought = "oweing", i.e. to be debited.

Losse by herring	88:	10:	11	Gaines by wine	46:	2:	4
By tarr computed	13:	0:	9	Losse to ballance	55:	9:	4
Totall	101:	11:	8	Totall	101:	11:	8
of which your losse being ½ it is					27:	14:	8

which to the best of my knowledge is true, yet neverthelesse if you please what moneyes I have had of yow if you shall allow it in part of the 600^l for the peere and take this 27^l 14^s 8^d losse in our owne handes rather then you beare it. The coles betweene Mr Wibergh and me are now quieted, my father haveing this last weeke bought them out of him, so now all is now in our owne handes, and I doubt not but that yow shall se[e] good profit for you and Mr Marris. The 20th of December last your 200^l in the salt panns was increased to 272^l 7^s 1¾^d and I thinke I have now better ordered them then ever heretofore haveing eaven in the wages, which were 31^s 2^d per weeke to six salterers, brought them to five and but 24^s per weeke besides payeing them by the number of weighes of salt that they make, which will make them labour harder, being a thinge not used in these partes and which I have beene this year about ere I could effect it and so our collyers they are nearer hand then we have had them formerly so I hope there will likewise be more profit in them, soe I feare nothing but vent, and all by reason of the rubidge not taken up yet within the peere; the peere itself being reasoneable secure and fit for greater shippeing. It hath alreadye cost above 420^l, neither do I thinke that if you se[e] it that you would imagine that over 600^l would have done that which is done, at wherefore I pray yow let me know whether I may expect any aide from you aboute the peere to finish it and for the salt and cole when we have it. For coles we must thinke of some way to git them carried by great shipping and stored up at Dublin against winter and for salt if we could have but 9^s per Bristol band barrell with two shakes we should profit well by them, which might be done I thinke if my lord would prohibitte the sayle of French salt, while English salt were to be had at 10^s per barrell at Dublin. And then if we could have 10^s per barrell we could give my lord 12^d upon everie barrell we should so sell, and then I doubt not but I could bargaine good quantities of salt in this countrie to sende over by which I thinke we might profitt alsoe. And this would bring a great increase to the King's Customes both heere in England and at Dublin; and it would enrich the English, lessen the vent of French salt and be a more certaine way for Ireland.

Soe haveing nothing more but desireing to heere from you I rest, being tomorrow bound for London to expect my Canarie adventure and take my freedome of the Merchant Adventurers' Companie, the King haveing lately renewed unto them and inlarged there Charter,

Your verie loveing friend and servante,

Christopher Lowther

[There are no further letters in the letter book for the period 1634 to 1638, the next letter chronologically being dated 7 April 1639. Some drafts or copies of letters, or rough notes of or for letters which help to bridge this gap were found in three of Sir Christopher's small notebooks, extracts from which are to be found in Parts II and III of this edition].

From my lorde Clifford's[86] secretary   *Page 88*
Mr Lowther,

My lord haith commaund from the Kinge to stay my Lord Deputy's shipp for defence of this coast til another be provided. And soe my lord hath sent a warrant for her stay accordingly, which you will receive herewith, and alsoe another letter to my Lord Deputye which his lord[ship] desires you to send away with the other by the first that goes, and that in the interim the shipp may be stayd and unladen againe.

And concerninge what yow writt about the Scotch goods and money, my lord hath notnor knowes of any order or commaund for it and therefore will not give any order for stay of anythinge, yett his lord[ship] thinks it not amisse if the shipp be stayd till the ordnance be landed and in safetye, and soe in great hast goeinge to church, I rest,

Your lovinge freind,
Ro. Robotham

Workington this 7th of Aprill 1639

Laus deo in Whitehaven the 8 Aprill 1639   *Page 87*

Right hono^{ble.},[87]

May it please you to take notice that the 6th instant I beinge with my Lord Clifford at Workington, and all of us rayzed out of our bedds with an alarum, that the citye of Carlisle was burnt and the Irish soldiers all slain by the Scotts,[88] insomuch that the beacons were lighted, and the contrye arose, which putt my lord and all men into such an amazement, that he had given me comaundment to rayse what strength about me as was possible for our defence at Whitehaven and to send for the traynd band of Lancashire to be readye at Lancaster, but God be praysed the alarum being false, and all safe, I sent after the alarum and stayd it, and the same day I received one of these letters inclosed from my lord wherein I doubt not but that he hath better certified yow of all, which makes me shorter. And yesterday I received another letter from him to your lordship and another to myselfe with a warrant to the captain or master of your lordship's shippe, supposinge that she had bene ungone from hence, yett I tould

---

[86] This superscription was in Christopher's hand. The letter in a clerk's hand. Henry Clifford, Fifth Earl of Cumberland, Lord Lieutenant of Northumberland, Cumberland and Westmorland until 31 August 1639. In April 1639 he was at Carlisle Castle in command of local levies. He was Wentworth's brother-in-law.

[87] No addressee but obviously to Lord Wentworth in Ireland.

[88] Clifford's local levies had been stiffened by some of Wentworth's Irish soldiers.

my Lord Clifford that both his Majesty's pinnace the *Confidence* and your honour's pinnace the *Phoenix* were gone, but it seemes multitude of busines caused his lordship to forgett and therefore I have likewise sent yow the warrant to the captain and his lord[ship's] letter to me that your honor may be better informed. I expedited this barque away of purpose for the speedye convayance of these letters. My Lord Clifford departed yesterday imediatelye after dinner towards Carlisle, and since this morninge came a warrant from my Lord Marshall to stay all Scotch shippinge till further order, which here I have done. My Lord Clifford and all the countrye are much affraid of this port of Whitehaven being the best landinge place for the enemie,[89] if they should come with any force by sea, wherefore I have bought two peeces of ordinance (2 sacres) of Captain Bartlett and his brother, and tenn musketts with furniture from Newcastle all at my owne chardge and I desire that your honour would be pleased to send me two peeces of ordinance more to these two I have, and I shall with thanks either pay for them, or when these troubles are quieted send them back againe; for I will presently make a fortification for them on the peere. And if your lordship will be soe pleased to send me them I doe intreat you that I may have some powder, shott and other materialls belonginge to them, and soe I humbly take leave and rest,

Your honor's most obliged and devoted servant,
Christopher Lowther

A Coppye of the warrant from the lord Clifford to the Capt. or Master of the lo. Deputyes shippe at Whitehaven, under his seale;

It is His Majesty's pleasure signified unto me by my Lord Marshall Generall of His Majesty's Armie that yow continue with your shippe here upon this Coast. And His Majesty hath caused Mr Secretarye Cooke to write to my lord Deputye soe much, and that he should send allsoe 2 or 3 shallopps for His Majesty's service upon this coast allsoe. Theese are therefore to require yow that accordinglye yow make your stay here on this side where you shall receive from time to time further orders for His Majesty's service as occasion requireth, and here of yow must not faile. Given at Workington this 7th Aprill 1639.

T. Clifforde.

Whitehaven the 17th May 1639

Loveinge Brother:[90]

I have received the inclosed touching Robert Bradley who I perceive by Robert Bradley's wife sonne is drowned and therefore his wife as it seemeth thinketh to be restored to the land which was surrendred by him. If it appeare that Robert Bradley's estate of it was but duringe his life or

[89] I.e. the Scots.
[90] Probably William Lowther.

inter marriage with his wife I doubt yow cann have it noe longer, if it be true that he be drowned; howsoever, since it now concernes yow and not me I would wish yow to meet the Referrees mentioned in this inclosed at the day appointed and gett Mr Midgley with yow, if yow hope to doe any good. I have noe papers nor writing touching Robert Bradley at all but yow have what I had, and therefore goe not unprepared and I pray yow lett not me suffer who was never but a nominall instrument in this matter. I have writt to them the inclosed which when yow have read yow may seale and send it then with what you thinke fitt to write yourselfe. Your wife was well at Meaburn[91] and all there on Tuesday last. I meane to see yow at Meaburne at Whitsontide.

Your lovinge brother,
Christopher Lowther

[Enclosure]

Whereas we have received a reference from the King's most excellent Majesty directed unto us Abraham Sunderland, Esquire, Richard Marsh, doctor of divinitye, Isaac Naylor and George Fayrbanck, gentleman or to any two of us for to call yow Christopher Lowther, gentleman, and Joseph Denton and all others whom it may concerne, tenants or undertenants, whom have the possession of the goods and lands of Margarett Bradley widdow and her children, and upon the examination of the premisses to mediate some conscionable end and agreement, as we shall thinke fitt accordinge unto equitye and good conscience or els to certifie in whose default the same is. These are therefore to give yow notice that we intend to sitt upon the said reference at Sunderland in the Towneshipp of North-owrum in the parish of Halifax upon the tenth day of June by nine of clock in the forenoone of the same day when and where we desire your personall appearance. Fayle yow not hereof or will answer the contrary. Geoven under our hands at Sunderland the 13th day of May and in the fifteenth yeare of our Majesty's raigne that now is 1639.

Richard Marsh   Abraham Sunderland

To our welbeloved freinds Chr. Lowther, gentleman, Joseph Denton.

Whitehaven the 12th of June 1639   Page 57

Honest Archie Myllan,

As I have ever found you to be an honest man, soe am I willinge to deale with yow before any other man. I have undertaken a partnership with Mr Christopher Sandys[92] of Maynewater,[93] Ironworker, toucheinge the worke

---

[91] Mauds Meaburn Manor, Westmorland, a Lowther property.

[92] Sandys is sometimes spelled Sands, or Sand's.

[93] Now Randalstown, but in seventeenth century called Mainwater or Ironworks, Co. Antrim, 17 miles NW of Belfast.

and I am to furnish iron myne yearlye and if yow please I am willinge to give yow the carryinge of it before another, for I perceive yow have 2 or 3 close barques which if yow follow bringinge of cattell the whole summer time yow may easilye carrye 200 tunne for me this summer and God willinge your barques shall at noe time neede to stay above 2 dayes here for takinge in their loadinge. Nay I hope in two tydes to loade any barque for my myne is at my ore steere fast by the harbour, and for your fraight I am to pay yow for this loadinge being six and twenty tunnes five shillings sixpence the tonne carriage to Four Myle Water[94] soe neare as your barque will fleet towards it. Yow see that I am likelye to be out a greate deale of money about this iron myne, soe that if yow be content to carrye it for me, yett I must condicion with yow not to pay yow till the latter end of sommer your fraights when yow leave off tradinge hither with carryinge cattle, unless yow will take iron of me d[elivere]d to yow at Four Mile Water at such rate as you and I cann agree of, and howsoever, I must intreat you to vent for me what iron yow can about yow, soe it be not within the Countye of Anthrum[95] and some iron I thinke to transport hither from thence, and I hope yow will use me kindlye for that, soe it may lye under the beasts' feete without hindringe anything, and since I am willinge to employ you wholye, I hope yow will thinke that 5^s 6^d per tunne will be sufficient for fraight, for 6^d in a tunne is a small abatement of your old rate to have a full imployment and an honest paymaster. I desire your answer herein by the first, that if yow like not my proposicions I may conclude with some other, soe rest your lovinge friend to his power,

                                                            Christopher Lowther

To Archie Myllan, Merchant at Dunnawhadie in Ireland[96]
[Immediately following this letter on page 57 is the following note:]

                                                    The 12th June 1639
I[97] writte likewise to Mr Chr. Sandys with George Hewetson for to ayde George in his entries and business about the iron woorekes and that I had discharged 3^l for him to Robert Copley, my cousin Pennington's man, which I wished him to repay to George to whom I alsoe writte that I had paid him more 10^l in his pursse.

Page 94   [c. June 1639]
Richard Powley,
    I expected ere this to have heard from the[e]. I hope that thy imployments are so urgent that thou hast not leisure once in a fortnight to write to

---

[94] Unidentified but on an inlet of the sea about 15 miles from Mainwater, see below p. 72.
[95] I.e. Antrim.
[96] Probably Donaghadie, Co. Down.
[97] Here the clerk's hand is replaced by Christopher's.

me to lett me know thy proceedings. I pray God direct thee in all they actions and give the[e] grace with diligence to performe the dutyes of thy callinge. I pray thee serve God and observe my directions, and thou shalt assuredly finde the comfort of it in thy conscience, which is not to be valued with any treasure. Leonard Ribton dep[ar]ted hence towards Wales on Thursday next after thou went hence. When thou hearest from him lett me know if thou hast had a good markett for thy salt and hast bought any commodities for the shopp. Thou may send them over by some of our neighbors. After thou went hence I concluded with Mr Chr. Sandys of Maynewater for a partnership in his ironworks, soe that I shall have need yett a while to pay moneys in the north to furnish my p[ar]te of my undertakings there. I have sent George Hewetson over with 26 tons of iron mine on a barque of Archie Millan's and given him 20^l with him to pay customes and carriage. Thou must provide for him 100^l soe shortly as thou canst to pay for chardge of 9 score tunns more that I shall send him this summer, and therfore what moneys that George Hewetson writeth to thee for, or doth chardge on thee by his note for that purpose, I pray thee see dischardged. I meane to write to Mr Roger Lindon, the collector of the customes at Knockfergus to furnish him with money, and that thou shalt repay him at Dublin whither he useth to retourne his customes yearly. I send thee the coppy of my articles by which thou may see my bargaine, and what I am bound to; take a coppie of it to keepe by thee and then write to George Hewetson into the north and send it him, havinge not els, I rest

Thy lovinge master,
Chr. Lowther

July 3rd

This letter should longe since have come to thee but the wind served not, and Will Nicholson did promise to call for a letter to thee before he went but did not, and since I received thy letter of the 18th June being all that I received from thee yett, and touching the sellinge of thy salte I hope it will mend now that there is a certaine peace concluded, but that I refer to thy discretion as thou forecasteth for the best of which write me. I send thee a certificate for Hen. Tubman's beasts landed here to cleare thy bond. I am fearfull of thy falling to drinck at Parkers, and though thy table cost 10^l per annum at a civill house where is noe drinck or wine sold I care not, which thou maist enquire after, as at Mr Newman's or such like. Be careful to further in old debts and new, and to sell what can be to Belter-bett[98] and Etley men or barter with them. I like not for barteringe for those wines which thou writest of, unlesse thou knowest where againe to sell them there, and that to good men. Mr Williamson promiseth me to satisfie the 4^l to me, soe you may acquaint them to whom thou sold that salt. We have

[98] Belturbet, Co. Cavan, market town 67 m. NW of Dublin.

received the rundlett of sack and barrell of tarre but noe candles, noe tobacco pipes, which was carelessly done by which I perceive thy unsufferable negligence, for we neither have nor can gett one candle for money. The boy encloseth a particular of what things he wanteth, of which fitt him with by the next, and slipp not time as thou hast done allreadye.

Page 95

9th July 1639

Since I have received of Edward Lancaster of Askham the sum of fower and thirtye pounds and eighteene shillings for James Taylor dwellinge at Maydowne in the Countye of Armagh which when he calleth to thee for soe much pay it to him and take his acquittance, for I have writt to him of the receipt of it here.

Portus Whitehaven

Know yee that Richard Powley for Chr. Lowther, merchant, hath here unloaden from the *Micheal* of Workington, Henry Simpson master, 24 cowes and steres granted by cockett dated at Dublin the 10th of this instant June as wittness our hands and seal of office, this 20th of June 1639.

| Lancelott Fletcher | Jo. Gurnell | Rowland Jackson |
| p. Customs | Collector et searcher | pr. Compt^r.99 |

Whitehaven the 9th July 1639

To James Taylor at Maydowne in Armagh in Ireland
James Taylor,

The 7th of this month Edward Lancaster did bringe over to me fower and thirty pounds, eighteene shillings which I have received of him, and have writt to Richard Powley this day to pay it to yow when you call for it of him, which upon sight of this my letter, and deliverye of it unto him, I require him hereby to dischardge honestly to yow, which I doubt not but that he will doe, and soe I rest,

Your lovinge freind,
Chr. Lowther

[p.s.]   Edward Lancaster kept back 2ˢ as I perceive by my man unknowne to me; he should not have done it if I had knowne, but if I can hereafter gett it you shall not want it.

Chr. Lowther

Sent by Thomas Dawson

Page 96

The 9th July 1639

Directions for Will. Atkinson goeinge for Belfast and Knockfergus and to George Hewetson

1. Enquire at Jo. Pennington's for George Hewetson.
2. To informe George to take out his bonds of imploym[ent] when he hath

---

99 Abbreviation for "Comptroller".

disbursed as much as the bonds is, and that from time to time as need requireth.

3. To go to or with G. H. to the ironworks and by the way to marke the length of the way and goodnes, and how or where the ure leaders live from the ironworks or Four Mile Water.

4. To speake with some of the principall ure leaders how carriage will be every month in the yeare both for price and plenty and the manner how.

5. Know what course is taken for sellaring of his iron at Four Mile Water or elswhere against conveniencye of shippinge.

6. Speak to Mr Roger Lindall to fitt George with money and tell him that Dick Powley shall repay it at Dublin, which I have directed Dick to doe to which end, if he desire my letter to him, I shall write to him.

7. To consider of all things at the ironworks how the waterweares and dams are in repair (and the houses) and what may yearly repaire them.

8. To examine how the calculation of Mr Sandys to me is, whether true or not.

9. To enquire well of Mr Sandys' condition, whether litigious or faire; and readye to further and not to quarrell.

10. View all the woods and consider them well both for last, and nearnes and goodnes.

11. To call in for my specialtyes of Mr Foster or Geo. Jackson and deliver them to Geo. Hewetson and give him information of all the debts and debtors and make him follow them earnestly.

12. To knowe what hearths are up and how much iron each hearth will make a weeke.

13. Know what drought or backwater hinders the ironworks, or is cost to us and at what tymes.

14. To know what yeelde the iron ure that George carried maketh.

15. If George have begun to make iron of my ure, and have made any, then to bringe it with yow what yow cann.

16. If that George have gotten sufficient ure thither and doe nott enter to make iron of it, but that I lose my time, then if the bargaine be not likely he refuse holdinge on:

17. To bring one coppye of Mr Sandys' his lease from Sir Henry O'Neill:

18. To enquire well of Mr Sandys' meanes and estate and power and ability to performe the articles on his parte.

19. To knowe whether washinge my ure in salte water doe hurte the ure or not.

20. To bringe over what iron that George hath readye made.

21. If that noe iron be brought to Four Mile Water send for as much with all hast to pay the Lancashire man his fraight out at 15^s per hundred, 20^s he shall have here.

22. If Mr Atkinson's barque chance to goe thither abouts, take what money of them they cann spare to fitt your turne.

23. Enquire how I may have tunne timber from thence to Four Mile Water or Knockfergus, or the like, as pannell.

These directions are for Leonard Ribton, 20th September '39

Page 96 ends

Chr. Lowther

Page 97

An answer of directions given me by my m[aster].

1. I did enquire for George Hewetson and Jo. Pennington[1] tould me that he did not know him, and then I did write for him to come over to speake with me, and then I went over to the Four Mile Water and got Mr Boyd to unload.
2. For bonds of imployment they will ask none, and we have gott the other in.
3. The way is very deepe in wett weather, and none cann be led in the winter time, and the leaders lives here and there, and the way is 15 miles long.
4. And I spoke with 10 of the leaders and there, is noe good to be done but in June and Julye for price and plentye.
5. For sellaringe I have agreed with Mr Boyd to finde a roome, and to carrye it aboord for 1ˢ per tunne, if we cann take noe better course.
5. Mr Lyndell will lett George have money if your worship will send your letter.
7. Things are in indifferent repaire but what will uphould them I doe not know.
8. And I heare that Mr Sandys is well conditioned, but I think that if he had not dealt with your worship there had bene a fault.
9. For Mr Sandys's relation is very neare the right.
10. I viewed all the woods, and there is wood enough, but they take of the nearest first.
11. George tould me that he had gott in all the specialtyes.
12. There was 3 harths up, and they will make 7 cwt ech hearth in the weeke, and they have made 9 cwt in the weeke and more.
13. For droughte I thinke it will doe some hurt in a dry summer, but backwater will doe little hurt, for they say that one day is the most in the greatest raine.
14. The iron ure doth yeeld out of 2 tonn and ½ one tunn of iron and good iron.
15. They have made out of your owne ure when I was there about 3 tonn.
16. They have gotten all they had of the first over, and some of that which went last.
18.[2] Mr Sandys hath some creditt but small meanes but I see in the wood good store of wood cutt, and some 4 coale pits, and the workemen tould me that there was 500 cords.

---

[1] Spelled here "Peniton".
[2] No answer required by question 17.

19. Wash ure in salt water doth noe hurt.
20. I have brought 3 tonn, it was all that there was ready, but there is more 3 tonne.
21. We have payed the wyremen in iron.
22. Wm. Atkinson barque came and they lent me 3^l.
23. Noe timber cann be brought to the Four Mile Water, but it lyeth dearer then in England.

20th January from Whitehaven 1639/40   *Page 58*

To Mr Andrew Lyndsay at Awkenskewth in Galloway in Scotland
Worthy Sir,

I received your letter of the 2nd of January instant and I humbly thanke yow that yow would be pleased to give me notice of this shipp's furniture which yow write of to me. I heard of the castinge away of the shipp before, but it is the humour of many not to meddle with anythinge of a lost shipp, as holding it unfortunate, but yett I doe not allwayes comply with their opinions in that espetially if the shipp be honestly come by and noe curse be upon her, wherefore I thought fitt to lett yow know that the bearer, my servaunt, who being fraighted hence for Drumfreyse³, shall come to see such furniture and geire of the shipp which yow write of, and if there be either masts, gunnes, anchors, ropes or sayles that may be fitt for me I am content to buy them, provided that the owners of them come to deliver them before William Atkinson, this bearer, depart from those parts with his barque and if it may be soe, then I have authorised him to bargaine for what he liketh for me, and accordinge as he agreeth for payment it shall by God's permission be punctually performed, and if the owners feare payment for their geare lett them send anyone along with them in the barque, and I shall pay for all before I receive anything, and soe I rest wishing to be able to doe yow the like favour wherein, God willinge, you shall not want what lyeth in the power of,

Your lovinge freind,
Chr. Lowther

Orders sent herewith by William Atkinson
1. Deliver this letter to Mr Lindsay and speake with him yourselfe.
2. If neither Mr Lindsey nor any nearby have order for sellinge the shipp geare gett Mr Lindsey to send imediately to the owners to lett them know that upon his letter to me I am pleased that thou buy such of the geare as thou thinkest convenient if thou may receive them before thou depart thence.
3. If thou comest to buy any of the ship furniture give not above 30^s per hundred[weight] for anchors, not above 16^s for gunnes and murderers, not above 30^s per hundred for such cables as are new, or noe worse and

³ I.e. Dumfries.

see them from end to end, and for masts and sayles as thou seest them worth.

4. If they hold them dearer then thus buy onely the anchors or what els is very good cheape.   Chr. Lowther

Page 58 ends

Page 59

Whitehaven 24th January 1639/40

To Mr Henry Pearson at Dunthwaite

Mr Pearson,

     I received your letter by your man, and thanke yow that yow would be pleased to remember my busines as you have directed me. I have caused your man to serve the subpaena on William Towerson and Robert Milholme; on the other two, viz: William Hodgson and Anthony Gosforth your brother James the[m] served the writt

1. formerly, and now I send you my bill against them ingrossed and signed which I pray you putt into the Court and bring me the copye of their answers, if they putt any in this tearme, but if they doe not, proceed against them to gett an injunction for possession which I thinke is the course.

2.   For Osborne if she proceed to renew her commission take care of it and if she take out a new commission I pray yow putt in commissioners for me, Gyles Moore and my cosen Mr John Senhouse of Seascayle; if she take any other course doe for me as you thinke may be for the best.

3.   I pray you call to Mr Jo. Wells, Judge Vernon's man, for my recqverye of Sockbridge etc which he promised should be under seale and finished this tearme. My brother William Lowther's factor will pay him all that is dew to him about it.

4.   Deliver my uncle Richard Lowther this letter and call for an answer when yow come away.

5.   I have paid your man eleaven shillings sixpence upon your letter. If it be not enough I shall give yow more in your next accompt, which I shall thankfully repay.

Page 59 contd.

Whitehaven 24th January 1639 [1640]

Lovinge Uncle,

     I received your letter of the 3rd July last in August after with a letter from my brother Sir John in which yow and he write to me to take your bargaine of Sandwith and Cowthertons[4] tithes off your hand, the which I answered my brother then, and wished him to lett yow know that I was so content to doe it, but whether my brother lett yow know as much I know not and therefore I thought good to lett yow know that I am content to take them, hoping that yow will helpe to establish me to the tithes or my money, and therefore if yow continue your purpose to lett me know by this bearer, and send your reckoninge downe what it is that yow doe demaund

4 Sandwith and Coulderton were closes of St Bees demesne.

(which I pray lett it be such as my cosen Wibergh cannot denye) and I shall pay it to yow at Whitsontide at the furthest with the use, soe expectinge your answer I rest, etc, your lovinge nephew,

Chr. Lowther

For Mr Richard Lowther, Esquire

*Page 59
ends*

[c. April 1640]

(Directions for John Wood goeinge for Dublin with a ladinge of salt and coales in Richard Richardson

*Page 100
begins*

1. Carry your two best suites of apparrell with the best of your shirts and bands.

2. If you be putt into the Isle of Man by the way and make any stay, if you can sell any salt for money, though but $\frac{1}{2}$ a dozen of barrells, be doeing to gett money, but forecast your busines and runne noe danger for not enteringe, but in all things ask councell of divers, and marke how they agree in opinion and follow the best.

3. But if it please God to bring yow safe to Dublin first enquire after Richard Powley, my servant, at John Parker's the gaberman or els-where, and if he be in towne, or be not farre absent, as maybe at Tredath, then find him out or send for him presently, and lett him know that yow have a loadinge of salt and coales to sell, which he must dispatch off and lett him and yow sell them for ready money though cheaper, or at time to currant honest, able and good paymasters, and then come yow back by the first shippinge, and leave things in order, and lett Richard Powley goe and take the chardge of the iron workes of George Hewetson and' carry some money whither as I did last direct him.

4. And if yow find Richard Powley at Dublin lett him show unto yow and make you acquainted with all the debtors and such as are our chapmen to sell salt to, and merchants to buy our commodities on, and all other wayes and things that he knoweth if needfull for yow to know, least perhaps I send you shortly thither againe.

5. But if soe be that Richard Powley be gone into the north of Ireland to George Hewetson then enquire whom he hath left his busines withall as his bookes and debts, and salt, if any be unsould, and do yow gett them if they be merchants to helpe yow to enter your goods in the custome house, and to helpe yow to sayle of them, and receive the bookes and spetialities from them, which keepe in like order as they have bene till yow have sold all.

6. But if Richard Powley be gone in to the north, and that he have left none in trust behind him then deliver this my letter to Mr John Bamber or in his absence to John Parker who I hope will helpe and further yow both to enter and sell of the salt and coales and to helpe yow to hire sellers for such of your salt as yow cannot sell of presently.

*Above all
things serve
God daily
and things
will prosper
with you.*

7. But if none of theese wayes happen right then must yow advise with your owner Richard Richardson and gett him to helpe and direct yow, or some of our contrymen if there be any. For your coales I suppose yow will gett ready money about 5^t, and sell of[f] as much salt at such poore rates as it will be to pay the owner out his freight which is ten pounds if all be safely dischardged at Dublin and sell likewise the rest goe soon as thou canst.

8. When thou hast sold all or p[ar]te so that thou hast money then buy for me for my shipp the best Frensh canvas for sayle cloath, about 300 yeards in which take good advise of seamen and merchants as alsoe 3 anchors, prime good ones one of 4^{cwt}. 0. 0., another of 3^c. 2^q. 0. and a third of 2^c. 2^q. 0. weight. I suppose they will be about 1–6–8 the hundred weight or it may be more or lesse for I know not certainly.

9. If Richard Powley be at Dublin lodge with him, or if he be not, yett enquire outt his lodgeinge and lye where he did last, unles it be a druncken expensive house, and then learne out a better and change the sooner.

10. Write back so soone as yow can possibly of your arrivall and voyage lest anything crosse yow soe that I may sooner advise yow back againe what to doe.

Page 101

Thy lovinge master as thou shalt shew thy care and honesty,

C. L.

Whitehaven 20th Aprill 1640

To his lovinge friends Mr John Bamber, merchant in Dublin, Daniel Hutchinson, chandler, John Parker, gaberman, or any of them,
My Lovinge friends,

I have lately directed my servant Richard Powley to goe for the north of Ireland not thinking to have had occasion soe shortly to have sent to Dublin and in regard the man I now send is younge and hath never bene abroad, I desire your helpe and furtherance to him, both in enteringe and selling his goods, and in reimploying the money, and yow shall not onely find me ready to acknowledge your kindness, but likewise to requite it to the utmost of my power, and in confidence that you will grant me my requests I rest, Your assured lovinge friend in the utmost of my power,

Christopher Lowther

Page 67 begins

[16 May 1640]

Coppy of a letter to Ewan Christian,[5] Esquire, Deemster in the Isle of Man. Worthy Sir,

I received your letter from your sonne Mr William Christian[6] of the 17th

---

[5] Ewan Christian of Ewanrigg, obit 1653, a Deemster, one of the Tynwald's two law givers and judges. He was the ancestor of Fletcher Christian of the *Bounty*.

[6] William Christian, third son of Ewan, illegally executed 1662 for his part in surrendering the Isle of Man to the Parliamentary forces in 1651.

April last about the wreck which did happen within my libertyes which (I hope your sonne is or at least may be satisfied) by the law falleth to be mine, and therefore am I not soe sleightly to give it away, not is there reason for me to hearken to any other meanes then a loveing intreatye from yow that I should retribute any part of your losse unto yow, espetially since it is legally my owne by the common and statue lawes of this land by both prescription and grant, and besides it is but a small recompence to 2,353^l odd money lost by me and my youngest brother at one shipwrack, neither is it any such great matter but my chardges of buildinge a harbour to bringe in trade to this country and customes in to His Majesty hath bene very much more and God be praised, yow are as well and much more able to spare this losse then we the 2,353^l and odd money; howsoever, if without more stirr, trouble or question yow will be pleased to take soe much money as freely given yow by me meerely as a curtesie and free pledge of my bountye, being in tender comiseracion of your losse, and in hopes that yow will not be backward to affoord me and my freinds the like curtesies if we be thereunto necessitated, which sume I have acquainted your sonne, whose civill, discreet and modest carriage hath drawne me to more, I must assure yow, than I either had or was resolved on; he promising to referr it (after that I had showne him the strength of my title) wholey to myself which nevertheless I will yett performe if yow doe the like; but if you have any hopes to gett anythinge from me by suite in law then understand that I shall, as touchinge my profitt be better pleased, but as touching the firmer unitinge of our loves weighinge that much more, I shall be best of all satisfied; the consideracion of which referringe to yourselfe expectinge your answer when you please, I rest

> The same as yow have professed yourself to me, your kinsman and assured lovinge freind,

> > Christopher Lowther

> > Whitehaven 16th May 1640

[On pages 61 to 65 are copies of papers relating to the affairs of Deemster Christian which one Christopher Crapples was carrying at the time he was cast away. See also letter on page 79 below.]

1640: July 7: Cumberland   Coppy of a letter to the Deputy Luietenants   *Page 89 begins*
Right Worshipful,

My humblest and best respects presented to all of you. May it please yow to take notices that though I am at this time not well able to ride[e] and therefor cannott waytt one you myselfe as I desire yet would I not soe farr neglect my dutye but present my requests and I hope just excuse. About this time twelve munth weare some of the Debety Liuetennants pleased to impose the charge of a light horse upon my cosen Mr Wibergh and me and though I and he both for our lands in this countye being onely heare for which we are freed of all chargis and incumberance, etc, except the payment of His Majesty's fee farm rent of 1^l 4^s 0^d and ode money and severall cuerats' wadgis, might justly thinck of ourselves free of this charg, yet for my part then was and still am ryde[7] to the outmost of my means to joyn and dowe as other the naburing jentry doe and have I all this yeare by past been obsairevant of your warrants and showne both horse and man compleat though I had not any assistance from my cosen Wibergh at all and indeed considering he is put to the charg to find a light horse in Westmoreland and that his ingagements and charg of childeren are much more, I believe, then aneythinge he hase in this countye can defray I could not well in concience to[o] much urge him nor doe I hope you will, yet that His Majesty's sarves may not be hindered I have thought of towe able men my negboars who are not barened with this charg videliset: Thomas Benson of Skallgill and Anthony Bend[8] of whom my [whom I] desire may joyn in lue of my cosen Wibergh. I moved it formerly when the horses wear shown at Cockermouth and then Sir Nicholas Bevan and the Debety Louetennants who weare theire wised me to let it alon till the next metting, and I should have redress and; if this may please you, that I may have each of theme to joyne with me to find a quarter part I shall find the other halfe and lett [them] find man and arms or horse and farniter[9] as you please soe I shall doe other, and yet if I doe that it will fall out after my unckell death I shall find a whole horse for Sokbedg[10] and halfe of one for this which is a dearer charg then most men beear and if you plese you may consider both my charg and danger leveing heare to defend myselfe and the cuntry about me which might chaleng some favour if it please you to grant my recuest. If this note like yow you may signe it of what other you please and let me knowe your comands and upon reset I shall doe my best to obay theme, hoping at this time, it being the first, you will excuse mee,

Your most affectioned friend and sarvant,
Christopher Lowther

Page 90 begins

The copye of the warrant sent hear with:
[There followed a copy in the same hand of the warrant to Benson and Bond that on receipt they were required to join with Lowther to find a light horse, man, arms and harness for the royal service, the two bearing a quarter part and Lowther the other half. If unprovided with arms for the man or harness for the horse Lowther would furnish them with these at

---

[7] I.e. "ready". Neither the writing nor spelling is Christopher's, apart from the superscription.
[8] "Bend" probably should be "Bond".
[9] I.e. "furniture".
[10] Sockbridge Manor occupied by his wife's uncle, Mr Lancaster.

cost. The light horseman was to be in readiness to be sent when and where they should in future be directed. Dated 8th July 1640.]

the 8th of August 1640   *Page 102*

Worthy Sir,[11]

You knowe and if you please yow may remember your protistations to give me satisfaction touchinge[12] the singeing the acquitance that I showd unto you before your departure hence but in regarde of the suddenness of your goeing away I must hould you excused whearefor I thought fitte to write to you now that you will be pleased that your father may signe this acquittance which as I conceave, and if you will mark it, it is accordinge to your intention as well as myne, I haveing in noe wise tyed your father to aney further discahrge then the hundered and seventeene pounds eighte shillings and nine peance either to me or Christopher Crapples soe for any further reckeninge betwixt Christopher Crapples or his sone and your father, your father is still at libertye to take his best corse. Sir, I pray yow forgitt not to gitt your father to signe and deliver this receipte inclosed and sende it back by the bearer to me soe that I may have never other occasion to aprove myselfe otherwise then what I have allready begune to be which is,

Your affectionate frend and loveing kinsman,

Ch. Lowther

An accquitance sent hearwith Md. receved by mee, Ewaŋ Christian of the Isle of Man, Esquire, by the hands of my sonne William Christian, at and from the handes of Christopher Lowther of Whitehaven in England, Esquire, the some of foure score pounds sterling bestowed on me by him[13] and returned backe to me by my said sonne the 29th of July last past, it being in full satisfacktion and to my contentement accepted in full of one hundred and seaventeen pounds eight shillings and ninepeance being cast up as a wreck at Whitehaven about the 6th of March last past, which one Christopher Crapples, who then likewise perished, was to bringe over to me, being dew from him in parte discharged of sevarall reckning and accompts betweene us and in consideration of the saide some of fourscore pounds soe received by me I doe hearby for me my heires, executers, administrators and assignes acquite & forever discharge the saide Christopher Lowther his heires, executors, administrators, and assignes from all further tytle, clayme and demand, to be made ether by me, my heires, executers, administrators or assignes or the heires, executers, or administrators of Christopher Crapples deseased or of any other clayming by from or under us or them, or any of us or them, ór by our or theire

---

[11] To William Christian, I. of Man.

[12] southinge appears to be written.

[13] "on him by me" crossed out.

consents and procurements to anye further parte of the said one hundred
and seaventeen pounds eight shillings and ninepence and further alsoe for
the forsaid four score pounds which I have received soe freely from the
saide Chr. Lowther if it soe happen that clameing by a better title that then I
the said Ewan Christian doe hearby binde my heires, executors, administrators and assignes and every of us other to repay the fourscore pounds that
I have received or to keepe the said Chr. Lowther his heires, executors and
administrators harmeless and undamnified In witnes wherof I have hear-
unto set my hand and seale the day and yeare first above written, 1640.

Sealed signed and delivered in the presence of us.

*Page 98
begins*

Richard Powley   Whitehaven the 11th September 1640
    I received thyne of the 27th Auguste wheereby I take notise of thy
wand of money and that thou art 12^l oweinge and that John Hambleton let
the[e] have 40^s which he shall have when he will call. This of thyne of the
27th August was the first letter that I received from the[e] sence George
Hewetson came over save one of a former datte which I received sence,
beinge all to one affect for which slaknes I have not a litell reason to
blame thee besides they lithernes[14] when thou dost writ for thou never lettest
me knowe how much ure thou haste at the forge nor how much unled to the
fourge, which I most desired to knowe, or howe much iron you have
draune into barres and howe much into cowps; nor hast thou sent me like an
idle raskall the coppy of thy journall since the 26th of February, nay not
soe much as a balance of thy leager when thou camest from Dublin as a
merchant would have done, which I charge the[e] send me by William
Atkinson, but like a geddy headed foole writeth to me that I must send
the[e] accompt what the ure I have sent with all charges cometh to, which is
unnessessary for the[e] to know. Take thou notice what thou receavest
and how thou wilt make accoumpt of it to me and trouble not thyselfe
whether a tunne of ure stand me to a penny or a pound. Follow thou thy
busines which is not soe great and be sure thou send by Will Atkinson all
the iron thou hast made and if thou sendest me iron I will nether faile the[e]
of money, nor ure, without which after this I will doe neither, nor indeed can
I, or at any time this sommer could I send you any ure as yet though I have
earnestly desired both our owne cuntrymen, wyremen and the Irish Scotch,
and that by reason of the great rate that coles beare at Dublin all this year
and the multitudes of fraughts of catle, yet for this time I have sent the[e]
tenne pounds by this bearer Will Atkinson, and have ordered him to give
the[e] ten pounds more to put the[e] out of debt; alsoe Mr Thomas Dawson
to let the[e] have if it be twenty pounds and I shall repay it him heare
againe, by whom I write to the[e] when he went hence with his hoye and soe
soune as I can I will send over more ure which I hope will be shortly but

[14] Idleness (dialect).

these Scotch warres hindereth us in all things soe that I cannot doe as I would and if Mr Sandys can doe better when that ure is wrought I shall relinquish my partenershipe if he thinke I ame any hindrance to him, and if he doe not, let him leave off his complaints, and I shall doe my best, for I will not endure causelesse complainings, I having reason onely to complayne if any have, and of this I expect his answer, soe rests, thy loveing maister yet if thou mend,

Chr. Lowther

Page 103
begins

Whitehaven the 4th November[15]

To Mr Josua Carpinter at Knockfergus by Ad[am] Warckman

Worthy Sir,

Yours of the 15th of Octo[ber] I have received and to helpe to satisfie your desires I have incoureaged this bearer, Adam Warkman, my sarvante who exerciseth tanneinge to fraight over this littell barqe of about 15 tunes burthen with coles and a litell salte to you, who is willinge that you have theme at the price currante whith you and if you and he can agree, he will buy the hides of the beasts which yow slaughter soe farre as he hath money. Fraught is verie harde to be gotten and at unreasonable rates, for barques of twentie tuns aske 1^l 6 frayght to Knockfergus but if I can gitt my company ventor[16] to you I shall make my shippe ready with above 40 tuns of coles and neare 20 tuns of salte but unless God send them good wether it is a question whether they will goe because she wanteth yet much of her riggeinge for want of mastse but I hope if she come you will dispatche her and you shall chuse whether you will tacke her loadeinge on your owen adventer at the rates currant heere and pay 10^s per tune fright or take the coles at the [rates] currant with you and give me for my salte 8^s per barrelle, Bristoll-bounde of 32 gallons, with a shake, of which resoulve the bearer whether you will chuse and I will stand to it. Soe rests, thankinge you kindly for your loveing profer,

Chr. Lowther

Page 103
ends

To Richard Powley[17]   14th February 1640/1 By Robert MackConnell

Page 98
contd.

I sende the[e] by the bearer 20 tunnes of Iron myne which is very good and well washed and because thou haste solde 3 tunne of iron for money I leave thee to pay theire fraighte which is 5^l 10^s 0 at 5^s 6^d per tunne and 12^d for a messenger to bringe thee a letter to Mayne Water if thou be theire; more thou art not to pay them. We received the trifle of iron which thou didste sende by Adam. Sende me a coppy of the journall, etc.

Chr. Lowther

---

[15] Probably 1640.

[16] [*Sic*] to venture? "Company" probably means ship's company or crew.

[17] For two letters to Lowther from Powley in May and October 1641 see below pp. 220–1.

August the i6th 1642

To Mr Thomas Felps at Wentworth Woodhouse in Yorkshire
Sir,

I perceave youe are steward to that noble sweete lord the Earle of Strafford whom I both knowe, love and honour and this bearer saith youe have imployed him to fetch some goods away from hence for your lord, which one Browne (as I have just occation to say an evel and crost wicked, unconscienable base fellow and ungraitfull) lefte heare for I have suffered more then is fitte from him as the bearer knoweth from me, and yeat for my lord's sake soe I might have my reasonable parte of my losses by him I could be well content to suffer more, but pardon me I pray youe in staying these goods brought by my shippe, which I perceave ar safe, till I have my freight paid and some part of my costes of suite. If you yourselfe come with authority and if the goods be my lord's I doubt not but wee shall soone conclude, though my losse by him be very neare 300^l starl. In the meane-time my care shall not be wantinge to see your goods in safety, and theirfore I rest as you shall find mee,

Your loveinge freind,
Christopher Lowther[18]

---

[18] Pages 113–127 of the text contain legal questions and answers on Christopher Lowther's title to St Bees, 1638–1662, copied about 1662.

SECTION TWO

NOTEBOOK A, 1631–1634

from 21 November 1631

$\frac{1}{3}$	London expenses till the $\frac{1}{3}$ in anno domini 1632	48	5	0
	Irish and English expen. from $\frac{1}{3}$ untill the $\frac{12}{7}$	13	13	8
$\frac{12}{7}$	Disburssed till the 12 7ber	61	18	8
	For my dyet at Mr Thompson's from the $\frac{22}{7}$ to the $\frac{2}{8}$	0	12	0
$\frac{3}{8}$	For bringing my books from my Ant's house to			
	Mr Newman's	0	0	4
	For a pound of candles	0	0	4
$\frac{9}{8}$	For washing my clothes	0	1	0
$\frac{13}{8}$	For a knyfe	0	0	6
$\frac{15}{8}$	Pd. for a lb of candles	0	0	4
	Pd. for mending my boots	0	0	3
$\frac{25}{8}$	Pd. for a seat in Christ Church	0	0	4
	Given to Jo. Nicholson's men	0	0	6
	For mending a pair of spurs	0	0	2
$\frac{6}{9}$	Pd. for a lb of candles	0	0	4
	Pd. for wine to Mr Newman	0	0	5
$\frac{11}{9}$	Pd. for a payer of shews	0	2	6
$\frac{21}{9}$	Pd. for mending a pare of boots	0	0	2
	Pd. the joyner for makeing a boxe	0	4	6
$\frac{24}{9}$	For a book of rates and Harris his booke	0	2	6
$\frac{5}{10}$	In beer to him that set the grate	0	0	2
	Pd. for a lb of candles	0	0	4
	Pd. for a hatband	0	2	0
$\frac{11}{10}$	Pd. for a lb of candles	0	0	4
		63	7	8
$\frac{11}{10}$	disburssed as on the other side	63	7	8
$\frac{12}{10}$	For soleing a pare of bootes	0	1	0
	Pd for a lb of candles	0	0	4
	Pd for a knife sheath	0	0	1
$\frac{22}{10}$	Mending my bootes	0	0	2
	Pd for woormseed	0	0	3

$\frac{27}{10}$	Pd for a candle cheist	0	1	6
	Pd for mending bootes	0	0	2
$\frac{18}{11}$(19)	A buckle for my girdle	0	0	3
	Sooleing my boots	0	1	0
	Isabell's New Year's gifte	0	2	6
	For a girdle	0	4	6
$\frac{21}{11}$	The landeresse washinge clothes	0	4	0
	For shewes mendinge	0	0	6
$\frac{22}{11}$	For silk, eyes, hooks and fustian	0	2	0
	For black thread & mending boots	0	0	8
$\frac{24}{11}$	For spurr leathers	0	0	6
	Loupe lace and buttons	0	1	6
	To Mr Newman in wyne	0	1	0
	Oysters to me and lemons to Mr Weldon	0	2	6
	Beer to my Uncle Lancelott	0	0	2
$\frac{1}{12}$	To the joyner for half a day work	0	0	6
	More in ernest of a chest to him	0	4	0
	To the sawers of dale boards	0	0	6
	Beer to Mr Derensa	0	0	2
$\frac{18}{12}$	For mending boots	0	0	2
	Bringing a boat from Lowsey Hill	0	0	6
	Pd the landeresse	0	2	6
	In beer with Mr Bouskaile	0	0	4
$\frac{4}{1}$(20)	For mending my boots and shews	0	0	4
	For a lb of candles	0	0	4
$\frac{13}{1}$	For 3 oyled skines	0	2	4
	For port of letters	0	0	6
$\frac{15}{1}$	Loupe lace and buttons	0	8	2
		65	12	7

Page 3 $\frac{15}{1}$	Disburssed in chardges per contra	65	12	7
	In needles to the taylor	0	0	2
	Beer to Chr. Grayson	0	0	4
$\frac{21}{1}$	Walting and sooling boots	0	1	6
$\frac{22}{1}$	Pd the taylor for makeing my suite	0	10	0
	Given to a poor man	0	0	$0\frac{1}{2}$
	Fringe and a button for my cloke	0	2	8
	Given to the taylor's men	0	0	6
	Beer to my Ant Lowther	0	0	3
	For a payer of belly peeces	0	0	10
	For a payer of spur lethers	0	0	2

[19] I.e. 18 Jan. 1633.
[20] I.e. 4 March 1633.

	£	s	d
For my dyet from Michalmasse till our Ladie Day followeinge to Mrs Newman	6	0	0
For a chamber for 17 weeks from June till October last to Mrs Lowther att 3^s 6^d per weeke and 6^d over	3	0	0
Mr Cook's bill of parcells for makeing upp my cloth suite	1	13	0
Seaven yards of cloth for my saide suite at 14^s per yard	4	18	0
$\frac{24}{1}$ For 2 dozen of poynts	0	5	0

	£	s	d
Somme totall	82	5	0$\frac{1}{2}$
In guiftes to Mr Newman's servants at my goeing for Eng[land]	0	10	0
2 yardes of cloake bage stuffe	0	4	0
3 yards of ribbaninge etc	0	2	0
Cloacke bagge stringes	0	0	4
Makeing a girdle	0	1	0
Beer to taylor 2^d, makeing stockins	0	1	8
Sattan & silk for stockines	0	2	6
Payre shewes and laste	0	16	6

1 18 0   84 3 0$\frac{1}{2}$

March 24 1633

	£	s	d
Broughte from thother side	84	3	0$\frac{1}{2}$
Soleing my Mrs shewes	0	1	0
In tabacko on Mrs Newman	0	2	0
In wine to Mr Newman at dinner	0	1	0
In bayze for my stocking tops	0	0	6
Apr/3 A quarte of beere with Myles	0	0	8
On Mr Adney my fayre well	0	0	2
A payre of gloves	0	1	6
. . . .[21] of my cloathes aboarde	0	0	10

	£	s	d
4 Aprill disbursede 0^l 7^s 8^d	84	10	8$\frac{1}{2}$

	£	s	d
21 Aprill receaveinge the sacram^t.	0	1	0
16 dayes dyet & charges	1	1	6
Given in ribbeninge to our comp[any]	0	1	0
25 3 days charge at Whitehaven	0	3	0

[21] Smudged out.

		£	s	d
30 Aprill.	Given salters & workman	0	2	0
2 May	To the collyeres at the pits	0	0	6
5 May.	With my cousin Wiber[gh] in beere	0	0	6
15 „	A ladle at Leades[22]	0	7	0
20 May	7 dayes in my way from Cumb.	1	15	6
22.	Sockes and Boote house[23]	0	1	8
	ad 4:2 ad 22:3: 3:13:8			
	Pulling of the mayre shewes	0	0	$1\frac{1}{2}$
	Comeinge by water from Lowehouse[24]	0	0	4
	To Thomas Vayray and walers beere	0	0	6
	Swoard scabord & bootes mendinge at Whitehaven	0	0	6
	To a scholler at St Bees schoole	0	1	0
24	A tytheinge table	0	0	10
25	Bootes	0	8	6
	To French marriners	0	0	6

Ad. 22: 3; ad. 26: 3: 12^s: 3$\frac{1}{2}^d$		In toto	88	16	8

April 4 : 1633

		£	s	d
26:3	Totall disburssements per contra	88	16	8
28:3	To Sara my uncle's mayd's wedding	0	5	0
29:3	Two foldeinge bandes	0	7	0
	Barbeinge	0	0	6
1:4	Lethor sockes: 3 payer	0	1	6
	A jugg of beere abroade	0	0	2
2:4	Watch mendeinge	0	6	8
	My meare bloode letteinge	0	0	6
	Wyne at home with uncle	0	0	6
	My bootes coloureing & oyleing	0	1	0
	To Mr Denny's coachman	0	0	6
	Coarall for my mother	0	0	0[25]
	Grayne weightes	0	1	6
	Byndeing: G.J.	0	6	0
4:4	Search Yorkshire auditor	0	1	4
	Oleron Lawes	0	1	0
	Golde weightes	0	2	4
6:4	Meare sheweinge	0	0	8
7:4	Sea mirror	1	0	0
	Bible & Practisce of Piety	0	18	0

[22] Leeds?
[23] I.e. boot hose.
[24] Smudged.
[25] Coral? Figure given as 5^d but crossed out.

	A prayer booke & Marcham	0	0	8
	A foldeinge bande	0	5	0
8:4	Porte of my father's and Gyles' letters	0	4	0
	My bootes mendeing	0	0	3
	Swoorde mendeinge & scaberd	0	2	4
8:4	Port: 2: letters to Hamburg	0	0	6
	A map: Uncle Robert hath it	0	1	6
	By water to Westminster	0	0	6
	Add. 26: 3; ad. 8: 4; 4^l: 8: 11	93	5	7

1633

	Broughte from the other side	93	5	7
8:4	Broughte from the other side	93	5	7
10:4	Gloves to the children	0	4	2
12:4	Meere grasse: at 3^s 6^d per weeke	0	12	0
	To my uncle's servantes	0	4	8
	Goeinge by water to Westminster	0	0	3
13:4	My meare sheweinge	0	0	9
	The boy rideinge	0	0	3
	At Ingerston, 20, our charges[26]	0	4	6
14:	At Colchester 23 myles nowne, our charges	0	3	6
	The salters theire, Mr Stirckson's	0	1	0
14:	At Ipswitch 12 myle, nighte charge	0	5	2
15:4	At Dersam 22 myle, nighte charges etc	0	5	0
17:4	At Bettles, 10 myles nowne[27]	0	2	0
	At Yarmouth 10 m. nighte and nowne	0	4	6
	To Mr Matford's salte woorkes theire	0	0	6
18:	At Norridge[28] 16m nighte	0	4	8
19:	At Lynn 30m nighte's charge	0	4	7
20:	Ferry boate passadge	0	0	3
	Guide over the 5 myle eashes	0	0	8
	At Dinnington nowne[29]	0	0	10
	At Sleaford: 30 myle nighte charge	0	4	0
	13 July to Uncle Robert my dyet & the boy's 3 weekes & 3 dayes	2	0	0
21:	At Lyncolne 14 myle nighte	0	4	6
22:	At Doncaster 24 myle	0	4	8
	At Wentworth 10 myle nighte	0	5	0
23:	At Leeds 18 myle nightes charge	0	7	6

[26] I.e. Ingateston, Essex. The 20 refers to miles.
[27] I.e. Beccles. There is no indication where 16th spent.
[28] I.e. Norwich.
[29] Probably Dunnington, Lincs.

88

25:	At Giggleswicke 25, night's charge	0	3	6
26:	Drincke by the way to Lancaster, 35 myle	0	0	2
	Add. $\frac{8}{4}$ ad. $\frac{27}{4}$: 6^l 7^s 11^d	99	13	6

Page 7

27:4	Broughte from the other side	99	13	6
1:5	To the peere men in ayle	0	0	6
12:5	About 12 July at Kirckby[30]	0	1	0
15:5	On John Fletcher & Ch. Grayson in beere	0	0	4
17:5	On my Cousin Wibergh	0	0	4
13:Aug.	In expences at Cockermouth	0	0	4
14:	At Thomas Gatesgarthe	0	0	10
5:6	Aug. At my brother Kirckby's	0	1	0
6:6	My bootes mendeing	0	1	6
7:6	At Thwaytes, charges	0	1	6
	On Hensingham colliery	0	0	3
	A payre of gloves	0	0	8
15:6	from the 27:4 total 0 : 8 : 3	100	1	9

20:11	In expenses proprio till the 20 January from 16 November in my owne accomptes onely	1	0	0
15:12	A silver girdle 6^s 8^d; an ivory water triall, 1^s 6^d; a swoorde girdle, 2^s 6^d; a payre of Northampton bootes 6^s 8^d; a payre of brasse, sylevered spurres 2^s 6^d; bandes ruffes 5^s; a mathematicall booke 3^s	1	8	4
	Other smalle trifles then as in memoriall	0	4	5
	$5\frac{1}{2}$ yardes blacke broade perfurmed Spanish cloath	4	19	0
	Bootes mendeinge, inckhorne & pay paper booke	0	1	2
21:12	3 necklaces of Bristol pearlle	0	6	0
	2 bandes; 2 payre of ruffes & bootehose tops	0	9	3
	1 payre fulled boote hoose	0	5	0
	2 lytle brasse candle stickes	0	1	4
	For a white hatte & band 15^s & one other dresseinge	0	17	0
	For the watch mendeinge	0	3	0
22:12	1633[31] totall disb. Disburssements proprio	9	14	6

Page 8

22:12	1633 broughte per contra	9	14	6

[30] Kirkby-in-Furness, home of his brother-in-law Roger Kirkby.
[31] I.e. 22 February 1634.

24:12	Sutton's bill of my suite & satten	1	0	6
	For 3½ doz. of blacke silke & 3 silver poyntes	0	12	3
	For black silke ribbon garters & stockings	0	12	8
27:12	For ribbaninge to my white hatte	0	0	6
	For a truncke: 3 quarters longe	0	4	8
	For the 10 Commandements	0	0	6
1:1	For scoweringe my swoord	0	0	6
23:1	Of the firste for a swoorde blade	0	6	8

23:1	1633[32] disburssed in toto 12 : 14 : 9	

1634	For my bootes, shewes and varnisheing, etc	0	14	8
July				
16:	For gloaves 2 payre & a letter case	0	1	8
17:	For pursses, 2 to the children	0	5	0
3 Aug	Given them in money with them	0	5	0

16:	Auguste. Disb. from 23 March laste for my accompte proprio 1 : 6 : 4

17:	Disburssed for lynneinge cloath boughte by Gyles for shirteing at 15[d] per yarde	1	5	4
September 7th	To a gatheringe at St Bees church	0	1	0
11:	To Raynes the mathematician for a quadrante	0	2	0
	For a pare of gloves at Cockermouth	0	0	6
Oct 21	from 16 Auguste 1^l 8^s 10^d			

Decem				
20	For a fustian money bagge	0	1	0
	To a poore man at St Bees church	0	0	4
	For a veste of flatt cloath for shirtes	0	0	6

Page 8 ends

Pages 9, 10 blank

March 25th	Receipts of Money 163⅔				*Page 11*

25:1	M[oney] in proprio pursse then	8	0	2
3:2	Recd. of Richd. Wibergh at my departure	95	0	0
	Of Myles for yarne	1	0	7
25:3	Of Wm. Atkinson in full of his debts to me	1	2	0
	Of my mother to buy hollands	0	10	0

[32] I.e. 23 March 1634.

		£	s	d
	For broken silver of hirs	0	1	4
	Of Whitehaven marriners	1	0	0
25:4	Reste of my uncle Robt debte to my father	75	5	1
25:5	Of the beaste money at Ravenglass	76	2	8
6:6	Thwaytes rentes for my father	21	10	9
	For 1 pounde of tabacko on my mother	0	2	6
	Earnest of wheat solde	0	1	0
12:5	Receaved in toto then: 279^l 16^s 11^d	279	16	11
	Receaved in accompte of Will Atkinson			
	12 Aug 33 besides what he had of mee	86	16	0½
	15 Auguste 1633 totall receaved facit	366	12	11½
	Totall disbursed then	364	19	9
	Soe restes in my hande of which John Musgrave			
	hath 20s	1	13	2½

Page 12

		£	s	d
15:6	1633 Rested in my hande the 15 Auguste and Jo. Musgrave's broughte from the other side at the cleeringe of our accomptes	1	13	2½
2:7	Receaved of Lancelot Harbert for 41 t[ons] 3 c[wt] of coles bought of W. Atkinson	2	16	6
10:7	Recd. of Richard Wibergh at Dublin at 2 severall tymes as in the margent	0	10	0
16:7	Recd more of him at twice	112	0	0
25:7	Recd of George Jackson	6	0	0
1:8	Recd of him more	1	0	0
11:8	Recd of him more at Carrickfergus	15	0	0
8:9	Recd of Richard Wibergh at Dublin	0	15	1
9:9	Recd more of him of L[ord] Baltinglasse's money	157	11	11
30:9	Recd of Christopher Wharton at Whitehaven	5	0	0
27:11	Recd of my brother Will & Anthony Cowper	11	8	6
22:11	Recd of my father at Lowther	10	0	0
20:12	Recd of Mr Sanckley of Castle Taverne for 6 pypes of Canarie sackes	63	0	0
24:12	Recd of Mr Chesleyne, Cowper, in Roode Layne for 10¼ pypes of Canarie	116	16	6
14:1	Recd of my mother: to Bennet for Ro. Simpson	1	0	0
23:1	Recd of my mother at Lowther	5	10	0
	Recd of etc appointed[33] Richard Wibergh the 11 9ber laste to give & allowe Mrs Newman for my dyet theire one month from the laste of			

[33] Probably means "of that which I appointed" (i.e. instructed).

	Auguste before	2	0	0

24 March 1633/34 totall recd by me C. Low.		512	1	8½	
24: March 1634 Recd broughte per contra		512	1	8½	*Page 14*
	Recd of Will Atkinson money which I had formerly disburssed of my owne for the peere	3	13	0	

24: March 1633 Total received		515	14	8½
	Total disburssed then	515	0	7½

25: March 1634: restes in my hande		0	14	1	
21: May. Recd of Will Atkinson		5	0	0	
25:	Of my mother at Lowther	2	0	0	
	Of my mother then from brother Will	5	0	0	
26:	Of my father firste Rossley Munday	40	0	0	
27:	Of Carlisle men in parte herreinge	44	0	0	
30:	Of Margaret Dodgeson of Ouston in parte	14	0	0	
4:	June of Walter Becke	20	0	0	
	Of Ned Bayteman	5	0	0	
	Of Barnard Benson in parte prunes	3	0	0	
12:	Of Uncle Fallowfield in parte	0	15	0	
13:	Of Mr Walton	45	5	0	
14:	Of Peter Huggins	10	0	0	
	Of Will Wickeliffe for tabacko sent by W. Atkinson	0	7	0	
20:	Of Barnard Benson cleered	11	8	0	
	Of Mr Becke then in parte of 45^l 5^s	10	0	0	
	Of George Jackson	14	0	0	
21:	Of William Dodgeson	4	0	0	

21: 1634	June 1634 Received in all	234	9	1	
21:	June. Broughte from the other side	234	9	1	*Page 16*
	Of Mr Preston of the manner	8	10	0	
	Of Richard Wibergh per James Crosstatt[34]	155	0	0	
6;	July, of Will Atkinson	20	0	0	
	Of Carlisle men	20	0	0	
	Of Mr Cape for prunes	3·12	0		
	Of Mr Emmerson, Canary accompte	44	10	0	
	Of Mr William Carre for 3½ pypes of Canarie sackes	28	10	0	
	Of my mother for spices	0	5	6	
	Of Michael Gybson for wyne	18	0	0	
	Of Mr Becke by Rowland Wife	15	0	0	

[34] Probably Crossthwait[e].

27:	July, of my mother & father to pay Tubman	20	0	0
27:	July Totall receaved ad. $\frac{25}{1}$	567	16	7
1	Receaved to ballance the accompte to this day, that I have spente lesse then 3^s per diem in my travell with that which Jo: Musgrave oughte me, viz 20^s: now in my mother's hande	1	7	1
6:	Auguste Totall received then 1634	569	3	8
	Disburssed then	568	3	8[35]
6:	Auguste 1634 Remayninge then	1	0	0

1634

16:	Auguste remayninge then	1	0	0
17:	Receavede by Gyles Moore of Mr John Cape for his laste of the prunes & delivered me the money	2	0	0
21:	September. Receaved of my partener Rowland Jackson the use of 300^l dew the 29 of September nexte to my father out of his stocke	24	0	0
21:	Sept. Receaved of Rob. Wilkinson for his tyme & charges	23	6	6
29:	Recd. for Lowdemayne rente	11	0	0
	Recd. of William Dodgson by my cozen Senhouse	15	0	0
	Recd. more by him of Lawrence Haworth by my cozen John Senhouse	38	0	0
	Recd. in Christo. Lowther's bonde of Leeds accepted by my father in pte of money oweinge by us to him	49	0	0
11:	October. Receaved of my brother Kirckby in full of halfe a tunne of wyne, iron, etc	1	11	0
13:	Receaved of Rayslacke farmers in pte.	10	0	0
13:	Receaved of John Rostall in pte.	10	0	0
14:	Receaved Of Rich. Maberrie in full	8	8	6
14:	Recd. of Peter Huggons in full	36	10	0
15:	Recd. of Edward Bayteman in full	6	14	0
15:	Recd. of Walter Beck in full	12	14	0
15:	Recd. of Mr Rich. Walton in full	22	9	0
16:	Recd. of Nicholas Egleston	30	0	0
17:	Recd. of Mrs Hodgekinson of Garestange	1	4	6
18:	Recd. of Mrs Conell[36]	4	0	0

[35] For disbursements account see below pp. 93–9.

18:	Recd. of Edward Lawrence of Ebell	4	9	8
18:	Mrs Conell to pay the reste of the bonde to my cousen Senhouse	4	0	0
21:	October. Totall 1634	315	7	2

1634

Page 24

Oct 21	Recd. from thother side	315	7	2
Auguste	2 laste paste receaved of my father for a hghd. of wyne then put to accompte	3	0	0
Oct 21	Receaved in accompte of my mother which she receaved of Will Ion for parte of our 54 beastes solde by him	32	4	3
21:	Appoynted my mother to receave of Will. Ion for 5 beastes at Burgh fayre solde	8	5	0
24:	Recd. of Lawrance Lancaster for John Roskall of Dalton in full of his bonde 20ˢ abayted	12	0	0
25:	Recd. for cordage of Lawrence Lancaster then beinge 1ˡ 2ˢ 12ᵈ	3	4	0
27:	Recd. of Will Fletcher in full of his bonde in suite[37]	11	16	11
Nov 6	Recd of Will Wickeliffe from Widdowe Askew of Kirckby in full[38]	4	5	0
Dec 3	Recd of And. Davy for John Sand for 5 bush. salte oweinge by him in Aprill	0	8	6
Dec 5	Recd of Will Atkinson to pay Steph. ....howe[39] & John Creswell	1	9	4
	Of Will Atkinson warfage money etc	0	10	0[40]

15:6	1633	Disburssementes			

Page 13

2:7ber	For 35 bunches of lathes and portage	0	7	8
3:7	For 10 dozen of cask hoopes C J	0	7	9
	For ½ C. broad cask hoopes	0	4	0
4:7	For 5 beefe barrells	0	7	6
	For 1,200 brll hoopes for Jam. Gyles	1	5	6
6:7	To James Gyles at Fraythinge earnest	0	1	4
7:7	Earnest of Sir Jo. Gypson's woolle	0	1	0

[36] Followed by "in parte" crossed out.

[37] Followed by "to my cousin Senhouse 11.0.0" crossed out.

[38] There follows, but crossed out, "Recd by my cousen John Senhouse of Mr Lawrence Haworth at R. Stone as by Mr Lawrence Haworth's letter to me sente me by my cousen Senhouse's man the 13th 38   0   0.

[39] The first part of the name is illegible.

[40] This is the last receipts entry in the notebook and there is no final total.

8:7	To Rich. Wibergh in money	0	10	6
9:7	More to him in money	0	2	10½
	Disburssed to Mr Younge earnest of 50 hghds of salte	0	2	0
16:7	In . . . . . . of the horse . . . . . [?][41]	1	16	2
24:7	To George Jackson at Belfast	110	0	0
25:7	For 10 flote of linninge cloath	0	14	2
	Earneste of 3,000 of tyles to Mrs Hermon	0	5	0
	Earnest to Jo. Whappe, cowper for Gylles	0	1	0
1:8	Butter to Mrs Letherborrowe	0	18	10
	Butter to Cayte's syster for Whitehaven	1	1	3
	For 4½ dozen of poles for peere[42]	0	18	6
2:8	Custome of salte out of our barq upon a poste entrie: 2 laste and fees	0	8	6
	Cloath for Steven at Lysnagarne	0	3	6
	Custome of caske & entrie to the fishinge	0	13	0
	Carriage of the caske to the barqs	0	2	2
	Dresseinge Mrs Hermon's caske to Whappe	0	7	0
9:8	Gyven to James Gylles and company at the headeinge and packinge theire salte	0	3	6
11:8	For 120 barrell staves for Ja. Gyles	0	4	0
11:8ber	disburssed	120	19	0½

Page 15

		l	*s*	*d*
11:8ber	1633 Disburssements			
	Broughte from the other side	120	19	0½
15:8	Given to James Gyles' companny at theire goeinge to the fisheing	0	2	6
	Sente by James Gyles to Myles	10	0	0
23:9	Pd in Will Atkinson's caske	157	11	11
	My owne charges a die 24th of Auguste at which tyme I parted Whitehaven to fitt the herreinge voyage for Ireland till I returned backe againe 16:9ber at 3ˢ per diem myselfe and horse	12	12	0
26:9	To my partner Rowland Jackson	1	0	0
Woolle	In barter of 3 stone of woolle valued at 8ˢ per stone and 18ˢ of money for a lether coloured dozen price 2ˡ 2ˢ	0	18	0
W.	In my journey to Leeds about the woolle 14 dayes	2	2	0
	In expences proprio till Jannuary	1	0	0
8:12	For my father, Atkins rente and fees	3	1	4

[41] Illegible.
[42] "For peere" is crossed out.

	For 1½ dozen alkumie spones for him	0	6	0
	For pynnes to my mother	0	1	7
	For 30—¾ of an elne of Hollande	6	15	0
	For 18 yardes Turkie grogram and lace	6	11	0
	To my brother William	4	0	0
	A fyrkin of pippins	0	6	0
10:12	For 2 lockes on seller doores of the Canary wynes[43]	0	2	0
	On Sanckley the Vyntener in a capon, etc	0	6	0
24:12	For a but of Malligo of Mr Humphrey Slayney	15	0	0
24:12	1633/4 Totall disburssed	343	14	4½

1634

Page 17

24:12	1633 Broughte from the other side	342	14	4½
	To Uncle Robert Lowther then	140	0	0
	Mr Cowper Woodcocke's bill	3	10	0
27:	A transire to Newcastle	0	3	0
1:1	For porterage 4^s 6^d; shippeinge 8^s 6^d; carteinge 5^s 4^d; craynage 2^s 8^d and watchinge 2^s 6^d	1	3	6
21:1	At Catterick to Save my meare	0	8	6
23:1	My charges from the twentieth January till the 23:1 nexte after	9	3	0
	To Rowland Jackson at his house	5	0	0
23:1	My owne charges proprio from $\frac{20}{11}$ till $\frac{23}{1}$	12	14	9
	1 ounce camfora 6^d and one ounce of Opium	0	1	6
	6 Alqumie spoones for Whitehaven	0	2	0
24:1	Totall disburssed the 24 March	515	0	7½

23 May	Disburssed to George Jackson	4	10	6
26:	Disburssed at Rossley for my father	31	18	6
	To my father in money 17 June	8	1	6
30:	Disbd to George Jackson at Peele[44]	49	8	0
	More to him then by Mr Hunter	14	0	0
	To Mr Lawrence Parcke in all	43	6	6
	To Will Atkinson to pay Chalmeley	7	0	0
	To Mr Beck's manaporte of 20 cwt	0	1	0
	To George Jackson at R...coats[45]	27	19	0
4 June	To Tho. Britton's man parte of 10 hoghds	0	11	2

[43] At London see Notebook B below p. 133.
[44] Northern Ireland.
[45] First syllable illegible.

14:	To John Jackson for his master at Ambleside	5	0	0
17:	To Will Atkinson	39	0	0
	To my mother then	2	0	0
	Cartage 10 hghds to Milnethorpe & sellering etc	0	7	2
	To George Braythwaite, Searcher	1	0	0

17 June	Totall disburssed 1634	234	3	4

1633 Disburssment Generall[46]

3:2	To the 4th Aprill nexte foll. 2				0	3	2
3:2	Sesse to the troope[47]				0	9	6
	To Mrs Newman ¼ rent before				5	0	0
10:2	To Myles in accompte, viz: Anchorage at						
	Douglasse 8^d powder 1^s				0	1	8
14:2	To Myles in money				2	12	7
16:2	For Thomas Keaninge				0	0	4
	For fish				0	1	2
19:2	More Myles himselfe in money				0	10	0
19:2	Goods boughte in the Ile of Man as in booke of						
	accompte follio 23				8	5	2
	Goodes in peere accompte fo. 8				0	16	4
23:2	Whitehaven voyage by C. Lowther onely, follio 27				0	4	2
6:3	To Myles Bateman in money				5	0	0
7:3	To him more in money				13	9	1
7:3	More to him on a new accompte				5	10	0
7:3[48]							
7:3	To William Atkinson for the *George* his loadeinge in pte, viz:						
	16 tunnes 6 loades of coles	1^l	18^s	1^d			
	512 bushells salte, bearinge	0	9	0			
	drinke 2^s 8^d; a lifter 8^d	0	3	4			
	loane of caddowes[49]	0	0	6	2	10	11
7:3	To William Atkinson for the *Mayflower*:						
	26 tunne of coles at 2^s 4^d	4	5	0			
	fees of entrie	0	8	4			
	salte bearers	0	2	2			
	drinke	0	1	3	4	16	9

	49	10	10

[46] Originally headed "Extraordinaryes" but crossed out.

[47] [*Sic*].

[48] Entry scribbled out but read "from the seventh May ditto to Mr John Williamson in parte salte 6 score bushel at 20^d per bushel   10   0   0".

[49] A coarse woollen cloth.

1633:   May : 7

	Broughte from the other side				49	10	10
	Pd to Mr William Atkinson for the *Lyons* etc:						
7:3	6 tunnes & 3 loades ouer coles	0	14	3			
	Fees of entrie	0	8	4			
	Salte bearers	0	5	4			
	Drinke to the mariners	0	0	3	1	8	2
	To Will Atkinson the *George*'s entrie to & from				0	14	0
	Hir custome in & out to him				1	0	0
	Towards answering Cholmely				0	5	0
	Charges in shippe goods in Rob. Bankes				0	3	8
	A reade sente for the boye				0	8	0
	Stockinges for him, 22 May				0	1	4
7:3	To Will Atkinson to buy coles for me				32	12	6
7:3	To George then with 5^l the day before				5	7	6
22:3	From the 4th Aprill till the 22 of May now instante						
	as in follio the 2nd of this booke in expences						
	p[rop]rio				3	13	8

| 25:3 | 973 3 5 | 86 4 8 | 10 18 9 |

5:3	Earnest of coles to Chr. Grayson	0	1	0
7:3	On the *George* company at theire departure the			
	7 May from Whitehaven, in beere	0	1	0
23:3	Search of St Bees in the Rowles[50]	0	1	4
26:3	Disburssments proprio ad. 22:3 ad 26:3	0	12	3½
27:3	A corrall for my mother	0	6	8
29:3	To Mr Tho. Sledayle for Whith[aven] marriners	1	0	0
30:3	Porte of my brother's bookes	0	0	8
1:4	Bargayneinge about herringe	0	0	6
8:4	To Mr Rayleton for the peere	2	0	0
	For 38 glasses, boxe & corde	0	15	0
	Porte downe to Uncle Robert's	0	0	2
	A boxe for the gloaves	0	2	8
	For porte of the glasses & gloves to carrier	0	0	8
	Porte of my brother's chiste & cordinge	0	1	0

| 8:4 | Totall disburssed facit | 100 | 7 | 7 |

[50] I.e. in the Master of the Rolls archives.

1633

8:4	Broughte per contra	100	7	7
8:4	2 ells of Holland for my mother	0	10	6
8:4	Disburssements proprio from $\frac{26}{3}$ till $\frac{8}{4}$	4	8	11
23:4	To Ch. Lowther at Leedes	68	0	0
26:4	Disburssements proprio from $\frac{8}{4}$ till $\frac{27}{4}$	6	7	11
1:5	To our marriners in ayle	0	0	6
2:5	To the salters in drincke	0	1	4
	To our owne marriners the day the[y] went forth	0	1	0
12:5	In ayle on the wrightes at Calder	0	0	6
16:5	On Mr Hudson at Edgarmont[51] about salters	0	1	6
	More on him then at Tho. Fishers	0	0	4
17:5	On the peere men in beere	0	0	6
13:6	For a congar to the commissioners	0	1	6

		180	2	1
	Disburssed for netts & in other charges about sayle of our catle	0	10	4
12:6	Disburssments proprio a die $\frac{27}{4}$ till $\frac{15}{6}$	0	8	3
	Disb. in discharge of W. Atkinson's accompte of this 12 instant	147	1	10
12:6	More to him then in preste of salte	15	6	6
	Disb. to Mr Layton of Delinayme	19	18	6
	More for fees to Judge Vernon's man	0	11	6
	In a pursse with the Thwaites note	1	0	9

15:	Auguste 1633 disburssed in toto	364	19	9

1634

1634	Broughte from the other side			
17 June	disburssementes	234	3	4
16 June	To my brother Will for uncle Robert	156	0	0
16 July	Mr Gray his note of grocery for W. Atk.	9	13	0
	Mr Davison for the beste steele beinge 2 [q.] 1 [lb.]	1	8	6
	Disburssed to Mr Emmerson for his account whereof for honey and sugar 21. 4. 8.	44	10	0
	More to Cudbert Carter, cowper for caske	0	4	0
20 June	More to my father in parte of oweinge him	93	0	0

51 Egremont, Cumberland.

For my systers wyne	0	15	0
My charges 30 dayes from the 20 of May till 22 June about French wynes sellering	4	10	0
My charges to Carlisle about herringe money received twyce $3\frac{1}{2}$ dayes	0	10	6
My charges about Canarie wynes from the 8 July till 22th of the same	1	19	0
16 Aug. My expenses proprio for an iron Bitch for Cole Woorckes	0	4	0
Pd. Tubman for beastes for my father	20	0	0
16 August 1634 disburssed	568	3	8

16:    Auguste   1634   *Page 23*

18: To Mr Pearson for breakeinge up Wilkinson's writte 2^s; spent with him 3^d	0	2	3
18: September; to Burneyeate for sendinge my cousen John Senhouse letter from York posted	0	1	0
20: To the bayliffe's fees upon a proces at suite of Will Fletcher	0	4	8
To Antho. Grigg 1^s; ... d^{52}	0	1	0
21: Disbursed for my partener to my father the use of his 300^l borrowed of my father put in stock with me	24	0	0
21: John Musgrave's charges about Wilkinson's arreste	0	13	0
7: October; disburssed for 19 gallons & 3 quartes of tarre	1	6	6
At Wigton for 7 declarations	0	7	0
More for putteinge in the allowing	0	2	6
Given Mr Edw. Orpheur to look unto them	0	5	0
My charges that nighte & day & nexte	0	3	0
6: October. Disburssed to my cousen Jo. Senhouse in money at sealeinge	30	0	0
Disbursed to my cousen John Senhouse in Dodgeson's & Haworth's money	53	0	0
Delivered my brother Will, Christopher Lowther's bonde of Leedes for my father	49	0	0
18: Delivered my cousen Senhouse Mr Edmond Conell's bond to receave of it for bringeinge one hogsheade of wyne from Powton[53] to Lancaster	0	2	6
For lockes, sneckes, gemmers, etc	0	6	8

[52] Blotted out.
[53] Poulton.

21:	Payd to my mother in money	140	0	0
21:	October 1634 totall	303	15	1
	October 21st Disb. broughte from thother side	303	15	1
21:	then more my expences proprio	1	8	10
Auguste 2	disburssed then to my father in wyne	3	0	0
October 21	disburssed by my mother to mt brother Will to pay my Uncle Robert the laste of my bond to him for 100^l dew 20 Aug	30	0	0
21:	More payde to my mother the 44^s she had in hand & William Ion's 8^l 5^s, she to receave	10	9	0
23:	Payd by me to my cousen Jo. Senhouse besides 6^l 6^s 8^d W. Atkinson pd him then	7	0	0
23:	My charges goeinge about to sell off the wyne at Lancaster & receave in the moneyes dew 13 out[54]	1	19	0
27:	To my cousen Senhouse by a boy	6	13	4
31:	To my cousen Jo. Senhouse	10	0	0
	To Will Atkinson then	10	7	7[55]
18: Nov	Dis. to my partener to pay Jo. Wibergh	1	5	0
20:	More to him to pay John Love, etc	3	0	0
16 Dec	Pd. to Phillip Pickeringe for the upper parte of the steeple wyndow	0	10	0
10 Dec	To Andrew Dawes Decem. 10th	1	0	0
8:	To Thomas Reede sayler—8th	0	5	0

This page of rough notes was written with the notebook turned upside down on the penultimate written page.

to Myles	5	10	0
to Mr Williamson	10	0	0
the *George* cole etc	2	10	11
the *Mayflower*	4	16	9
the *Lyon*	1	8	2
½ fees the *George* out	0	7	0
custome of hir salt & cole out	0	10	0
sewet money	0	5	0
George Jackson York. cloath	0	2	8
Boy sewte	0	8	0
Boy stockinges	0	1	4
Will Atkinson	23	12	6

[54] Probably 13 days.

[55] The next entry, later crossed out, read: "November. Disburssed by Mr Lawrence Haworth as per contra to my cousen John Senhouse of Seascayle 38   0   0".

George Jackson	5	17	6
Expenses proper	3	13	8
	48	14	6
Earnest coles to Chr. Grayson	0	1	0

$\frac{15}{5}$ 1^l 13^s $2\frac{1}{2}^d$ remayned in my hand whereof John Musgrave hath 10^s

Roapemakinge

Number of woorkemen	2: Spynners & to dresse 1: wheele turner
What ropes they will make in the weeke spinning and dresseinge three dayes; tarreinge one day; makeinge up two dayes	Those three folkes will spin 2^c of white yarne which will take 1^c of tarre & will make 3^c of roapes
What hempe in a yeare that is & what tarre	10,000 weighte of hempe & 5,000 wheight of tarre

Fisheinge lynes & sayle twyne

Number of men	2: spinners & to dresse 1: wheeleturner & to dresse
What hempe those three will dresse & spin a day & five dayes a weeke and one day to lay in it	9^{lbs} of raw hempe which will waste $\frac{1}{3}$ soe maketh 6^{lb}
What hemp it is a a weeke and yeere at 40 weekes, because the roapemakers must leave theire roapeworkeing to lye the lynes for twine & the lyne spinners againe to lye the roapes	they will woorke of rawe hempe 3^c 0^q 2 which will make of lynes made 2^c 0^q 1^{lb}

NOTEBOOK B 1633–1634

Transcripts from Sir Christopher Lowther's Notebook "B"

[The first page contains rough notes badly discoloured, some in Latin. The lower half of the page contains the following memoranda:]
706 bushell at 22^d per bushell is 64^l 2^s 8^d.   16 laste:[56] 67^l 4^s 0^d at 7^s per b[arrel].

[Below is the following memorandum:]
To knowe the tare of a caske of butter, tallowe, oyle, herringe, beere, tarre, haveing the net content I devide the net content by 9, the quotient is the tare soe multiply the tare by 8 & the producte is the net content.

[On page 2 under the heading "Remembrances" is] 1. Call to Hutton of Cockermouth for 24^l 10^s dew to Gyles. [Below it is the roughly drawn diagram of a pumping engine.]

[On page 3 is a set of notes in Latin.

On page 4 is a diagram, apparently the roughly drawn ground plan of a building. Below it is written:]

Jame[s] William at 6^s per weeke	15	12	0
James Fayrer at 5^s per weeke	13	0	0
Christopher Wharton 4^s per weeke	10	8	0
Rich. Pruddey—4^s per weeke	10	8	0
William Dickson 5 per weeke	13	0	0
Troughton; Bradley; ⎫			
2^s 4^d ⎬ at 3^s 6^d	27	6	0
Huetson; Andrewes ⎭	6	1	8
3 Stewards	39	0	0
Totall	134	15	8
deducte wages	45	0	0
Rest for housekeeping	89	15	8

[Page 5 contains notes in Latin, which continue to the top of page 6, then:]

From $\frac{4}{3}$ till $\frac{21}{6}$ '33 Myles Bateman's reckoning

[56] I.e. 12 barrels.

| $\frac{21}{6}$ 33 | Recd. by him as appeareth in that tyme viz: from the 4th May laste till the 21 Auguste 1633 the somme of 49^l 6^s 3^d | 49 | 6 | 3 |
| | Disburssed ad. $\frac{4}{3}$ ad. $\frac{21}{6}$ | 42 | 19 | 1 |

	Restes the $\frac{21}{6}$ 1633	6	7	2
15 October recd. here as per accompte		86	11	2

	92	18	4

$\frac{22}{6}$ 33 Myles Bateman's reckoning add $\frac{4}{3}$ 33   *Page 7*

$\frac{21}{6}$	Disburssed by Myles in the said tyme:						
	Petie charges add. $\frac{4}{3}$ ad $\frac{19}{3}$	1	15	0			
	Victuallinge then	2	13	7	9	3	1[57]
	Weare & teare	2	14	0			
7	Wages of men	2	0	6			
	Petie charges add. $\frac{19}{3}$ ad $\frac{4}{4}$	0	10	6			
	Victualls then	1	12	6	3	19	10
	Weare & teare	0	0	0			
7	mens wages	1	16	10			
	Pet. charges add. $\frac{4}{4}$ ad $\frac{19}{4}$	1	3	4			
	Victuallinge then	2	3	8	5	12	9
	Weare & teare then	0	12	2			
7	Men's wages	1	13	7			
	P. charges add. $\frac{19}{4}$ ad $\frac{4}{5}$	0	19	10			
	Victualling then	0	12	4	3	10	8
	Weare & teare then	0	4	6			
7	Men's wages then	1	14	0			
	Pet. charges add. $\frac{4}{5}$ ad $\frac{19}{5}$	1	19	4			
	Victualls then	5	6	2	9	3	8
	Weare & teare	0	4	2			
7	mens wages	1	14	0			
	Pet. disb. add. $\frac{19}{5}$ ad $\frac{21}{6}$	1	2	1			
	Victuallinge then	3	17	3	11	9	1
	Weare & teare	1	18	0			
	Men's wages then	4	11	9			

	Totall charge 3 months 17 dayes	42	19	1[58]

[57] Error for £11?
[58] Error for £44?

Customes in the Ile of Man

		s	*d* $\frac{1}{2}$
Page 9	Sylver the pounde exported	0	2$\frac{1}{2}$
	Ayle the barrell	0	1$\frac{1}{2}$
	Allome the Cma.[59]		
	Anchorage of any vessell with a boate	0	8
	without a boate	0	4
	Barly the bowle in bulcke of the strang.[60]	0	1
	In caske the brll.	0	2
	Beefe the carkasse	0	2
	Beefe quicke to { strangers	2	0
	{ Islanders	1	0
	Boardes sowen or cloven the Cma.	0	6
	Butter the barrell	0	1
	Beere the barrell	0	2
	Brasse the Cma.	0	8
	Cloathe: broade { the Cma.	2	0
	of wollen { the dozen	0	2
	narrowe { the Cma.	0	8
	{ the dozen	0	1$\frac{1}{2}$[61]
	Coales the boate one barrell	0	4
	Cloath of lynnen, Irish, the Cma.	0	6
	Pouledaines the boalte	0	6
Page 10	Pilteras the boalte 0	0	6
	Calfe skins the dozen 1^d ob & the Cma.	0	6
	Cheese the wey cont.: 256 lbs	0	6
	Caddowes	0	2
	Hapins the dozen[62]	0	6
	Mudfish the dozen	0	6
	Drie fish the Cma.	0	6
	Eyles cayme the Cma	0	8
	Fysh the tunne	1	0
	Flesh the barrell	0	2
	Fledges	0	2
	Flocks the stone	0	1$\frac{1}{2}$
	Flaxe the bayle	0	1
	Fethers the stone	0	2
	Goates quicke the dozen	0	4

[59] I.e. cent. maximum, or "great hundred", which is 120.
[60] I.e. strangers to the Isle of Man as distinct from inhabitants.
[61] Illegible but probably 1^d is meant. The $\frac{1}{2}^d$ is clear.
[62] Coverings.

Goate fells	{ the Cma.		0	6
	{ the dozen		0	$0\frac{3}{4}$
Geese the dozen			0	3
Hydes of oxen 8 to a dicker	⎫ [63]			
of cowes 10 to a dicker	⎬			
to the stranger			0	6
to the countryman			0	3
Haberden the Cma.		0	0	6
Herreinges the tunne			1	0

2 dum caput

Page 11

Horsses the peece	{ Islanders	6	6
	{ Strangers	[blank]	
Herreinges the maze		0	1
Hopps the Cma.		0	6
Honey the fyrkin		0	$1\frac{1}{2}$
Hens the dozen		0	2
Iron	{ the tunne	1	0
	{ the Cma.	0	$0\frac{3}{4}$
Kiddes the dozen		0	$4\frac{1}{2}$
Kidde fells	{ the Cma.	0	3
	{ the dozen	0	$0\frac{1}{2}$
Lambes quicke the dozen		0	4
Lyme the bowle or barrell		0	$1\frac{1}{2}$
Mather the Cma.		0	5
Maulte the bowle	{ the Islander	0	1
	{ the Stranger	[blank]	
Mantles the peece		0	2
Nayles the thousand		0	3
hundred		0	$0\frac{1}{2}$
the laste		2	0
Oake tymber, bares, shaftes, sparres, plowe beames & all other kinde of tymber the Cma., three peeces of a kynde custamd.			8
Oates the bowle { Ila.		0	1
{ Str.		[blank]	
Pitch the Cma.		0	$1\frac{1}{2}$
Packs { the footepack		0	6
{ the horsse packe		1	0
Plancks for shippes the Cma.		1	0
Pewter the Cma.		0	8
Powten the dozen		0	2
Ressen the Cma.		0	$1\frac{1}{2}$

Page 12

[63] I.e. ten.

Roapes of hayre the dozen	0	1½
Roapes Brittish the Cma.	0	6
Rugges the Cma.	0	2
Rugge freize the dozen	0	1½
Raysins the frayte or heade	0	3
Ryse the bowle	0	1
Sheepe the dozen	0	4
Sheepe skins the Cma.	0	6
Swyne the dozen	0	4
Salte the tunne	1	0
Shippes with salte British or Portingall inward shall pay ¼ of a tunne before the maste & an other above the maste if it be 20 tunnes or els the halfe		
......[64] the dozen	0	3
Salmon the butte	0	6
Salmon the barrll.	0	3
The fyrkin of salmon	0	1½
Soape the Cma.	0	4
Sacke a butte, Ilander or Stranger	1	0
A smalle boate or pickard loaden with white or gray English salte, one fyrlatte before the maste, another after the maste	[blank]	
Tallowe the Cma. weighte	0	6
Tarre the Cma.	0	1½

Page 13

Tanned lether the dicker[65]	Ilander	0	6
	Stranger	1	0
Wyne the tunne		2	0

Prize wynes in the Iland is if they sell 10 tunne, ½ a tunne for prize wynes; if they sell 20 tunnes then a whole tunne for prize wynes or if they sell more then 20 tunnes but one tunne still for the reste of the wynes sold besides the prize wyne given. The custome is 2^s the tunne for what they sell onely; for what is shipped out without sayle, if once landed yet it payeth custome 2^s per tunne though not prise wynes, but if yow change your wynes into other bottomes without landeinge for that, neither price wynes nor custome is payd.

Page 14

Woolle the stone 20 lb to the stone	Islander	0	2
	Stranger	0	3
Wadde the bayle		0	6
Wheate the boale[66]	Islander	0	1
	Stranger	[blank]	

[64] Damaged.
[65] I.e. ten.
[66] [Sic] Bowl?

C.L. to pay L. B. 500^l per ann, to take a lease theireof in Chalmley name and mine. Chalmley to release his title therein; & I to give him for his services in collectinge 100^l per annum if the profitts amount soe much above 500^l per annum; if amounte to lesse then 600^l he onely to have what more they [make than?] 500^l; if to more then 600^l I to have it.

the 19 November, 1633, per me Douglass   Chr. Lowther.

[Page 14 ends. Page 15 reflections in Latin which continue to top page 16 then:]

28 10ber Goods on the other side	1633		
Remayninge in November	2,093	16	8
100 more in cloaths since by my ptener. Rowland	200	0	0
In hoppes	140	0	0
In Rowland's horsse 6^l, brass peece 18^s	6	18	0
Salte pannes & house	280	0	0
Peere	100	0	0
Osburne's lande	81	0	0
Cole woorkes	100	0	0
Deducte with Rowland's 120^l	3,001	14	8
Restes	2,981	14	8[67]

A Rude coniecture what our Stocke amounteth to $\frac{2}{9}$ '33.   *Page 17*

Herreinge voyage			574	7	11
Woole in England			160	0	0
Cloathe in Ireland	{ Dublin		83	8	2
	{ Belfast		38	13	10
Salte	{ Dublin		1	7	0
	{ Belfast		[blank]		
Coles in Dublin			1	10	0
Caddowes in Dublin			10	12	9
Canarie adventure					
Rowland for Hopes					
	Cloath England				

Herreinge Voyage		574	7	11
Woolle in England		160	0	0
Canarie		550	0	0
Dublin	Goods	156	10	4
	Debts & ready money	134	16	6$\frac{1}{2}$

[67] Probably an error for 2,881.14.8.

Belfast	Goods	110	3	10
	Debts & ready money	237	18	1
Whitehaven		50	0	0
Rowland Jackson in England		120	0	8

2,093 16 8½

Page 18

A cloath suite

Dublet a britches 2yrds ¾ } Coate 2 2⁄4 }	3	10	0
3 doz ½ loope lace for boath	0	14	0
3 dozen buttons for coate	0	3	0
5 dozen do. spare for dublet	0	3	0
2 yardes stuffe lyninge	0	6	6
3 oyled skines	0	3	0
bayze	0	1	6
silke one ounce ½	0	2	6
1 yard ¾ plush	0	15	0
canvesse stiffeninge etc	0	2	6
Fringe and button	0	1	10
Taffaty	0	1	6
poyntes 2½ dozen	0	7	6
hookes, eyes, tape	0	0	7
makeinge	0	10	0

My suite	7	2	5

My mother's 18 yds grogram	5	8	0
Crteny.[68] satten 1 yrd ½	0	12	0
lace	1	10	0

19: september

Page 19

Our fisheinge

Caske	76	{ 20 the *George*
	66	{ 20 the *Barronet*
		{ 26 the *Margaret*
	10	Casks remayninge which if can get at 50ˢ per tunne. pilotage in Rich. Bell to goe to fraighte him or if not then to ly them up either for nexte yeare or make beefe here of them.
Salte	240	brlls. of white salte
	130	brlls. of Spanish salte
	370	

[68] [*Sic*] Cretonne?

13	French salte

383	brlls. in all salte, of which we shall neede for the:
280	brlls.

Reste 103

$$\left\{\begin{array}{ll} George & 80 \\ Barronet & 80 \\ Margaret & 120 \end{array}\right\} \; 280$$

To sell: the French 13
To carry overplus salte: 30

To make Jo. Boyde & Poake make 2 cisternes for makeing herreinges in;   *Page 20*
To bargaine 60 dozen candles with John Laythes in pte. of his dbts. of 18 &
   20 in the pounde: 30 dozen and of (12:16: & 14) 20 dozen & of (6:8:10:)
   10 dozen.

Debts

John Laythes yet oweth	2	0	0[69]
Anth. Freeman oweth	31	0	6
Alexander Thompson	0[70]	13	10
John Quarton per 2 bills	{ 9	10	0
	{ 4	3	4
Wm. Gilbarte per bill	20	14	4
Mr Foster per bill	18	2	8
Nicholas Ecleston bill	4	10	0
Wm. Couley of Strangford	1	14	6
Robert Rurneleys bill	8	12	8

Oweinge this $\frac{20}{7}$th 1633 totall	128	1	8
Onyon reds[71] sugar & molasses etc	[blank]		
Mr Thompson salte	15	6	0

Caske   *Page 21*

Laste
40   at Belfast with   { John Boyde
 5   { Quinton Gathergoode
——

45	laste in all at Belfast the 25th September			
	Put aboard the *Henry* of them	17	0	0
	George	16	4	0
	With Wat Rowlandson	0	5	0

[69] Formerly 20.0.0 but inked out.
[70] Formerly 25 but crossed out.
[71] Smudged or damaged and illegible.

With French salte	1	1	0
With White salte	67	1	0
With Mrs Foster one brll. loste	0	2	0
42:2: ber with Robert Nevens	0	2	0

William Roger's barque	7 laste of salte
Our owne barque	9 all white
James Gylles	10 Span. salte
	—
Salte in all	26 laste

William Roger's caske	17 laste
Our owne barq. new caske	18 laste : 8 barrells
boarde caske olde	00 :6
James Gylles hath	27 :6
Totall caske per account stated	63 :2
Bulke herreinge: W. Rogers	1 :4
	64 :6
May be God blesseing us	64 :2 of
	herringe

26th of September 1633

Cloth resting unsould att Belfast vallue worth as followeth:

1	Crowne rash	4	0	0
1	Moheire	2	8	0
2¾	yards of Spanish cloth	1	6	8
4	Yorkshire dozens	14	13	4
1	Kersie	2	6	8
9	yards Kersie prest	1	1	0
44	yards Pennistone	4	15	4
84	ore therabouts yrds. of baise	8	10	10
64	yards of Kendall cotten	3	6	8
	In toto	42	8	6
	Mohayre & Spanish remnent solde	3	14	8
	Restes goods theire the 17 October	38	13	10
	Spa. salte 18 brlls; Fren. salte 13 brlls. at 12^s	18	12	0
	White salte 49 brlls. at 8^s 6^d	20	17	6

Empty caske 52 brlls. 1^s 6^d	3	18	0
14 tallowe caske, Quinton	1	5	8
Given Quinton, etc, in pte. caske for Whitehaven	6	10	6
2 rundlets butter	2	13	6
Earnest tyles 5^s pooles[72] 15^s	1	0	0
Shovells 5 dozen a marke	0	13	4
Hempe	6	0	0
	100	3	10

Disposeinge of the Herrings

Page 23

1.   The *George* for France viz: Rochell to sell the herr. & thence to Bordeaux for wines. Theise herringes to be made with halfe Engl. & halfe Spanish, wholy repacked[72]; the wines discharge at Douglas all but 9 tunne 3 hogshds. that to Whitehaven; reste to be selerred up if barques of Whitehaven or Workington or others be not theire to carry some more along with the *George* but not above 9 tunne 3 hogshds. in a bottome.

2.   James to touch at Knockfergus according to charter party for advise and for to goe as advized; not to France if noe advice at Belfast, then to Whitehaven; to picke of this barqe's loadeinge.

3.   The *Henry* to come to Knockfergus for advice, to packe hirs piccled & make bulk herreinge good store. *Page 24*

4.   To get John Boyd's adventure of 8 laste from him upon an accompte if I like it.

[There follows in a different coloured ink:]

1.   On Friday our barque departed the bay of Knockfergus beinge the 4th October, reached that day Olderfleete and deptd. thence upon the 9th of October in the morneinge by cockcrowe.

2.   The *Henry* departed the Bay of Knockfergus the 4th of October, by tempest driven in againe upon the 6th & upon the eighth departed againe with a southwest winde with which it is thought she is got ($\frac{15}{8}$) to Ila..[73] Our owne barq & the rest of the fleete from Olderfleete in number shipps, barques & fishers about 40 at leaste.

The *Margaret* 40 tunne upon our accompte of caske put aboard hir 1200 *Page 25* hoopes 10^l sterling sent Myles for further provision, 1 shovelle, 12 dishes, 12 dayle boardes, 10 laste herringe barrell packed salt by hande &

[72] These two words interpolated.
[73] [*Sic*].

Addiss...[74] She departed the Bay of Carrickfergus the   [75]October & came in thither from Dublin the 8th October.

$\frac{15}{8}$ Myles, mak 6 barrells of herringe with Spanishe salte & 6 with white salte onely in every barque for experience if yow have leysure repack wholy & pickle all your herreinge. I have sente yow here by James Gylles 10 ^{l}. Enquire of the herreinge sommer fisheing, & cods and lynge the tyme when, the place & how we may compass this & for the makeing oyl of the guts of herreinge & learne what goode the Londoners did this yeare in theire fisheing. Make much of the company. Play the good husband but not to nigardly as neither to lavish, but discreetly I pray yow.

16 October. Goodes left at Knockfergus to be sente by the nexte shippeing for Whitehaven, viz: 2 ryderkins of butter at John Pennington's and at Mr Letherborrowes 4 dozen & 3 polles of ash, 5 doz. of shovells,

Page 26

matts of straw & French matts and 6 barrells of Spanish salte and 200 at 6 score to the c. or thereabouts, of hoopes for barrells; and about 600 hoopes more to be had at Mrs Herman's & 2,000 or as many more as would freight out the barque to Whitehaven of Dutch tyles of Mrs Herman for which given her in earnest 5^s and 300 ash bended butt hoopes of the cowper over against Jo. Pennington's, given him earnest 1^s, at 10^s per cwt and a waynescott bedd of the sayme joyner at 10^s noe earnest given him. Buy more poles if Will Tippin have any or any other; Ryll Young's beefe barrell it up, sell of the Spanish salte or make beefe with it; & send it to Whitehaven but howsoever send about 10 or twenty barrells of beefe and about 2 brlls. or 3 of candles of which take one brrll. of John Laythes, the rest at Knockfergus at 3^s 6^d per doz. cotton weebe, of the Londoner.

Page 27

1. Sell the cloath as yow can.
2. Make a slaughter to get in money: of Mr Foster

Mr Foster	50	beastes
John Laythes	30	beasts
Anth. Freeman	30	beasts
& of those who furnish your beste	10	b. more

Totall of beastes in all	120		160^l
To pay for the same 120 beastes	160	0	0
You have Mr Foster for	237	18	1

			77	18	1 to be for
Rem. Spanish cloath	1	5	0	to buy meale, paying
Wyne	48	2	8	for tyles, hempe,
Seeds	8	15	3	candles, lynnen, yarne
John Laythes	20	0	0	in the voyage with the

[74] Damaged abbreviated name.
[75] Blank.

Anthy. Freeman	31	0	6
Alex. Thomp[son]	0	13	10
Josuah Wharton	13	13	4
William Killcarte	29	14	4
Nicholas Ecleston	4	10	0
Will Couley	1	14	6
Robt. Turley	8	12	8
Mr Thompson, salte	15	6	0
Younge's cour.	1	10	0
120 hydes to be solde	33	0	0
in money in pursse	50	0	0
	267	18	1

beefe or more slaughter, cheifley tallowe

Write over all your bookes fayre and send me them over, both your cash booke, pety charges journall, etc; the particuler of your debts: the rests of your money in pursse.   *Page 28*

Of Mrs Herman Caske

16:	laste & one barrell over at 18^s per laste.
50:	John Boyde at 17^s 6^d.
6:	James Mackmeter at 17^s.
5:	of Quinton Caterwood[76]
77	laste boughte in all: whereof forth to the fisheinge new caske besides 5 or sixe beere barrells etc of our owne: 62 [laste]: 8 [barrels]: soe rests of the 77 laste, viz:
14:4	which are as followeth:

Rests with John Boyd	1 [laste]	10 [barrels]
with Sp[anish] salte	1	6
Fr[ench] salte	1	1
White salte unsoulde	4	1
Whith Mrs Foster	0	2
Robert Nevins	0	2
Broughte from 4 Myle Water	2	2

L. brlls.
14:5

Unsolde for beefe	11	0
Solde with salte Mr Thomp.	83	0
To Wat Rowlandson barrell	0	5

[76] [Sic] but more often Gathergoode. Mrs Herman is sometimes spelled Hermon or Hermonn.

The 20th October

1. To pay my Uncle Lancelot his annuity.
2. To set downe a computation owne of our fisheinge voyage & showe it to Mr Radcliffe. ·
3. To make Rich. Wibergh keepe his accots. by memorial journall & leadger, cashbooke, pety charges, acquittances.
4. To knowe of Mr Radcliffe what my lord or he will doe for serving the soldiers' coates & transporteing woolle.
5. Whether he will joyne in a lynge & cod adventure this spring for the Isles & talke with him about the sommer herreing fisheing.
6. To advise with Mr Radcliffe how farre I may adventure to trade by vertue of the Statutes or my charter.
7. To advise for the buyinge a shipp to trade in the fisheinge or salte & coles; in what I will he will joyne.
8. To take a tyme to caste & write downe theise foresd. and other projects.
9. To know what favour to have in prohibitions for transportation, as corne, yarne, popest wool.

10. That Rich[ard Wibergh] buy 12,000 barrell hoopes & send to Whitehaven by the firste.
11. That we buy some beefe & barrell it up for Whitehaven & 1,000^{wt} of tallowe, a fyrkin of soape, 200 lbs of prunes; 100 lbs of raysins of the Somme; 200 lbs of Malligo[77] raysins & 200 lbs of currants; 2 barrells of apples; 2 barrells or more of tarre; 2 rundlets of sacke.
12. To write to Mr George Lane of Bristol.[78]
    George Jackson, roapemakers bonde.
13. To goe through our debtors & get what is owne.
14. To sell of our cloath & stuffes if we can or let Mr Bamber have them.
15. To call to my partener Radcliffe for the lease & the rest paprs. of the salte pannes.
16. To speake to him that we have the onely selleinge of salte or noe foreigne salte to be solde, while is English.

The 2: November 1633
Goods at Dublin
Span. cloathes

1 Clay. 19 yrds $\frac{3}{4}$	9	12	7
1 Clay. 19 $\frac{3}{4}$ more	9	12	7
1 Spiers 20$\frac{1}{2}$	8	9	4
Yorkshires			
1 dozen wrapper	3	0	0

[77] I.e. Malaga.
[78] For letter see above *Page 61*.
[79] For *Page 31* see below p. 116.

Stuffes

6 Crowne rashes			24	0	0
2 Peropasses blew and black			6	15	0
4 damozellars		1 ashcolour	2	16	9
	W—	1 crimson	2	11	9
		1 crimson flored	3	0	9
	V—	1 greene flored	2	11	9

Whitehaven:

2 Mohayres	1 Mo. W		4	16	0
2 Carthages	1 Car. W		4	14	0
1 Figuraney	1 C Wen		1	7	0

For Whitehaven 11 14 10

83	8	2

58 stone at 15^l to the stone			
2^c of Eng. woolle of Mr Baker	33	10	0
9 sets of & 23 single caddowes	10	15	0
16 brlls. of beefe	16	0	0
3 brlls. salte	1	7	0
Hoopes 3^l 12^s; tymber 2^l 8^s; lathes 15^s	6	15	0

151	15	2

Goods at Dublin broughte from the other side	151	15	2

Page 34
top[80]

Under deducte for Whitehaven	11	14	10
Then restes goods at Dublin	140	0	0
Waxe about 3^l besides my mother's	3	0	0
Coles 2 tunne besides the Mayor's	1	10	0
Given beforehand of tallow 2 tunne	10	0	0
The blacke nagge	2	0	0

156	10	4

The 2 November 1633
Debts at Dublin dew to me

Page 33
top[81]

Will Weston Easter	3	0	0
James Browne, cornemrcht,	3	4	0
Rob. Wadding, etc, Easter & Trinity	6	11	0
Edward Carney $\frac{14}{7}$	11	18	10
Kedagh Goughaghan $\frac{11}{7}$	11	5	0
Chr. Honicocke $\frac{24}{9}$	14	5	0

[80] For remainder *Page 34* see below p. 117.
[81] For remainder *Page 33* see below p. 117.

Mathew Browne, clarke, $\frac{Mich.}{22}$	4 10 0	
Hutchingson 20 brlls. salte: present	9 0 0	

Totall debts	63 11 10	
Rich. Balle stuffe	3 13 4	
Mr Andrew Caddaylle, Crowene R[ash]	4 8 0	

71 13 2

Page 35 top

$\frac{11}{9}$ Debts broughte from thother side yet remayninge	63 11 10	
Mrs Newman { Elder ½ tunne coles	0 7 0	
{ Younger 1 tunne coles	0 14 0	
Mrs Thompson 1 tunne of coles	1 0 0	
Mr Bamber 2 brlls. salte	0 17 0	
Mr Benteley 2 s.½ coles	0 5 7	

$\frac{11}{9}$	66 15 5	
In money with Rich. Wibergh this 11 Nov. 1633	42 5 7½	
$\frac{11}{9}$br More with him which I gave him	24 15 6	
More with him for coles	1 10 0	

Page 35 ends

134 16 6½

Page 31

Dublin.   Directions lefte with Richd. Wibergh the 11th November 1633

1. Hercafter to keepe bookes of memoriall journall, leadger, cash, peti charges on merchandizes, invoizes, acquittances, charges generall, coppis of letters & remembrance booke, in severall quiers of papr.; and to sende me coppies of them over from tyme to tyme, especially ledger.
2. To send in your letter full intelligence of the rates of commodities & other notes or prohibition or lycence to transporte.
3. To write to George Jackson & know of him his proceadinges as also let him know of yours.
4. To send the tallow, 54^l:13:4; woolle 33^l:10^s; caddowes 10^l:15^s; yarne 18^l:10^s; beefe 26^l & if yow like a pack of skins and my letter to Mr Layne[82] with them.
5. To save bloode in barrells for Whitehaven.
6. To alter the seller as directed.
7. To get mandates for insolvant debtors by Mr Edmond's meanes & satisfie him.
8. As yow here of the herreing fishinge let Mr Radcliffe knowe of it, and the money of the hopps keepe by yow for the discharge the herreing fisheing that if need be George may charge yow from Belfast.

[82] See above *Page 61.*

9. To buy to the 4,000 of hoopes that yow have other 8,000 & send them for Whitehaven as yow can, and send tarre, pitch, etc.   *Page 33 lower half*

10. Sende the tymber & lathes to Whitehaven & hempe if at $3^s 4^d$ (16 cwt) and steele if about 4^d per pounde & northrèn broade iron, if about $13^l 10^s$, & cheese.

11. If the proceade doe returne hither of the goods sent to Bristol to sende them to Whitehaven, such as are for that place.

12. To alter my redd cloath suite, to turne it, satten edge it and send it to me over & to buy poyntes for it.   *Page 34 lower half*

13. To sell of the cloathes & stuffes if yow can or els let Mr Bamber sell them.

14. To bargaine us what salt yow can at $8^s 6^d$ from the shippe or gabers and 9^s or $9^s 6^d$ out of the seller, beforehand.

[Page 37 contains a diagram and an incomplete description of an "engine for drawing water…" as follows:]

To make an engyne for draweinge water out of colepits or for salt-woorkes: Firste, make a frame of woode 6 foot square (A) [on the diagram]. Then make 3 axeltrees 2 inch square or more of iron, whereof let the 2 higheste have a greate wheele at the one ende and a litle wheele at thother ende; all the lytle wheeles yow see are to be 12 inches about with 12 teeth a peece, the greet wheeles 60 inches about and 60 teeth a peece; the outmoste crosse-barred wheele of wood with a handle at the side almoste to turne the iron wheeles about by a man; for …[83]
[Page 38 is blank.]

The 20 Febr. 1633/4   *Page 39*

1. To sell of the 10 new pypes of wyne if I can or soe many as I can.
2. To speake for a but of Malligo for the 7 olde pypes to mix with them.
3. To get them sent to Newcastle.
4. To get Will Atkinson bounde to me.
5. To buy my mother hir Turky grogram and sende all thinges into the country.
6. To give my Uncle Robert his olde indentures and take in myne of him.
7. To see at Mr Cosbie's the Engine.
8. To speake to Uncle Richard[84] concerninge William Fletcher, etc.
9. To deliver Mr Littleton's letter.
10. To speake with Chalmley this 21st at night.
11. To deliver Lucy's letter and gynger bread.
12. To speake to my Lord of Berkshire.

---

[83] Ends in mid sentence.
[84] Probably Richard Lowther, Sir John's younger brother, who was a barrister of Greys Inn, and lived in Cripplegate, London.

13. To write to my ptner. Rowland Jackson.
14. To make Mr Battie a letter of atturney and take in that other from Uncle Robert.
15. To knowe whether matter of forgerie and riot may be both in one bill (4 charges maybe).
16. To knowe whether any extent against Crosby demayne.
17. To speake to Mr Popham about Newley.

10 March 1633/4

1.   I, C. L., to goe tomorrow being the 11th March, toward Whitehaven where to be on Friday, and theire to take some coursse with our herreinges and for our goods at Bristol and for imployment for our barques for Dublin; and to order the collyerié & salterie and what money we can make here in England or Ireland to write to Richard to imploy it in woolle for Leeds, and trayne if it may be easely done from Bristol.

2.   On Monday nexte to set from Whitehaven to Newcastle where to be on Wednesday, 19th, and theire stay till Monday, 24th, in selleinge of our wynes or giveing order for to Mr Emerson if they then be not come and to vew the cole woorckes theire and saltewoorckes perfectly, to which end to carry with me my laste booke of Newcastle directions.

3.   Either to holde on to Edinburgh the 24th being Munday where to be on Wednesday and Thirsday and Friday. Speake with Mondy and get the money owne and see theire saltery and collyerie and thence to be backe at Lowther by the 2nd of Aprill at farthest or from Newcastle come directly home, and then for Whitehaven.

4.   My brother Will to stay at Leeds and theire gette in the debts and to buy more cloath till have gotten a sortement for Hamburg of about 500^l woorth to be returnned in dyeinge stuffe which Anthony Cowper to manage & he oversee and for the woolle busines I shall drawe out 400^l to the 600^l at Leeds soe will be for woolle 500^l at present and for cloath and a dyeing stuffe shoppe 500^l more, with which till my father get in money we must be doeinge with; & whether the dyeinge stuffe and cloath or woolle & cloath be better to-imploy it, that to followe moste.

A computation for the makeinge of caske by 50 laste the 20 September as is undertaken by Quinton Gatherwood.

1. 50 laste of scrowes with theire headeinge at Belfast at 11^s
   per laste halfe ready money given him the reste when
   finished at midsommer   27 10 0
2. Custom & carriadge to Whitehaven at 2^s per laste   5 0 0
3. Hoopes from Dublin at 3^s per laste   7 10 0

4. Setteinge up in England at 2ˢ 6ᵈ per laste   6 5 0

5. House rent for the cowper at Whitehaven   1 5 0

---

6. 50 laste soe made at 19ˢ per laste   47 10 0

   10 laste more soe bargayned   9 10 0

   Totall 60 laste bargnd. with Quinton & And. Crumey[85]   57 0 0

   The scrowes to be ready per $\frac{1}{1}$ 34

---

272 inches and $\frac{25}{100}$ pte. of an inch in an ayle gallon

7,616 inches in a barrell of 28 gallons

8,704 inches in a brrll. of 32 gallons

1,728 inches in a foote square

       5 barrells & one pynte in a yarde square.

A computation for the makeinge of caske by 20 laste the 1 of October. *Page 43*
Jo. Poake

	l	s	d
5,000 at 6 score to the hundreds[86] of staves in the woodes of Kilwarden of Mr Arth. Hill's at 17ˢ per mille	2	11	0
1,200 of headeinge at 17ˢ per mille	1	0	4
Scroweinge of the 20 laste at 3ˢ per laste	3	0	0
Porteage of 20 laste of scrowes at 1ˢ per laste	1	0	0
Portage of 1,200 headeing at 1ˢ per hundred	0	12	0
2,000 of unslit runges in the woodes at 9ᵈ [per] 120	0	15	0
slitting and shaveing at 12ᵈ the C[120]	1	0	0
Carriage of the runges at 8ᵈ the double hundred	0	13	4
20 laste of caske wth. runges which is 10ˢ 7ᵈ per laste at Belfast.	10	11	8
Carriag & custome etc into England	2	0	0
Setteinge them up in England	2	10	0
20 laste sett up in England which is 15ˢ 1ᵈ per laste	15	1	8

	l	s	d	
Recd. per Row. Jackson or reste	109	13	10	*Page 44*
Of James Bennet	100	0	0	
Of Mr Marris	150	0	0	
For pte. paymt. of 20 stone of woolle of Wm. Close at 13ˢ per stone, the reste per bill cost	3	0	0	

[85] May be contraction.

[86] I.e. "great hundred", 120.

For 2 stone of woolle	1	6	0
For 2 pounde of woolle	0	1	6

Recd. the 21st November 1633	364	1	4
Of Mr Thomas Foster for Robt. Foster	13	0	0

12 buttes

400 of 120 pipe staves	3	0	0
200 hoopes	1	0	0
Screweinge of the 12 butts	0	16	0
Carriage, custome, etc	0	4	0

Page 45

For 16 baggs hopps cont: 35 cwt 1 q 22[87]	115	6	8
Carriage of the 7 bags of 17 cwt 1 q 5 lbs	7	13	0
Carriage to White[haven] 19 baggs cont: at 18 1 q 17	10	16	10
Porteradge Sturbidge[88]	0	3	4
Porteradge etc at Liverpool	0	5	0
Entry and custome at Liverpool	0	13	0
Sellaradge	[blank]		

	134	17	10

*Page 46
blank*

Page 47

Hen. Boylen.   Roape makeinge at Whitehaven in England

1. One heade roapemaker with the helpe of a boy & 2 days woorke of an ordinary man will woorke each weeke 1 C weighte; in a yeare 52 cwt of hempe into cordige	60	13	4
2. Tarre if tarrd cordige in a weeke: 43 lb weight in a yeare 1 tunne	8	0	0

3. Totall hempe & Tarre 72 cwt	68	13	4
4. Woorkeinge the hempe & tarre at 8^s 6^d the hundred	30	12	0
5. Waste in weighte before sayle at 50 lbs weight in the cwt: 3 cwt 24 lbs	5	2	6

6. Totall 68 cwt 3 qt 4 lb weighte in cordige	104	7	10
7. Which at Dublin may yeelde at 36^s per C weighte	123	16	0
8. Soe rests profit. towards adventure above what it standeth to 5^s 8^d upon a cwt in a yeare	19	8	2

[87] "Firste penny" crossed out.
[88] Stourbridge, Worcester.

9. Custome of cordage in Ireland tard or untard 6^d per
   C weighte of 112 lbs   [blank]

1633 $\frac{24}{8ber}$ Slaughtering of beefe   Page 48
1. We slaughtered anno dm. 1632 164 beeses at Belfast to
   take up debts theire at one penny a pounde, the
   beefe, hyde & tallowe 12^d in a beaste abayted. They
   amounted to in all 117^l 2^s 7^d which is:
2. uppon 1^l 6 6 per beaste   1   6   5$\frac{1}{4}$
3. 164 cowes made beefe in all   366 . 3 . 20
   482 cwt 0 q 16 lbs   hyde   59 . 1 . 23
   totall weighte   rough tallow 55 . 3 . 1
   which came to at a penny per pounde twelve pence
   in a beaste abayted   117   2   7
4. The whole weighte of each beaste was 329 lb subtill
   and $\frac{1}{4}$ of a pounde
5. which was at 1^d per pounde 12^d abayted   1   6   5$\frac{1}{4}$
6. But beefe at 1^d per pound without any abayatement pro
   rata per dicta will amounte to per Irish cowe   1   7   6
   equallinge the other rate of buying beefe at $\frac{3}{4}$[^{d}] per
   pounde wt. 250 lbs   0   15   7$\frac{1}{2}$
   hyde at $\frac{6}{4}$ & $\frac{3}{4}$ of a farthing, 40:   0   5   7$\frac{1}{2}$
   tallowe at 2^d per pounde wt. 38:   0   6   4

   a beaste soe rated facit   1   7   7
                                                       _____

                 Slaughteringe   Page 49

7. 164 carkases of beefe weyed laste year 366 C 3 q 20 lbs
   and made out 159 barrells Scotch gage dried packed.
8. Soe each barrell weyed 2 C. 1 q. 6$\frac{1}{2}$ lbs which at $\frac{3}{4}$[d]
   per lb is per barrell   0   16   2
   The caske   0   1   6
   The salte   0   3   0

   A barrell of beefe at $\frac{3}{4}$^{d} per pd.   1   0   8
                                                       _____

9. Tallowe rough at 2^d per pounde is per Cwt 0 : 18 : 8
   Rendringe & makeing weighte againe at   0 : 5 : 0
   1 C weighte refine tallowe   1 : 3 : 8   1   3   8

A forecaste of furnishing 60 tunne of beeffe and tallowe for Amsterdam.   Page 50
Beeses 420 will make 400 brlls of beefe at 20^s 8^d facit   413   6   8

& of tallowe will make 142 C 2q 0 lb	133	0	0
Ren[d]ringe & restoringe weighte for weighte at 5^s per C	35	2	6
Hydes at 5^s 7^d per peecke	118	2	6
besides salteinge at 4^d per hyde	6	3	4
	706	15	0[?][89]
300 hydes custome at 9$\frac{1}{2}$^{d} (?) per hyde[90]	11	10	0[?]
Custome of the beefe at 2^s per barrell entreinge $\frac{3}{4}$	30	0	0
Custome of tallowe at 1^s 6^d per Cwt $\frac{3}{4}$ entred	8	0	0
Fees of entrie	1	0	0
Guiftes amonge customers[91]	2	10	0
Craynidge, lighterage, portige, warehouse roome and peti charges	6	13	4
Ensuerance at 3^l per cent	24	0	0
Factorige at 2$\frac{1}{2}$ per cent	20	0	0
Fraighte at 40^s per tunne	120	0	0
Custome at Amsterdam as here	65	13	4
Factoridge theire	20	0	0
	1,015	1	8

Page 51   [N.B. The accounts on pages 50 and 51 face each other.]

Sales per Contra

400 brlls. of beefe at 40^s per barrll.	800	0	0
420 hydes at 10^s per hyde	210	0	0
142 C 2 q tallowe at 40^s	285	0	0
	1,295	0	0

Page 52

Herringe Voyage Anno '33

Betweene the Lord Deputy [and] Mr Radcliffe who have put in 200^l & Christopher Lowther & Rowland Jackson his partener who have layde out the reste of the stocke.

---

[89] All figures marked ? are conjectural because either barely legible or totally smudged out.

[90] Lowther expected to sell 420 hydes but only to pay custom on 300 apparently.

[91] I.e. customs officers.

Caske

16 laste of Mrs Hermon Knockf[ergus] at 18s per laste firste penny			14	8	0
46 laste of John Boyd & wht. he procured at 17^s 6^d per laste			40	5	0

of which are in the ⎧ *George*   18   laste
    62 laste   ⎨ *Henry*   17   „
              ⎩ *Margaret*   27   „

Hoopes in the ⎧ *George* 1,200 ⎫					
⎩ *Henry* 200 ⎭			1	6	8
in the *Margaret* 1,200			1	5	6
Hogshd. staves: in the *George* 60			0	3	4
Barrell staves: in the *Margaret* 120			0	4	0

Salte

16 laste white salte in the   *George*   9
                    & *Henry*   7

at 7^s a barrell brought to Belfast			67	4	0
10 laste Spanish salte in the *Margaret* made out of 45 hhds. & 1 barrell at 22^s 2^d per hogsheade			50	8	7

Fyshers

3 fyshers given them beforehand 2 of them at 16^l 10^s per man, 1 at 17^l per man			50	0	0
			—	—	—
Totall caske, salte & fyshers, firste penny			225	5	7

Anno '33 Herreinge voyage		*Page 54*

The caske, salte & fyshers brought from the other side			225	5	7	*Page 53*
Advance money to the shippes, viz:						*is blank*

the *George*   92^l 18   4 ⎫
the *Henry*   8   0   0 ⎬   121 18 4
the *Margaret*   21   0   0 ⎭

Advance to the cowpers viz.

To John Boyd   1 . 0 . 0 ⎫
To John Poake   2 . 0 . 0 ⎬   4   0   0
To John Whape   1 . 0 . 0 ⎭

Advance to pylats

To Willm. Hyndeman   3 . 0 . 0 ⎫
To John Love   0 . 1 . 0 ⎭   3   1   0

Petye charges of my partener R. J. (6^l), myself (6^l), George (6^l)
and Richard (2^l) and Myles I immagine to be allready   20   0   0

374	4	11

Page 55
blank
Page 56

Our owne shippe in value   200   0   0^{92}

Rects. per my partener.

Feb. 28	Of Will Atkinson besides what repd. to him	2	5	0
Mar. 23	Of my partener. Mr Lowther^{93}	5	0	0
	Recd. at Bristol as in Myles Dickson accompte	68	4	6
Apr. 25	Rcd. of Mr Lowther my partner.	15	0	0
	Rcd. in Myles Bateman's accote. to Jo. Love and John Roe	0	18	10
June. 14	To my partener's wife^{94}	5	0	0

Totall   96   8   4

Of Wm. Jackson in cloath per contra   21   12   0

Page 57   For Norway.   Disburssed by my partner. R. Jackson.

	2	blacke doz. of Lancelot Glover^{95}	4	9	0
	1	black doz. of John Rosse	2	8	6
7	2	blacke doz. of Will. Smith	4	12	0
	1	blacke doz. of Will. Gylle	2	8	6
	1	black doz. of Brian Woormall	2	1	0
11	1	narrow reade 18 yrds., Anth. Martin	1	10	0
	10	reade dozens of John Greene	25	0	0
	2	Gray doz. of Mr Francis Jackson	6	6	0
	1	Sivet doz. Henry Powson	2	15	0
	2	one Gray cloath 26 yds. of Wm. Jackson	6	16	0
10	2	lighte coloured doz. of him	7	4	0
	1	leade doz. of him	3	6	0
	1	silke poynte 13 yards of him	4	6	0
	1	leade doz. of Thomas Benson	3	1	0
1	1	narrow codlin	0	16	0

^{92} This final note is in a different ink and may have been added later.

^{93} I.e. Christopher. The account is Rowland Jackson's but copied by Christopher.

^{94} Mysterious. Either this was an error for "mother" or Christopher in copying has switched "voices" and means Rowland's wife. Neither Christopher nor Will Lowther was married at this time.

^{95} This name crossed out.

3	{ 3 bayzes 124 yardes, sivet, deroy and gray, James Taylor at 20^d	10	8	4
3	{ 1 double shagge reade: 40 yds. at 22^d	3	13	4
	{ 1 single shagge reade: 25 „ at 22	2	5	10
	{ 1 greene cotton 40 at 22	3	13	4
8	8 colloured Kendayle cottones	7	4	0
43	Totall firste penny	104	3	10
	Carriage to Whitehaven	2	5	0
	Cords and towle[96]	0	4	0
	For a horsse to Mr Will Guy	7	0	0
	Myles Dickson's disbursts. at Bristol	8	11	0
	My parteners. charge from $\frac{27}{12}$ toll $\frac{25}{2}$	7	1	0
		129	4	10

Serveinge the soldiers of Ireland with cloath   *Page 58*

40: companyes of soldiers
10: dozens of Yorkshire to a company beinge 50 men; of colour betweene a gray & a browne & an eye of redde in it and shruncken to be betweene 6 & 7 quarters broade about 3^l a dozen firste penny.

The whole 40: companies will take at 10 doz. to a company, 400 dozens at 3^l per doz:	1,200	0	0
Custome & charges at 10^s upon a dozen	200	0	0
Profit at 10^s per dozen	200	0	0

For a triall to sende over unt..[97] Sir George Radcliffe 10 dozens   30   0   0

Page 59
blank
Page 60

Moneyes receaved per Rowland Jackson since our accompte in August 1633:

Imprimis upon accompte then due in my hande	109	18	10
Item of James Benet at Kendal	100	0	0
Item of Mr Marris	150	0	0
Item 2^{lb} of wool at Whitehaven	0	1	6
Item of Mr Tho. Foster	13	0	0
Item for wooll	4	6	0
Recd. 25/9 '33	377	6	4

[96] Toll? or wrapping?
[97] Smudged. Probably "unto" meant.

	£	s	d
[deduct disbursements opposite]	372	18	5
Reste the 25 November	4	7	11
Of me then recd.	1	0	0
Restes 29 9ber 1633	5	7	11
Of Rich. Wibergh at White[haven]	40	0	0
Disb. per Rowland Jackson since our last accompte w. in August 1633[98]	4	2	11
	3	11	0
		11	11
In Leadforth hoppes 134 . 17 . 10	115	6	8
In carriage of the hopes & cost of 7 bagges	19	11	2
	134	17	10
For cloth bought in Yorkshire	184	9	4
Carriage of the cloth to Whitehaven	3	6	4
Sent to Sir John Lowther	20	0	0
For pack cloths & cordes	0	17	6
For toule[99] of the cloth	0	2	6
For pack clothes for the wooll	3	5	11
For cariage of wooll to Leeds with 2^{lb} kept in Willm. Jackson's hands for to pay when packes comes	7	1	0
For a horse for my London jurney & other service	6	0	0
For a brasse peece which is aboard the *George*	0	18	0
In 2 jurneyes to Whitehaven	0	9	0
My owne charges since the 30th of August	11	11	0
	372	18	5

[Underneath is the following calculation:]

184	9	4
3	6	4
	17	6
	2	6
	9	0
11	11	0

200   15   8   cloath[1]

Page 61 (left margin)

[98] Like the account on preceding page this is in a different handwriting, perhaps William Lowther's.

[99] Perhaps toll, meaning "counting".

[1] Presumably meaning the cost of the cloth deal.

A note of how much Irish wool is sould since the 5th November 1633[2]

Page 62 blank
Page 63

9ber	5	To a hatter 2 stone 13^s per stone R. J.	1	6	0
	12	To Jo. Simpson 13 stone 13^s per stone	8	9	0
	12	to Wm. Close[3] 20 stone 13^s per stone[4]	13	0	0
	14	To John Kilburne 2 ston. 12^s 8^d per stone	1	5	4
	19	To Duke Sarvant & Will Clark 27 st. 12^{s}8^d per	17	2	0
	20	To Will Wright 3 st. 12^s 8^d per stone	1	18	0
	26	To money[5] 1 st. of the lockes at	0	10	11
10/3		To money 8 lb of the lockes	0	5	6
	3	To Will Wright[3] 4st. 12^s 8^d per stone	2	10	8
	3	To Widow Windaras[3] 3 st. 13^s per stone	1	19	0
	3	To Tho. Harrison[6] 1 st. 12^s per stone	0	12	0
	4	To Ro. Kilburne[6] 12 st. 12^s per stone	7	4	0
	10	To Wm. Wright[3] 2 stone at 12^s 8^d per st.	1	5	4
	10	To Jo. Simpson 32 st. 13^s per stone (10^l pd.)	20	16	0
	10	To Will. Armytage 17 stone	11	0	0
			—	—	—
16:10		Solde in all 139 sto. 8 pd. at	89	3	9

	Remaineing in Gyles his shop	51 sto.	0		
	Aboute Halifax	12	0		
	13 packes made out	202 sto.	8 lbs.		
	139: 8	the first Jan.			
17:11	3: 0 to Matthew Glover at 13^s 4^d per st.		2	0	0
	3: 0 to Robert Jackson at 13^s 4^d paid		2	0	0
	11:12 to Gylbert Walker 12^s		7	0	0
	3: 0 In Exchange of woolle for cloath		1	4	0
	16: 0 To Michael Storie		8	16	0
	26: 0 To John Benson for cloath		15	12	0
	—		—	—	—
	202: 4		125	15	9
	202 stone 4 lbs solde broughte per contra		125	15	9
	63 of woolle sold by Gyles		41	2	0
	10 to Michael Robinson		6	6	8
	one resteth of that packe & ......[7] 3 stone				

Page 64

---

[2] Not C. Lowther's handwriting.
[3] 1 January inserted above name.
[4] "3^s paid" inserted above "stone".
[5] "To a stranger" crossed out and "to money" substituted.
[6] "dew laste" inserted above name.
[7] Word illegible because badly smudged and overwritten.

3	st.	Irish sckin woolle to Rob. Walker of Woodhouse	1	19	0
4		more to Rob. Allan pd.	2	11	4
6		skin w. to Richard Ellyson	3	15	0
1		fleece woolle Will Clarck	0	13	0
3		Irish fleece w. Jo. Schedall	1	18	3
11		F. woolle to Michael Robinson	7	3	0
2		F. woolle to Jo. Schedall	1	5	6
7		F. woolle to Rob. Walker	4	5	2
3	9lbs	to Robert Glover	1	15	6
315:13		solde amounteth to	198	11	0

Page 65 blank
Page 66

Recd. by me at Leeds

17	of	December of Will Jackson	12	5	0
	3	Rcd. for 3 stone of Irish woolle of Rob. Jackson	2	0	0
18		Rcd. of Will Jackson pte. of note	4	0	0
	26	Rcd. of John Benson	15	12	0
19	3	Rcd. for 3 stone of unwashed	1	4	0
		Rcd. by Gyles & disburssed	29	5	8
		By my brother	0	15	4
		By Will Jackson paid my brother	11	0	0
		More Will Jackson's note of disb.			

[An isolated note foot of page states: Sir George Radcliffe 35^l 7^s.]

Page 67

	$\frac{17}{10}$	Disbur. for 1 lighte brown			
G	2	Gray cont. 24 yardes undressed	4	19	0
G	2	1 yrd. of a white Shergray	5	6	0
G	1	2 of a fyne lether colour	4	0	0
Jac	1	2 of the same colour, Will Jack son	4	0	0
G	2	4 of John Benson's lether colour	8	8	0
G	2	o^8 of ditto lether colour	7	4	0
G	1	o for 3 stone of bad woolle & money $^{C.L.}$ of a lether colour	2	2	0
G	2	Grayes oweing for to Gyles: 6^l	6	0	0
G	1	4 Michael Robinson's lether colour oweing for it to Gyles:	4	16	0
Jac	1	Candie browne with Will Jackson	3	7	0
	6	More with Will Jackson or theire abouts	22	14	0
	2	Grayes by Gyles	5	0	0
	2	Candie browne	6	10	0
	1	Gray	2	11	6

[8] Probably means ditto.

2	Grayes by my brother Will and dresseinge	5	15	0
28	11 yardes	0	11	0

	93	3	6[9]

deducte 22^l: 14: in Will Jackson's accompted by
   my partener reste 109: 6:

21	by me pd. for firste penny	70	9	6
	dresseinge	18	14	6
	Custome 3^l supposed	3	0	0

	92	4	0

Nicholas Eccleston Dr

Page 68

16 October 1634, to money recd. of Robert Nevins sente by Mr Ro. Jackson	11	0	0
Of Mr Rowland Jackson in money	10	0	0
Of the oates lycence money	9	11	8

	30	11	8

Some oddes not remembred which was 11^s 8^d as per R. J. 's letter Myles dew for lycence of 240 barrls. of oates at 4^d ob per brll. wch Myles hath unpayd, facit 4^l 10^s

More ditto Nicholas is dr. to money recd. of my partener. Rowland Jackson, viz: in his owne bill dew to us	4	10	0
More for licence of oates to Scotchmen about 400 barrells facit 5^l	5	0	0

Nicholas Eccleston, Creditor

Page 69

16. 8. By cash for 30^l paid to me at Lancaster	30	0	0
By cash pd. William Atkinson	5	0	0

[In original these two accounts above are on facing pages.]

Imployments per contra

Page 70

1. Imployed in cloath for Dublin	60	0	0
To have ready for London	130	0	0
2. Scarcely come in by Easter	550	0	0
3. Imployed for Bristol	156	0	0
4. & 5. For woolle and coles[10]	200	0	0

[9] 89–12–6 crossed out.

[10] "And coles" appears to have been crossed out and "& salte" inserted over the top, but this too may be crossed out.

6. & 7. In the voyage now to Bristol	218[11]	0	0
For Whitehaven tyles, beefe	30	0	0
Hempe; caske; herreinge	100	0	0
8. Hoppes to get herreinge forward	40	0	0

1. Herreinge imployed in wynes and the shippe	500	0	0
2. In oates for Norway	110	0	0
3. In coles	55	0	0
4. In coles for Dublin	134	0	0
1. In salte for Dublin	66	0	0
2. In a shipp:[12]	180	0	0
3. In woole for Leeds	430	0	0
4. In coles rests[13] in Woollragayne	120	0	0
7. In salte for Dublin	73	0	0
8. In wyne allsoe	44	0	0

Page 71

Betweene Christmas and Easter to receave:

1. For woolle to Leeds	170	0	0
2. I hope our Canarie adventure	550	0	0
3. In our Dublin goods	156	0	0
4. In cloath sente laste thither	120	0	0
5. In hoppes Dublin	100	0	0
6. Belfast goods	110	3	10
7. Debts and ready money	237	18	1
8. Hoppes	40	0	0

	1,484	1	11

Betweene Easter and Midsomer

• 1. Herreinge voyage propria	100	0	0
2. Cloath at Belfast & Dublin	110	0	0
3. Out of salte from Whitehaven to Dublin for goods theire now	50	0	0
4. f[rom?] cloth at Dublin	134	16	6

Out of goods rcd. in last qrter

1. for cloath out of woolle at Leeds	66	0	0
2. Out of Canarie adventure	550	0	0
Money ready for London	130	0	0
3 6 7 Out of Bristol adventure	430	0	0
4. Out of woolle (120[l]) & coles (90[l])	210	0	0
Out of Whitehaven tyles, beefe, etc	33	0	0

[11] The 8 is doubtful.
[12] After "shippe" figure 400[l] may be inserted and "in tarre" crossed out.
[13] Figure "90" inserted above "rests".

7.	Hempe, etc	40	0	0
8.	Out of herreinge more	44	0	0
	Caske	60	0	0
		2,357	16	6

For settlement in trade by me Chr. Lowther haveinge 2,000^l stocke Page 72

In three severall wayes or partnershippes:		2,000	0	0
1.	Whith Rowland Jackson he $\frac{1}{3}$ & I $\frac{2}{3}$, viz: I have	1,200	0	0
2.	In my house and Osburne's lande at Whitehaven, 200^l	200	0	0
3.	And a stock for a shoppe theire 200^l	200	0	0
4.	In salte pannes building	400	0	0
	Totall where to setle my stocke	2,000	0	0

How our partable stocke will stand

1.	Rowland $\frac{1}{3}$	600	1,800	0	0
	myselfe $\frac{2}{3}$	1,200			
3.	I myselfe $\frac{10}{12}$	200	240	0	0
	R. Wibergh $\frac{1}{2}$	20			
	Will Atkinson $\frac{1}{2}$[14]	20			
4.	I $\frac{1}{2}$	200	400	0	0
	Mr Marris	200			
			2,440	0	0

How my proper stocke will stande:

2.	In house and Osburne's land	200	0	0
4.	In salt pannes proper	200	0	0
		400	0	0

How to order my partable stocke; and proper & firste of my proper stocke, viz: beinge 2 folde: Page 73

1.	House and Osburne's lande to be answered out of: saltery, collyerie, Whitehaven trade, yearley for conveniencie sake	20	0	0
2.	Salte pannes proper, to be builte and served, with Davies's grounde which I hope will answer[15]	40	0	0
		60	0	0

[14] So written but should be "$\frac{1}{12}$".
[15] I.e. from the coal lying beneath Davies's ground, see below p. 214.

Nexte is our partable stocke which beinge 3 folde: Rowland's firste: viz: thirds;

1.	1.	Barque to transporte salte	200	0	0
	2.	Stock for salte	200	0	0
2.	1.	Shippe for coles[16]	400	0	0
	2.	Stock for coles	600	0	0
3.	1.	A stocke to carry beefe for Bristol to reporte trayne thence to Norway to reporte tarre & soe for beefe againe	400	0	0

Or to buy butter against September to fetch wynes and out of the produce of beefe to fetch trayne & out of it butter.

What the ordering of salte

Charge of the barques at 14^l per moneth, 12 moneths	168	0	0
3,000 barrells of salte carried at 5: returnes with a duble stocke of 200^l. 95^l for 300 barrells at a tyme at 6^s 4^d	950	0	0
	1,118	0	0
3,000 barrells solde at 8^s per barrell facit	1,200	0	0
20 p.cent Gaynes if please God	82	0	0
1,000 tunnes of coles Dublin measure or 1,500 Whitehaven tunnes at 2^s 4^d Whitehaven or 12^s Dublin	600	0	0
Porterage at 8^d per tunne and yard rent at 4^d per tunne and factoridge 4^d	66	13	4
Charge of 1,000 Dublin tunnes	666	13	4
Sayles at 16^s per tunne	800	0	0
20 p. c. Gaynes if please God	133	6	8
1,000 stone of woolle at 10^s per stone firste penny, custome 1^s, fraighte 4^d and lande carriage 8^d, paid warehouse roome and the factoridge 4^d	616	13	4

[16] Written over is a later entry: "It fails because of our Canary voyage".

		£	s	d	
	1,000 stone at a marke per stone	666	13	4	
	Gaine at 2 returnes, viz: 50^l	100	0	0[17]	

Disburssements $\frac{16}{9}$ '33

Page 81[18]

		£	s	d	
	Disb. to Rowland Jackson $\frac{26}{9}$	1	0	0	
	In barter of 3 stone of woolle valued at 8^s per stone, and 18^s in money for a lether coloured dozen price 2^l 0^s 0^d	0	18	0	
	In my journey to Leeds about the woolle 14 dayes	2	2	0	
	in expences proprio till January	1	0	0	
$\frac{8}{12}$	For my father: Atkins rent & fees	3	1	4	
	For 2 dozen of Alcamy spoones	0	8	0	
$\frac{10}{12}$	For 2 lockes upon the seller doore of the Canary wynes at London	0	2	0	
$\frac{15}{2}$	For my owne accomptes: a girdle silver 6^s 8^d; a water trialle of ivory 1^s 6^d; a swoord girdle 2^s 6^d; a payre of bootes, Northamp. 6^s 8^d; a payre of brasse gilded spurres 2^s 6^d; tynneinge a payre of spurrs 6^d; bande & ruffes 5^s; a mathematicall booke 3^s	1	8	4	
	The English Usurer a boocke 6^d; shewes soaleinge 1^s; bootes mendeinge 5^d; paper case 6^d, wafers, 200, 6^d; hard waxe 3^d; band stringes 3^d	0	4	5[19]	
	1 ounce of camfora 6^d & 1 oze of opium 12^d	0	1	6	
	5$\frac{1}{2}$ yardes blacke Spanish cloath	4	19	0	
	Bootes mendeinge 3^d; inkhorne 3^d; paperbook 8^d	0	1	2	
		15	5	9	
$\frac{20}{12}$ 33[20]	Disburssed as on the other side	15	5	9	Page 79
	For pynnes for my mother	0	1	7	
	On Sanckley the vintener upon the receipt of the 60^l in a capon, etc.	0	6	0	
	To my Uncle Robert in pt. paymt.	40	0	0	
$\frac{21}{12}$	For the children guiftes	0	6	0	
	For 2 bandes and 2 pre. of ruffes	0	7	9	

[17] I.e. the profit on two adventures of £50 each.

[18] The following accounts on *Pages 81*, *79*, *77*, and *Pages 80*, *78*, *76* are written in reverse page order. They repeat accounts set out in Notebook "A" above pp. 88–9, 94–5.

[19] Error for 3^s 5^d?

[20] I.e. 20 Feb. 1634.

		£	s	d
	For 1 payre of boot hosse toppes	0	1	6
	For 1 payre fulled boote hosse	0	5	0
	For 2 candle stickes	0	1	4
$\frac{22}{12}$	For 30 elnes $\frac{1}{4}$ of a yarde holland	6	15	0
	For a hatte bande and another dresseinge and lyneinge	0	17	0
	For the watch mendeinge	0	3	0
	For a butte of Malligo of Mr Humphrey Slayney	15	0	0
	To my Uncle Robert Lowther	100	0	0
	For our cowper's bill, Mr Woodcock and for his men	3	10	0
	For 18 yardes Turkey chamlet	5	8	0
	For 6 doz. lace 20^s & one ounce $\frac{1}{2}$ of silke	1	3	0
	For Sutton's bill of my suite	0	19	0
	For sattane to face my broade sleaves	0	1	6
	For 3 doz. $\frac{1}{2}$ of blacke poyntes	0	12	3
	For blacke garters & stockins	0	12	8
	For ribbeninge to my white hatte	0	0	6
	For a transire and entreing the wyne	0	3	0
	27 February 1633/4	191	19	10

Page 77

		£	s	d
$\frac{27}{12}$	Disburssed per contra	191	19	10
	For porterage out of seller and putting aboard a boate			
$\frac{28}{12}$	8 pypes Canarie	0	4	6
	For carteage of the 8 pypes	0	5	4
	For cranage of theme at 4^d per pipe	0	2	8
	For boateinge them downe to Wollage	0	8	6
	For a payre of slippers	0	2	0
	For a trunck 3 quarters longe	0	4	8
	For the 10 Commandments pict.	0	0	6
$\frac{1}{1}$	For watchinge the wyne in the boates	0	2	6
	For scowreing my swoord	0	0	6
3	To my brother William	2	0	0
4	More to him	2	0	0
$\frac{21}{1}$	Disburssed for a fyrkin of pippins	0	6	0
	Disb. at Caterick to save my meare	0	8	6
	My owne charges from the 20th of January till 23rd of March at 3^s per diem on Canarie accompte	9	3	0
	Besides my brother's charges 17 & his horsse 7 dayes		[blank]	
$\frac{23}{1}$	To Rowland Jackson at his house	5	0	0

For a swoorde blade	0	6	8[21]	
Receipts a die. $\frac{16}{9}$ber '33				*Page 80*
$\frac{30}{9}$ Recd. of Chr. Wharton at Whitehaven	5	0	0	
Rcd. of my brother William at Leeds 27 January				
in lighte golde solde at 11^l 8^s 6^d	11	8	6	
Of my father 22 January	10	0	0	
$\frac{22}{12}$ Rcd. for 6 pypes of Canary of Mr Sanckley of				
Castle Taverne	63	0	0	
20 February: summa totall	89	8	6	
My owne expence per contra is markd.	7	12	11	
Disburssed for my father per contra	3	9	4	
20 February 1633/4 recd. brought per contra	89	8	6	*Page 78*
Recd. in full of 10 pipes $\frac{1}{4}$ of Mr Chesleyne,				
cowper, in Roode Lane the $\frac{24}{12}$ '33	116	16	6	
$\frac{27}{12}$ 1633/4 Summa Totall	206	5	0	
Disb. my owne expence broughte on	7	12	11	
More my expence per contra	4	10	6	
Totall	12	3	5	
Disbursd. for my father broughte on	3	9	4	
More per contra	13	7	7	
Totall to my father	16	16	11	
$\frac{27}{12}$ Recd. as on the other side	206	5	0	*Page 75 blank* *Page 76*
$\frac{14}{1}$ Recd. of my mother, to Bennet for Robert				
Sympson of Egleston	1	0	0	
$\frac{23}{1}$ Recd. of my mother at Lowther	5	10	0	
	212	15	0	
Disb. my owne expence broughte on	12	3	5	

[21] Account ends here untotalled.

More per contra	[blank]		

Disb. for my father brought on	16	16	11
More per contra	4	6	0
	21	2	11

Page 82

$\frac{29}{9}$ '33 Directions for my partener R. Jackson at his goeinge home from Lowther to Belfast & for to Bristol.

1. At your arrivall at Belfast George will showe yow my orders to him & Mr George Layne's letter which I writte to him, by which yow will know as thinges goe.
2. If George be ungone to Bristol goe yow alonge with the gargazon thither and let George goe to Dublin & stay with Richard till further order, after the herreinges come to Belfast.
3. If your selfe goe to Dublin[22] either to fraight barqes to Bristol, or other business Rich. will bringe yow acquainted with Sir George Radcliffe.
4. Let good store of hempe be bargayned for the roape maker.
5. Let the tyles, poles, butter, hoopes be sente by the firste for Whitehaven.
6. If yow want money to pay the fishers at theire returne take it up & charge it on Richard Wibergh[23] for Sir George Radcliffe to pay.

Page 83

7. If can bargaine any herreinge over to Whitehaven & Milnthorpe yow may then send James Gylles to Dublin to sell there, carry Will Rogers to Bristol to returne your goods & the *George* for France.
8. If Richard have sente the goods to Mr Layne which I thincke will be: 2 tunne of tallowe, 30 brlls. of beefe, 60 stone of woolle, 29 rugges, 4 lbs weighte of yarne; in valew 150^l, then take yow order & accompte of them from Mr Layne.
9. If Richard have not sente the goods yow may then if yow like consigne them to Myles Dickson, soapeboyler, on the bridge at the sygn of the 7 Starres to remayne till yow get thither yourselfe and in the meanetyme to sell & bargayne trayne.
10. If the goods come not to Mr Layne yet returne some playte iron howsoever, about 5 tunne or lesse, if about 14^l a tunne. They are about 9 inch broade, a yarde long & $\frac{1}{2}$ an inch thicke, and some tarre.
11. If George be gone allready for Bristol then may yow stall till the herreinges barques be ordered away by yow. Yow may see how thinges are at Dublin & soe returne if yow please.

[22] "to Dublin" inserted.
[23] Wibergh substituted for "Sir George Radcliffe".

19 Novbr. 1633

Page 86 is
blank
Page 87

Mr Robert Quayle in Duglasse[24]

1.   I desire yow to be my factor for my tradeinge in the Isle of Man, wherein if in anythinge I give yow not full advise yet to doe for my beste advantage as yow shall thinke goode, but where advized to followe the same as God will give leave.

2.   Your factoridge upon all sayles & imployments I will allowe yow as of any other I have, being 2 per centum with all your extraordinaries in my busines.

3.   On the like tearmes as above sd. yow shall at all tymes, either by myselfe or factors, finde me ready to doe for yow.
For particulers:

1.   I desire yow if Myles Bayteman returne from France or any other vessell of myne with wynes comes to unload in your island that yow will seller up such wynes as they shall discharge with yow, and sell what yow can, if ready money comes, at 16^l a tunne French wynes and at 17^l three monthes to currante men, but what yow cannot soe sell to shippe them over in small boats or barques that passe for Milnthorpe 9 tunnes $\frac{1}{2}$ & the reste as yow shall be afterwards advized by us. Page 88

2.   As yow have any rise or falle in commodityes advize me of them and I will joyne with your pte. at any tyme if in adventures to or from France or ellswhere.

3.   If any goods of myne come to yow from Bristol shippe them for Whitehaven, especially the playte iron, Mr George Layne is my factor theire.

4.   For what busines yow doe for me beinge not in sayles and imploymts. I will gratifie yow to your owne satisfaction.

5.   For what other goods Myles bringeth to yow then wynes, if they will Page 85 make presente sayle to advantage sell them & imploy the proceade of them in the best likely commodites either natural or forreigne that will present sayle & some likely advantage &[25] England or Ireland & shippe them.

6.   Mr George Layne our factor at Bristol; Richard Wibergh at Dublin; Willm. Atkinson at Whitehaven; Lewis Thompson at Belfast; by Milnthorpe to Mr Rowland Dawson at Kendal to be sente for Lowther.

The orders above I lefte with Mr Robt. Quayle of Douglas drawne in forme under my hande the 19th November 1633.

[N.B. Page 88 is the final page of this sequence. The following pages,

---

[24] Douglas, I. of Man. Above the name Quayle is drawn the Manx symbol, only with four legs joined at the knee.

[25] "In" was probably intended.

containing mostly brief jotted entries, begin from the other end with the notebook reversed top to bottom. I have nominated the pages A1, A2, etc. They were not numbered by Christopher.]

Page A1	Receaved of Rich[ard Wibergh] the 14th of September at Dublin	112	0	0
	2 tunne tallowe	58	0	0
	30 brlls. of beefe	33	0	0
	60 stone of woolle	33	10	0
	29 rugges	11	0	0
	4 lbs wt. yarne	20	0	0
		155	10	0
	Profit if please God	10	0	0
	5 tunne of playtes	70	0	0
	2 tunne of tarre	14	8	0
	2 tunnes of forge hammers	20	0	0
	2 butts of cherrie	20	0	0
	2 cwt suger	16	0	0

[Beneath are only a few roughly jotted figures with the page reversed.]

Page A2	November	Receaved of my father's money of the Lord Baltinglasse	157	11	11
	21	Pd. out to Hen. Osburne	2	6	8
	23	Paid to Chr. Wharton	10	0	0
	23	to Henry Osburne's wife	5	0	0

The whole 157 . 11 . 11 cleared in Will Atkinson's cash booke the $\frac{23}{9}$ 33.

Will Atkinson broughte over with him an invayce of goods at	24	2	5

1633

Page A3	$\frac{8}{9}$ Delivered Randall five pounde	5	0	0
	$\frac{11}{9}$ To Rich. Wibergh H. Osburne's	5	0	0
	2 barrells of candles of 30 doz. and 3lb of candles at 3^s 6^d per dozen & cask 2^s	5	8	0
	3 setts at 13^s 4^d per peece	2	0	0
	3 Caddowes playne at 6^s 8^d	1	0	0

3 brlls. beere at 12^s 10^d	2	1	6
6 barells beefe at 21^s	6	6	0
29 oares at 11^d per peece	1	6	7
10 doz. caske hoopes	0	8	0
1 fyrkin of soape, Bristol	0	13	4
1 hogshead of bloode	0	6	8
⎧ 2 damozellas ⎰ flored crimson	3	0	9
⎨ ⎱ Green flored	2	11	9
⎪ 1 figwraynay	1	7	0
⎪ 1 mohayre	2	8	0
⎩ 1 carthage	2	7	4
2 doz. hoopes	0	4	0
1 Jugge bestowed on Mr Fletcher	0	1	6
21 quartes of honey	1	2	6
2 barrells of herreinge	1	17	2
1 barrell of honges	0	6	8
Custome & fees at Dublin	0	18	0
: 22.17.10[26]			

[Page A4 has an incomplete diagram of a cylinder or piston. Pages A5 to A13 and page A15 contain religious notes. Page A14 contains a diagram of a handdriven pump.]

50 tunne fraighte at 3^l 10^s	175	0	0	*Page A16*
49 pypes custome at 1–7	71	7	6	
430 Quintalls Barillio 6^d per C with charges	13	12	6	
	260	0	0	
Whereof ¼ facit	65	0	0	
of wch. pd.	57	14	6	
Restes by computation oweing	7	5	6	
to made goode out of Barillo or answered other-wise piedra piedrio. I pd. as above more than the wynes charges came to towards barillio	6	7	0	
They recd. for Barillio	32	14	5¼	
Besides Sir Rob. Manstead's debte				
Totall	39	1	5¼	
Mr Gylles recd. onely	20	4	2	
Restes toward laste wynes pd.	18	17	3¼	

[26] An isolated figure. No total is given for this account which probably lists goods brought from Dublin to Whitehaven in November 1633.

[Page A17 devotional notes continuing A18]

Page A18

	Receaved the 11th October of my brother Kirkby in full	1	11	0
13	Receaved of Thwaites fermers	10	0	0
13	Recd. of John Rescall	10	0	0
14	Recd. of Rich. Maberrie	8	8	6
14	Recd. of Peter Huggons in full	36	10	0
15	Recd. of Edw. Bayteman in full	6	14	0
16	Recd. of Walter Becke in full	12	14	0
15	Recd. of Mr Walton	22	9	0
16	Recd. of Mr Nicholas Ecclestone as in his accompte in this boocke	30	0	0
		138	6	6
17	Recd. of Mrs Hodgekinson	1	5	6
18	Recd. of Mrs Connell	4	0	0
18	Recd. of Ned Lawrence	4	9	8

Page A19

Orders and directions lefte and sente to others. To Mr George Layne, Bristol

Oct 18	Dis. for lockes and gemmers	0	4	4
	more then	0	2	4

Page A20

Wines solde by Ellinor Ecleston of Lancaster in sommer 1634

hghds.	galls.	qrts.	
2	0	0	Mrs Colville, Lancaster, one white, another claret.
0	22	0	White wine to her more.
1	0	0	Edward Lawrans of Ellell one hoghd. of claret.
0	16	3	Mrs Hodgekinson of Garstang, cl. wyne.
4	0	0	Jefferay Woodes of Preston for Mr Haworth, of white wyne.

Page A21

Incomplete jottings:

Rects. October 1634

Of Mrs Colville—
Of Edw. Lawrance the Lord Mollinaux his man—
Of Mrs Hodgekinson in full   1 5 0
Of Mr Larence Haworth—

SECTION FOUR

NOTEBOOK C, 1635–1637

First of 10 pages without nos.

May 22.[27] And my diett that weecke 8^d per meale	0	9	4
Washinge a shirte, 2 bandes, my drawers, cuffes, & nightecappe 9^d & given Frances	0	1	4
Given osteler, etc	0	0	6
Alteringe my clocke, satten edge taken over	0	1	0
Total expences after comeinge to Hull till set sayle	5	4	3
8–0–0 totall receiptes then.			

So restes to ballance carried into my manuelle or pocket
boocke B[28]   1 15 9

The five & thirty shillinges nine pence is carried to my new pocket boocke indorsed B in follio 2:a: which is Flemish money at 36^s the exchange three poundes fowre shillinges.

[There follows 9 pages which Christopher used as a rough index to the notebook. On several pages of this there are notes and the draft of a letter in what I take to be the childhood hand of Sir Christopher's son, Sir John Lowther of Whitehaven, 2nd Baronet, who inherited the book along with the rest of his inheritance on his father's death in 1644 when he was only in his second year. Thereafter the pages are numbered 1a, 1b, 2a etc. Christopher did not use the a and b at the top of the page simply writing the number in the corner of the right hand leaf, but from internal evidence it is clear that he regarded the number as applying both to the left and right hand leaves. Page 1b contains the sentence "On the 22nd of June being Munday I arrived at Dublin." The remainder of the page together with 2a, part of 2b, 3a and part of 3b are covered with the childhood notes of Sir John Lowther of Whitehaven.]

A cattalogue of Yorkshire debters runne into Ireland given me by my brother Will by May 1635 viz: *Page 2b*

Henry Scedule. C.		4	1	0
John Illingworth		13	11	1
Edward Altam(oe) or Altus or Moore	Edinburgh[29]	3	0	0
John Lambert		13	5	5
	Totall	33	17	6

[27] The reference to Hull makes this 1637.

[28] There is no correspondence between Christopher's book "numbering" and that used by the editor.

[29] Actually written in margin opposite "Edward".

Roger Bayteman a Yorkshire cloathier runne away for Ireland dwelleth at Athie able., as Robert Bradeley informed me the 11th of October 1635. He oweth 3^l 10^s 0^d for woolle as Robert Bradeley sayth to me.
Edinburgh: Mathew Glover fledde; he oweth me for my

father's woolle	2	6	8
for my Irish woolle solde to him			
by Gyles Moore 3 stone	2	0	0

Page 3a

Feb. 26 1635/6

Yorkshire debters

l	s	d	Oweinge Leeds & about	desperate		
2	0	0	Matthew Glover, Edinburgh	2	0	0
1	2	0	Thomas Dickson	0	0	0
0	15	6	Robert Glover	0	5	6
1	15	0	Mychaell Storie	0	5	0
			Halifax			
5	19	0	John Howcker of 9^l 2^s 0^d	0	19	0
3	0	6	Gylbert Wacker 7 2 6	0	10	6
11	0	0	William Armitage 11 0 0	11	0	0
25	12	0	Totall	14	0	0

Page 3b

[Opposite the names of some of these debtors on the facing page are the following entries:]

Michaell Storie pd. to my brother for me	1	15	0
Gilbert hath pd. all but 20^s in difference betweene Thomas			
Reame and my brother.			
Will Armitage taken goods to the valew of 2. 10. 0 at 3^l soe			
loste besides charges 0–10–0.			

Page 4a

Aug. 29	Broughte remayneinge over from 0^l 7^s 0^d the other side in pursse.
30	Beinge Sunday at nighte invited to the Lord Chichester's where supped.
Aug. 31	I lefte Belfaste; lefte orders with Mr Lewis Thompson, the coppy in
Munday	George's Mannual Journall.
Sep. 1	I came to Downe from Kilmore with Mr Robert Turneley our debtor. I
Wed. 2	stayed at Downe, my horsse layme, & writte to Osburne & Mr Jo. Hawkins.
Thurs. 3	I receaved of George Jackson at Downe 24 6 3 for to pay to Dublin
	accomptes & gave George orders the coppy in my reade booke.
4	I came halteinge from Ralph Rillion to Dunda[lk].[30]

---

[30] Dundalk is a town 54 miles north of Dublin. Downe Patrick is 27 miles from Belfast, the capital of County Down.

I bargayned with Mr Patrick White of Dundalk for 400 brlls. of salte,   5
& hempe & 80 stone hempe to sende salte for presently, and thence I came
halteinge at night to my uncles.
Beinge Sunday I stayed at my Uncle Lancelot.   6
I came to Dublin from my uncle's that nighte.   7
I pd. over to Rich. Wibergh the northern money 24 6 3; spente in my   8
journey 12^s; Rich. repaid it me. That day I could not speacke with Sir
George.
Sir George went to Wickloe or theireabouts.   9
I was to speake with Lord Baltinglass.[31]   10
1 0 0 I recd. of Rich. Wibergh when I went with Mr Diet.   11
I disburssed in generall charges beinge with Mr Newman 1^s & with Mr   12
Diet 7^s 4^d 0   8   4 } Sept. 14
I boughte 2 payres of gloves coste   0   3   0 }
1 1 0 I recd. of Richard in 9^d pences to buy a hat. I receaved a letter
from my father of the 7th 7ber.

---

26 14 3 recd.   and disburssed   24 17 7 Sept.

Page 4b

The contents of a letter to my father sent by Sir Richard Diet   Sept. 15
My last letter from Downe Patricke 3rd instant.
1.   That the laste weecke when I came found Sir George gone to Wick-
       loe & returned on Saturday.
2.   That when I came hither I found your letters and for my boockéinge
       I hope shall not hereafter finde me faulty.
3.   This weeke I meane to have a mandat out againste all our debters
       here which will make them either secure or pay those that can.
4.   I have nothinge to doe with either Jo. Fletcher or Nicholas Egleston
       more then that I advised yow of my opinion at that tyme.
5.   At Dundalk I have articled for 400 barrells a year of salte for the
       nexte yeare; the one 200 barrells to receave ready money, the other
       hempe at a raite & soe I shall fitt him from yeare to yeare as we shall
       from yeare to yeare agree.
6.   Mr Diet beinge in towne desired my company 12 myles into the
       country to see it soe I went with him on Friday and Saturday. We
       returned on Sunday; he was knighted.
7.   On Munday morneinge I delivered your letter to Sir George Rad-
       cliffe. He told me he had written unto yow, but beinge soe very busie he
       appoynted me this day to speacke with him.
8.   Laste weecke I was to speacke severall tymes with Lord Baltinglasse;
       & all day yeasterday was before I could deliver your letter to him and
       he appoynted me to day or tomorrow to speack with him.

---

[31] For Lord Baltinglasse see footnote p. 62 above.

Page 5a

9.   I delivered your letter to Uncle Lancelot who promised to remember the house of Lowther and shall story more at large in the letter.

10.   That I have 100^l for Sir George as soone as I speacke with him in parte of theire herreing fisheinge adventure, if that they will not allowe it us in parte of the peere money.

11.   That within a fortnighte I expect George out of the north and after his comeinge meane not to stay a day longer then wynde serveth.

12.   I meane to bargayne what salte I can in this towne certainely for while wee keepe salte alwayes here they will but buy of us when they cannot have it of any other & then it sells but by barrell and barrell and not in quantitie.[32]

Sept. 15	26 19 3 recvd and disburssed	24 : 17 : 7	

Payd John Parker in pte. of lightera[ge] dew to him for twisce at 20^s per tyme   1   0   0

16   Payd for a payre of bootes   0   8   9

16   Wente to Lord Baltinglasse. Dyned theire. He continueth his demande for your other two hewers and would have had me to have referred it to Sir George but when I answered I woulde not by any meanes trouble him with it but if he would sewe us he should be answered, he then calmed; soe about a weecke hence when Mr Lowman cometh I hope I shall gett some ende made.[33]

Page 5b

Sep. 16
Wed.

26. 14. 3 recd. & disburssed broughte per contra   26   6   4

I spoack with Sir George Radcliffe who red my father's letter; fruitlesse labour remarkable in it, Sir [G.] not fully at leysure, on Friday appoynted to speake with him further.

I boughte a payre of kinnes   0   1   0

A payre of Kiltock gloves   0   0   6

Sir Richard Diet toocke shippeinge.

Thurs. 17   Yesterday & today the water up to shoppe doore & in seller but noe hurte. We changed dollers at 4^s 6^d to a grotte. Coulde not speack to Sir George. Followed our debters, gotte noe money.

Fri. 18   Attended our debters. Gotte noe money. Nowe a Wyreman with salte at key selleth at 7^s 6^d 2 shakes hindreth sayle of ours.

Agreed with Sir George for his quarter of the pannes at Whitehaven, & the herreinge voyage for him & my lorde,[34] viz:

Salte pannes, etc	143. 10. 4	
Herreinge fish.	185. 15. 7	

to pay 100^l in hande & the reste before our Lady Daye with intereste at 8 per centum. The coppy I have.

Sep. 18   26. 14. 3 rcvd. & disburssed   26. 7. 10

[32] Letter contents end here, and are succeeded by diary entries.
[33] Perhaps a late paragraph for the earlier letter.
[34] I.e. Lord Deputy Wentworth.

I solde 30 brlls. of salte to Mr Richardson the Dutchman at 8^s 3^d & two
shakes to be dd. tomorrow or Munday.
I perused our accomptes, visited greate Uncle Lancelot: bade comforte,
churlish. This nighte I satt up stayinge of Richard Wibergh till about one
o'clocke but he laid out, I suppose foxed and shamed to come.
Sunday, hunted out Richard after 10 of the clocke, at Mr Balle's, sitteinge.
St Matthias Day.   Ridded the seller for to measure salte out of & I redd
over the prologge Sea Mirror and talked with Mr Lowman & further
satisfied him about the salte pannes.
Dyned with Lord Baltinglasse & spente both forenowne & after about our
difference and offered ...[35] in lew of my 50^l dew to me & a peice of scarlet
which I value at 24^l being 14 yardes $\frac{1}{2}$ though we tooke it of Bobliffe
Johnson in parte of a desperrate debte at 29^l, but none here would give 24^l
for it or medle with it at any rate; could not speack this day with Sir
George.
Went to see Uncle Lancelot, the parson, sicke, he sayeth that my uncle Sir
Lancelot estate is woorth, viz:

Screne inheritance	250	0	0
Tythes theire	100	0	0
Enheritance per annum	350	0	0

26 14 3 recd. & disburssed broughte over per contra from the toppe 26 7 10
My uncle Sir Lancelot's inheritance broughte over per contra:

	350	0	0	Screene & tythes
His place of	200	0	0	Puines Barron
The use of his stocke	123	0	0	let out
Totall	673	0	0	per annum.

Besides plate & household furniture.
My uncle parson allsoe tolde me that Sir Gerrard Lowther tolde him that
the estate which he had made to my cousen Lancelot of Kirckbythore was
but condicionall & revocable; and that Sir Lancelot haith given his bonde
for the payment of the 50^l per annum to my Cousen George dureinge Sir
Lancelot life.
   A litle after nowne I perused over our papers to fynde Fytsgarret's
accompte to sew him by & new ordered all papers.
This day I attended Sir George about the note from my Lord Baltinglasse
who about 7 a clocke at nighte by his man approved of it.
I drew a petticion againste my debtors, had Mr Eddmonds to rectifie it, and
after I new writte it.
I was served with a warrant from my Lord. Dep. about forfited bondes of

[35] Too badly smudged to be legible, possibly "him".

employment which I beleeve were cancelled 10 dayes before, viz: 20th August theire warrant beinge of the laste of Auguste.

I solde 2 barrells of salte unfilled up at 17^s (6^d recd. earnest) repd. to Richard.

Page 7a

Sept. 24   26 14 3 rcd. & disburssed   26 7 10

25   I went to Lord Baltinglasse gotte his note for 65^l for my scarlet 14½ yrds. valued at 30^s per yarde & for my 50^l dew to me upon accompte; and I gave my acquittance to this effecte: "Recd. of the Lord Baltinglasse this day a note of 65^l and is in satisfaction of my 50^l dew upon accompte & 14½ yrds. of scarlet, if that the note be payd accordinge to its tenure to Sir George Radcliffe, witness my hand, Chr. Lowther."

The coppy of my lorde's note followeth:

"I doe hereby pray and appoynte his Majesties Vice Treasurer (for the tyme being) of this Kingdome of Irelande to pay unto the honble. Sir George Radcliffe, kt., one of his Majesty's honble. Privie Councell here the some of three score and five poundes of lawfull money of and in England, out of the firste moneyes which I am to receave out of his Majesty's revenue for the selleinge of ayle and beere within this Kingdome and is for soe much dew from me unto Mr Christopher Lowther, which by him I am assigned to pay unto the said Sir George Radcliffe, whose acknowledgment of the receipt of the said some, shall be unto the said Vice Treasurer a sufficient acquittance and discharge againste me, my executors and administrators for the same, as witnes my hande the 25th of September 1635. Signed in the prescence of Chr. Lowther and James Lowman, Baltinglasse.

Page 7b

Sept. 25   Recd. & disb. broughte over from the toppe of the other side:
           26 14 3   26 7 10

Friday   1. 0. 0. recd. of Richard Wibergh goeinge to Sir James Ware's.

Saturday 26   I & Edward Blennerhasset by note under his hande & myne in my custody have referred all our differences to Mr John Bamber & Edward Barrie on this day or Munday to be decided.

Edward Maghabe, a younge fellow with a Scotch cappe, a wanderer, suspitious fellow by our backside at Lowwater, dwelleinge at the paynter's in Copper Alley. I toocke the cash out of Richard's keepeinge haveinge found him come shorte.

Sun. 27   Beinge Sunday I visited my uncle & my goe over water coste 2^d.

I paide in likewise what money I had on me my selfe into the generall cash & soe for matter of receipte and disburssments I keepe it Richard's journall hence which was of   1 3 2

Posted 28   Pd. Mr Litle for Sir George   74 10 4

& dd. my lorde Baltinglasse note   65 0 0

28   I pd. for 2 bondes in the custome house cancellinge   0 7 6

And wayteinge on this was all my day woorke. I gotte the abstracte of what salte was entred in anno 1634 in Ireland.

I spente by tyme & tyme in generall charges		3	3	Posted 28
27 14 3		27 14	3	Sept. 28
				Page 8a

Per John ⎰ A perticuler of the saulte, etc, imported into Ireland at every
Halton ⎱ porte for which custome was paid for the yeare 1634.

	Barrlles weyges[36]	
	English	French etc
1. Dublin the firste of the portes & soe s:wards. about	1918	0725
2. Wexford	0000	$0093\frac{3}{4}$
3. Rossee	0002	$0118\frac{1}{2}$
4. Waterford	0303	$0925\frac{1}{4}$
5. Dungarven	◑000	0040
6. Youghall	0002	0175
7. Corcke	0023	0171
8. Kinsayle	0004	0656
9. Baltimore	0000	0289
10. Croockehaven	0000	0602
11. Bantre & Berchaven	0000	0436
12. Kylmac etc	0002	0148
13. Lymricke[37]	0005	0321
14. Gallway	——[38]	0303
15. Slygo & Mayne	——	0036
16. Calbeg	——	0104
17. London Derry	0356	$0478\frac{1}{2}$
18. Colrayne	0199	$0003\frac{1}{2}$
19. Ballantrey	0020	——
20. Carickfergus	0714	$0104\frac{1}{2}$
21. Bangor	0096	0025
22. Dannaghade	0073	0001
23. Strangforde	0413	——
24. Carlingforde & Dundalke	0256	0031
25. Drogheda	0018	0376
Totall of all	4404[39]	6163:1
White & forreigne salte totalle	Weyges	6603:4

[36] I.e. "weighes".

[37] No. 13 Lymricke and No. 14 Gallway are set down in reverse order by Lowther.

[38] A line drawn across in original but no indication of whether he lacked the figures or simply meant zero.

[39] This should be read as 440 weighes 4 lbs, see below.

Page 8b

pannes

The totall of the white salte per contra is weighes	440^w	4^{lb}
More that Lord Baltinglasse pannes make or may make per annum	300	0
he haveinge 4 pannes at Strangford, 2 at Newcastle, ...[40] at the Kerry.		
More that Colrayne pannes may make, 4 theire	260	0
White salte totall	1,000	04

And I suppose this is all the white salte that is spente in Ireland and admitte portige salte in respecte the pannes above in anno '34 were not perfected:

Then the totall French is	6,163	0
and more I beleeve that is not entred	837	0
Forraigne salte totall	7,000	0
English above	1,000	0
Totall of both	8,000	0

Againe theire is one fifte parte difference in the measure betwene the French & the English, soe by that accompte if all English should serve the Kingdome 10,000 weghes will but serve Ireland.

Page 9a

Sept. 29

Hence forwarddes I sette all my accomptes downe in the Generall Journall here at Dublin since Richard Wibergh fayled in his cash keepeinge.

Wedn. 30

I learned of Mrs Balle neere Newgaite, Richard Balle's wiffe, about makeinge of Usquebath, viz: 2 barrlles. of beere malte mashed as for drincke which let stand about 3 weeckes to ripen, after etc—loocke in my lytle reade clasped boocke. This day I perused and streyghted my accomptes in parte; by boocke should remayne—257 brlls. of salte.

This day I learned out of Thomas Hollyngworth, a cloathier in St Thomas Street, that Leonard Allane or Moore liveth in Edinburgh; Henry Schedule & John Illingworth live in Drogheda but poore both in theire trade. John Lambert loste at sea in goeinge back for England.

Memorandums

1. tomorrow to get Hutchingson's money which I gave him to change; 2. & to pay Sir George the 4^l, to gette him to give me an acquittance; 3. to tell Sir George about my greate uncle and Uncle Parson[41]; 4. to knowe his answer about the salte & to gette him to write of it to my father.

Page 9b

Sept. 30

5. to speacke to Sir George to helpe us about Fytsgarrette & the yealde;[42] 6. to exchange with Rickeseys salte for iron pannes & soape, etc. 7. to exchange with Chevers for rugges & caddowes; 8. to buy when have money

[40] Left blank.
[41] I.e. Sir Gerrard Lowther and Lancelot Lowther.
[42] Trinity Guild.

the whelles & carte flanges, 2 spoakes & a sett of fellowes; 9. to buy carte-horsse furniture; 10. to buy the mappe of Peter Wibrante; 11. to buy 2 dozen Irish stockinges & capes; 12. to buy some Irish lynneinge; 13. to give Mr Gibson salte for a rundlet of good sherreis or malligo; 14. to buy myselfe a hatte and see if can fynde a peece of cloath for my reade suite to buy it, & to dy my plush topps; 15. to leave a letter to Mr Johnes; 16. to pay Uncle Lancelot his annuity; 17. to buy 60 hydes or exchange; 18. to leave both Richard & George behinde till coles solde & noe longer which at furtheste shall be our Lady Day; 19. as they gette money to pay it in to Sir George in pte. of the herreing fisheing; 20. to gette a figge tree, younge damosell trees, damaske rosse trees, lavander Sp., severall sortes of Gylly *Page 10a* flowers at Mr Burns, turnip seds & artichocke plants at Mr Madder's; 21. to gette one to buy my horsse; 22. to gette out the mandat from Mr Edmonds; 23. to buy some vynegar white paper, a frykin of Sprickles soape, tabacko, nayles, honey, parchment, leather and what things ellse in Will Atkinson's note July 9th & 7ber 27th; butter if at 3^d.

This day Mrs Poore tolde me that our barque the *George* laste Wednesday   October 1
beinge the 23rd September was not gone from Belfast, that she had beene theire 10 dayes, within two dayes would be gone, that the tymber was troublesome to ship, that George would come as soone as she was gone away to Dublin.

Pd. to Mr Thomas Little for Sir George Radcliffe in full of the salte
pannes   4 10 0
Vide Richard's Journall.   Fri. 2
Recd. of Daniell Hutchingson   6 0 0   Satur. 3
on whom I wayted all day & neither eate nor druncke till I had recd. it which was by candle lighte.
Then I went immediately to pay it to my Uncle Lancelot haveinge paid   3
him 4^l before.

                                                                          Page 10b
My horsse in the pynfolde.   Sund. 4
Wente about my debters, gotte noethinge; ordered my trunckes againste I   Muny. Oct. 5
goe home.
2 barrlls. salte at 17^s solde to Walter Dunne.   Tew. Oct. 6
Gotte out my mandat from Mr Edmonds & pd. 12^s 6^d for it; 15 were in it,   Wed. 7
the coppy followeth; upon which I gotte of Mr John Whitmore 3^l 7^s 10^d Intr.[43]
clere, the wyne reckoninge 2^s 2^d pd. out besides.
I solde a brll. of salte to Widdowe Russell in St Thomas Streete at 8^s 6^d.   Intr. 8
I solde 2 hundred barrll. hoopes at 5^s.   Intr.
I writte in my reede boocke a consideration about waggon wayes & cattchinge the Powe[44] at Whitehaven, etc.
I made Richard serve the Lorde Deputy's mandat on severall of our debters.   Intr.

[43] Abbreviation for Intry, i.e. entry?
[44] The Poe stream which ran down through Whitehaven.

Intr.   Coste me 6^d in sacke at dinner with my landelady.

9   I boughte 4 peeces of lynninge of a Massarinde man,[45] 3 peeces qt. 50 yrds

Intr.   at 12^d, one qt. allmoste 18 at 9^d; in toto 3. 3. 6.

Intr.   I solde 2 hundred of hoopes at 2^s 10^d per hundred & 3 brlls. salte unfild at
                 25^s 6^d.

Intr.   Recd. from Mr Rellicke 2,000 hoope at 2. 6. 8.

                 George Jackson came this nighte to towne. This day I showed the bay
                 nagge to Mr Cardiffe & thinck to selle him.

                 Richard served the mandat on Fytsgarret.

Page 11a

Oct. 10   The coppy of the mandat followeth:

                 To the Right Hoble. the Lord Deputye, the humble peticion of Christo.
                 Lowther, merchant: Sheweth that the persons whose names to these presents
                 are annexed stand indebted unto yr. petitioner in severall somes of money
                 underwritten; all of which have bene longe since due, some by the space of
                 one, two or three years, most of which your petitioner haith specialtye for,
                 and for the best proofe reddie to be produced to evidence his just demands
                 when and where yr. Lordppe. shall require, therefore:

                 Yr. Petitioner humbly prayeth yr. good lordpp. for that he liveth in England
                 where his affaires by reason of his absence doe greatlye suffer, he haveinge
                 not other occation hearof abroade saveing the collecting in of these his
                 debts, that yr. lordpp. would be grateouslie pleased to comand the ptyes.
                 under written to make present payment of all such somes of money that each
                 of them are justlye due unto yr. petitioner or forthwith to shew cause to the
                 contrarie and yr. petitioner shall ever praye, etc.

Page 11b   Debts oweing to Yr. Petitioner

By the M[aste]r, Warden's clarke and fraternitye of the Guild	50	0	0
Mr Wm. Weston per specialtie	3	0	0
By John Tytlowe per specialtie	3	12	0
By Henry Radcliffe per specialtye	1	4	0
By John Clayton per contracte	8	13	0
By Rich. Balle per contracte	11	9	6
By John Briscoe per contracte	0	17	10
By Sir Robert Dixon for cooles	3	4	0
By Sir James Carroll for the like	1	12	0
By David Daniell	0	18	0
By Edward Blennerhasset	3	10	0
By Rich. Hatton	2	0	0
By John Illingworth	13	11	1
By John Whitmore	[blank]		
By Edward Rellicke	6	0	0

[45] Massarene on Six Mile Water near Antrim.

Dublin Castle the 2nd October 1635

The severall persons above named are hearby required either to give the petitioner present satisfaction of his just demands or otherwise to appear fourwith before us to shewe cause to the contrarie.

Wentworth.

Rcd. of Widdow Russell in full of hir brll. of salte 8^s 6^d solde before		Octo 10
Clered with John Tetlow, Water bayliffe 30^s recd. of him: new bill for		Saturday:
1–16–8 dew 20th December nexte, 4^s 8^d of it intereste		
I boughte a hatte & bande coste 17^s		Int^r.
8 10 8 this weecke recd. & disb.	4 19 3$\frac{1}{2}$	

3 11 4$\frac{1}{2}$ remaynder then.   Octo 10
5 18 9$\frac{1}{2}$ recd. of George Jackson out of the north of Ireland's accompte.   10
Disburssd. in generall charges this day   0 2 9   Sund. Octo 11
Richard Hatton served with Lord Deputy's warrant.   12
In generall charges disburssed   0 0 10
1 15 0 4 brlls. salte solde for money
0 3 0 A hundred hoopes solde for money
3 0 9 7 brrlls. of salte sold for money   13
0 5 0 Recd. in full of Edward Wesell.
1 17 0 Recd. in parte of the bay nagge of Mr Cardiffe 22^s behynde.
From this tyme he to pay for his grass.
This day I writte forecastes of our salte house at Whitehaven in my lytle   14
reade boocke.

3 14 6 { 9 brlls. of salte for money to Belturbet whereof 2 out of bulke
          17^s (5 with one caske powred out after fyllinge: 2^l, & 2 with
          caske fylled 17^s 6^d.

0 2 10   Recd. for a hundred of hoopes. Disburssed for
            candles by George   0 0 4
Recd. a letter from Tho. Gylliat from Will Atkinson   27 Sept.[46]
Disb. by Richard for my topps dyinge   0 0 6   [Oct.] 15
Given for bay nagg's grasse, at the boate, etc   0 3 5   15

Aprill 10 1621. A trew and perfecte note of all particuler charges touchinge the transportinge of fyer coles & pit coles out of the Countie of Cumberland into Ireland or Scotland.

Imprimis: for every tonn of coles to be rcd. into any barke   England
     or boate at anie port or creeke within the countie afore-
     saide   0 3 0
Item, for entry of every barke to the countie Costomer   0 0 5
Item, to His Maties. Searcher for every bark load of coes 0 0 8

---

[46] Probably the letter's date.

Itm. to the Deputie Costomer for every ton of coles, for the use of His Majesties great farmers	0	0	4
Totall	0	4	5

Ireland

Imprimis for entry of evry bark or boat at Dublin to His Maties. Costomer or his deputie	0	1	8
Item to the Costomer or his deputie for every tonn costome	0	0	3
Item to the officers at Dublin for the cyty's costome every tonn	0	0	1
Item for a note of every entrye	0	0	2
Item to His Mties. Searcher	0	1	6
Within the barr of Dublin, pertege[47]	0	0	9
Item to the Water Bayliffe for every bark or boate	0	0	10
	0	5	3

Charges as on the other side	0	5	3
Item more to the said Water Baliffe for a barrill to measure coles, two barrells of coles for every bark or boate, value	0	2	0[48]
Item to the porter for measuring every tonn	0	0	$1\frac{1}{4}$
Item for lighters or barges for cariedge coles upp the river to the Citie of Dublin every ton	0	0	6
Itm. chapmen gills[49] every bark or boat, once a year	0	1	6
Besids imposition now exacted by one Richard Baker of Newcastle every tonn	0	2	6
And likewise besids all charges for maintaining barks or boats and meat, drink and wages for men or laborers.			

1635
October 16

30 Whitehaven tunns is 20 Dublin tuns at $2^s 4^d$ at $3^s 6^d$	3	10	0
Imposte & custome a Dublin tunne at 10^s per tunne is	0	16	8
Fees, Customer, Searcher & Controwler	0	3	6
Keyage etc 18^d, ballaste $3^s 4^d$	0	5	0
6 men victualls: $2^s 6^d$ per weeck; 5 weeckes a voyage $12^s 6^d$ a man	3	15	0
6 men's wages at 11^s one with another	3	6	0
Weare & teare & profitt a voyage	3	6	8
Custome at Dublin 4^d per tunne & fees	0	12	5
Lighterage 9^d; measureinge $1\frac{1}{4}^d$; 2 brlls. of coles 4^s & 10^d toll to water baylife	0	5	$8\frac{1}{4}$
	16	0	$11\frac{1}{4}$

[47] [*Sic*] portage or peerage (as in keyage)?
[48] $1q^r$ (one penny quarter).
[49] [*Sic*] a fee.

Page 13b

A trewe and perfect note of the rates of coles sould, transported out of the ports or creeks within the Countie of Cumberland or Scotland.

At Dublin sometymes in winter when they ar scarce, for every tonn	0	10	0
At other tymes for a tonn	0	8	0
At other tymes for a tonne	0	6	0
At Carafargus[50] usually sould a tonn	0	5	0
At Scotland every tonn	0	4	0

A Note of Charges alonge the Coastes of England

To the costomers and other officers for fees	0	2	6
Item for bond to His Maties. use for returning certificate	0	0	8

The 20 tunnes of coles per contra[51] which is made out of 30 Whitehaven tunnes at 16^s per tunne is in all	16	0	0	1635 October 16
Loste to eaven the accompte if solde soe	0	0	11¼	
	16	0	11¼	

Page 14a

Theise five dayes loocke the com. journall for what hath beene done; Richard still amongste debters & I sometymes; the reste of the tyme directeinge Richard and George; George finisheinge his backward accomptes; I boockeinge what wee did; and forecasteinge.

October 16
17
18
19
20

[Remainder p. 14a and all p. 14b blank. Pages 15 a and b consist of a note of the ships "with their burthens and men that are to be raised in England and Wales", county by county, by the 1st March 1636.]

1635

Page 16a

Oct. 16

My desires to Sir George Radcliffe, Kt., to remember:

1. That the imposition upon the coles here may be as speedely as may be put on for the peere money at Whitehaven; for besides the 200^l that yow are out, the 30th of May I was 250^l more; and eare this I beleeve I am out 300^l of my owne.

2. That yow will remember what my father intimated to yow touchinge Sir Lancelot Low[ther], the barron[52], and what yow can make sure halfe shall be your owne, for unlesse yow helpe us here expecte noethinge.

---

[50] I.e. Carrickfergus, usually called by Sir Christopher by its alternative name Knockfergus.
[51] I.e. *Page 13a*.
[52] I.e. Sir Lancelot Lowther, Baron of the Exchequer in Ireland.

3.   That I may have your advice and furtherance to our 50^l the Cytty's desperrate clearke of theire Guilde hath cousened us of, wee nenver giveinge any credett as to himselfe, but as the Citty's servant, whose creditte by the lawe of merchantes, his M[aste]r the citty is to make good as I suppose.

4.   That I may have my lord's letter to the Councell at York to be carefull to punish condignely such ballaste casters as spoyle our key at Whitehaven.

[Page 16b blank.]

Page 17a

By vertue of a refferance made unto us Edward Balle of Dublin, Mayor, and John Haine, Masters of Trinitie Guilde, Richard Foster, Alderman, Exposer Foster and Exposer Handcock, Shirrifs Nicholas Stephenes and Patrick Gough, Marchantes, bearinge daite the 19th of October 1621 by the assembly then houlden for the vewinge mesurs and for redreseinge of misdemaners committed by the Waterbalifs and leyinge downe incertainties what there perquesites are, wee havinge perused and pondred the table made in anno 1558 and alsoe other ancient recordes of this cittie and sume statute lawes, for the certaine sealinge of the sade perquesites wee sett downe as followeth, viz:

Imprimis: the Water Baliffe shall receive and collect out of every shipp, barque, boate, or vessell of salte cuminge from beyond the seas unto this lande bringinge tenn tunns of salte or under, one penny English for each tunne belonginge to a freeman or upon his adventure, that upon a stranger's adventure they shall have two pence English per tunn; if the vessell or barque be above tenn tunns and under twenty then they shall have betweixt them one meseure of salte of the ^{53} saulte mesure which contains 20 gallons each water meseure which is 2 bushels and every bushell contains 5 English peckes, according to the Statute of Henry 7, anno 11 capp. 4 which meseure is accompted halfe a barrell. And yf the shipp, barque or boate containe above 20 tunns and under threscore, the Water Baliffe shall have 4 meseures of lyke meseure and yf the vessell contains threscore tunnes and above then they are to receive 8 meseures which make fower barrells of the sade messure of straingers onely and of free cytizens they shall have according to the aincient table, 1558.

Page 17b

Item: every barque, bote or vessell containeinge tenn tunns of coles or under shall have one penny English the tunne, as well free as unfree, and yf the vessell containe above tenn tunns and under 20: one barrell of the forsade messure betwixt them, and yf 20 tunnes or above then the sade Water Balifs shall have two barrells betweene them.

Item: as for the above Water Balifs duties and perquesites of heringe, millwell, linge, hake or any other fish wett or dry, flesh in caske or quarters to bee transported, oysters, apples etc, slatts to bee imported and discharged

^{53} Blank.

in the harbor they ar to have for the same accordinge to the sd. ould table in anno 1588 . . . .

Item: they ar to receive the same accordinge the forsade table & the bushell therin specified contained eight gallons of land messure at the raite of 32 gallons to the barrell.

Item: the Water Balifs are to have of all shippinge cominge from beyond the seas bringinge wine or iron twelv pence Irish for balnaige.   *Page 18a*

Item: they ar to have of every boate of fier wood that comes into this harbor to bee sould fourpence Irish but noe sticke of wood as heertofore.

Item: [they are to have of every boat]⁵⁴ that cometh into the market of the sade cittye to be sould, they shall have there dewe as alsoe of every freeman and woman according to the aincient table.

Item: accordinge to the lawes of this cittye that noe boates or other vessels bringinge comodities along the coast out of another harbor into this haven shall pay any other custome or duty heare butt chapman gield which is xviii^d Irish out of every boate and 21^d Irish out of each crossinge the seas, to bee payed but once a yeere to the Recorder, Shiriff & Water Baliffe, for keyage fowrpence, soe often as they come to the key, which we hould for good in regarde His Mtie. hath noe custome alongst the coast of comodities, yet because there is a reservation in the former table of anno 1558 concerninge salte comeinge alongst the coast we thinke fitt that Water Baliffs shall have the bennefit therof accordinge to the sade table, but noe other duty of corne, wine, iron or any other manner of comodities cominge alongst the coast shall they demand.

Item: for as much as all the citizens in generall doe complaine of the badnes of the messuringe barrel both of corne, salte & coles we therfor order that the Water Balifs make before the xxth day of November next 8 barrels for messuringe coles each barrel to containe 40 gallons of the standerd beeinge water messure accordinge to the forsade statute of H. 7.   *Page 18b*

Item: they shall make or cause to bee made 4 mesures for mesuringe of salte, each mesure to containe of water mesure aforesade 20 galls. which is halfe a barrell, all which vessells aforesade ar to be houped with iron both for cole and salte and ringed in the outside and sealed above the top and belowe by the chine with the King's marke in the presents of Mr Maior and Sherifes.

Item: they shall make or cause to bee made 4 barrels for mesuring of smith's coles and colme and other fower barrels for messuringe of corne all which must containe but 32 gallons each barrell of the statute messure, all which messures aforesade ar to bee made and presented to Mr Mayor and Sherifs by the foresade 20th of November by the Water Balifes otherwise they are to forfit forty shillings English to the use of the cittie and withall the law made xvi Elizabeth, Mr Christopher Fagan beeing Maior, that upon any misdemeanor comitted by anie of the officers the Mayor and Shirrifes

⁵⁴ This is left blank. The sentence begins at "that . . ."

have power of themselves to remove and displace them at their pleasures, and to put other in there places, the same to bee putt in execution against the sade Water Baliffes yf they shall transgresse or order or exact ani more duty or perquesites then is sett downe heere and in the sade table of 1558.

Item: wee thinke fitt that the Cranor shall keepe in the craine all the cole and salte messures and nott to deliver any of them without Mr Maior his directions given to the Water Balifs, and the sade Craner and Water Balifs shall permitt no man to messure coles till the Masterporters bee present and to deliver no barrell but to such owner as ar to discharge there coles at the key from Fian's Castle to the Bridge; and none to be sent downe the river or harbor to any vessell, which sendinge downe the river wee find to bee hurtfull to the Citizens and profitt onely to the ingrocers and retailers of coles.

These be all the fees and perquisites blonginge to the Water Balifes concerninge the shippinge and because all straingers that traffickes to this citie may know what they ought to pay wee order that the Crainer shall make a table of the dutyes belonginge to the Water Balifs accordinge this our leyinge downe and for the particulars not heere expressed to expresse them particularly accordinge to the table anno 1558 and the same to bee sett up in the Craine in a publick place to be seene and red by any of the King's subjects that have use thereof.

Hereafter followeth the raites dew out of every barque, boate or vessell and the goods and comodities in them contained which ar not particulerly prescribed above, which rates ar accordinge to the table 1558 as aforesade:

Imprimis: as touchinge the freemen, the Water Balifs of every freeman so often as hee loadeth saulte on any barque, bote or vessell into this haven, upon any of the freemen there adventure, viii^d ster.

Item: the Water Balifs ar to have out of every bote loade of hearings fresh, salte hundled or barrilled that they open them one hundred each of them.

Item: they are to have out of every boate of oysters 1c soe they bee not taken within the barr to freemen, viz 1c to each of them.

Item: that every vessell with milwell, hake, ling, or any fish wett or drye, that each Water Balife shall have a cheeife fishe.

Item: of every boate of slates 1c to each of the Water Baliffes.

Item: of any of our neighbours of Waterford, Drageda [Drogheda] or other townes by the coste to bring salte in boats alongst the coast, the Water Baliffs shall have one penny str. for every tunn, yf the loadeinge bee under 20 tunnes, and yf the loadinge bee above 20 tunnes they shall have ii^d ster. the tunne or one mesure beeinge $\frac{1}{2}$ barrell at the choyce of the owner of the sade salte.

Item: they ar to have out of every bote or vessell loaden with corne that cometh in to this haven upon a strainger's adventure two bushels, that is to say halfe a barrell.

Item: they ar to have of every stranger for every vessell loaden with flesh in quarters or caske ii^d ster. for every h[ogs]hd. and i^d ster. for every beefe in quarters, and this of straingers onely.

Item: they shall have of every owner loaden with victuals as the owner or they cann agree or els as Mr Maior shall ordder.

Item: yf any freeman doe bring a bargaine of salte alongst the coast and not from beyond the seas the Water Balif shall have noe salte but there duty of plankage, viz: where there plankes shall bee occupied soe there be no collution in the bargaine viii ster. for each loader.

Item: they shall have of every vessell loaden with apples two hundred.

Page 20b

The contents of a letter to my father the 21st of October [1635], per Thomas Gylliat.

1.   My laste per Sir Richard Diet 15 September.

2.   Have agreed with Sir George Radcliffe for his quarter parte of yr. pannes; have paid him 144^l : 0 : 0 and have his release and acquittance, and for the 185^l : 15 : 7 dew to them for the herringe accompte

3.   I am to pay at our Lady Day nexte or before and paying 8^l in the hundred for intrest till I pay it in.

4.   I agreed with Baltinglasse; have not yeelded to any of his demandes. I gott his note for the 65^l assigned over to Sir George Radcliffe in parte of the 144^l, before which was in full of my 50^l dew by him to me per the accompte, and for Babliffe[55] Johnson's scarlet taken of him in 29^l : 7; it was too deere.

5.   Soe soone as the nobility come to towne will have the peere money layd on if can.

6.   I have beene and am busie with our debts; have had warrants for 15 of them, have gotte money of some, gotte security of others, and of the citty for that 50^l hope litle good without my lord's[56] speciall favour which I doubte not but to have his warrant; I have served out some already.

7.   My uncle Sir Lancelot Lowther and cousen Richard here in suite; *Page 21a* hath offered to make my cousen Richard his heir. I beleeve he f[a]vareth him because of my Lorde Deputy's favour toward my cousen for my Lord Clifford's[57] sake, & for yourselfe or any of yours I beleeve will be litle better of anythinge that is his.

8.   Yet will I get Sir George to doe in it what he can.

9.   My uncle Lancelot parson I paid his anuity; he would desire you to paie him what yow thinck it woorth for it that he mighte have it to helpe to buy out the inheeretance of the lande he dwelleth on.

10.   My Lord Cheife Justice Sir Gerrard Lowther is thoughte that within this tenne dayes he will marry.

---

[55] [*Sic*].

[56] Wentworth.

[57] See footnote p. 65 above.

11.   George is come out of the north. Lefte our busines with Mr Lewis Thompson our factor theire, and I intend to leave him to keepe our accomptes for I cannot make Richard able to doe it; [he is] fitte onely to seecke chapmen for our salte and calle on debtors; yet till our coles be put off, thinck fitte to leave him to helpe to sell for he is misserable enough and honeste, but lither[58] to write.

12.   Coles are soe cheepe I feare wee shall loose by them this wynter.

13.   I have beene soe wearried to sell salte to the townesmen & wholesayle men of the towne & when solde to gett it in, that of late I have taken another coursse which I fynd better, and that is: I have gotten moste of theire customers, the countrymen to buy on as which pay us ready money; they are Belturbet[59] carriers that doe bringe butter weeckely to towne and carry backe salte.

14.   Yet whyle salte is but at theise ordinary rates it is not fitte to keepe servants and a house here for it, soe that at Our Lady Day[60] I meane to leave the house and to bringe home our servantes; for so smalle a quantity as we vente at present will not defray the charge.

15.   Here hath beene of layte such tempestuous weather that I like not to adventure in Gylliat's barq, or the like that are so small, but by our owne barq I intend to come.

16.   Yesternighte the marchants' quay was set on fyre and about halfe a dozen nearby houses burnte & if Sir George Radcliffe had not made greate helpe it had endamaged all the citty. I removed all into my landlady's garden & few expected safety.

17.   Robert Bradley and housholde dwelleth in Dublin. The inventory of his estate I sende that I may knowe your directions in it.

18.   I send yow a ballance of our estate heere inclosed which followeth:

Cash remaininge	24	14	7
Accompte of debts:			
Walter Fytsgarrds[61]	48	7	9
Richard Balle	11	9	6
John Briscoe	0	17	10
from accompte of the waiter	0	10	0
James Browne	4	13	10
Sir Robert Dickson	1	12	0
Sir James Carrol	1	12	0
Richard Hutton	2	0	0
Daniell Hutchinson	11	1	3
Edward Kellicke	13	6	8
William Weston	3	0	0

[58] Lazy.
[59] Belturbet, Co. Cavan.
[60] I.e. 25th March 1636.
[61] Fitzgarret?

John Clayton	8	13	0
Mr Thomas Gwilith	12	10	0
Walter Doyne	4	0	0
Richard Wibergh	11	15	$4\frac{1}{2}$
Redaugh Goughigan	0	17	0
Andrew Birde	0	2	6
Mr Henry Radcliffe	1	4	0
John Tetlowe	1	16	8
Rickards the Dutchman	12	7	6
Patrick Dillon	2	6	6
Christopher Lowther	102	18	8
Mr Clarke	1	5	6
Mr James Lowman	15	18	0
Andrew Bird	0	13	4
My father Sir John Lowther Kt	10	0	0

Totall debts heere	[62]284	18	$10\frac{1}{2}$

Page 22b

By goods remaineinge			
for 128 tns. $2\frac{1}{2}$ b. Dublin mesure steared in the yard	179	14	11
by salte remaineinge	59	12	4
by caske remaineinge	0	9	6
by household stuff	10	1	2
by cloth	1	0	0
by tarr remayning	22	19	0

Totall all godds rem.	273	16	11

Stocke ys debitor			
to barque *George*	19	6	8
to William Burton	5	0	0
to North of Ireland	63	1	$6\frac{1}{2}$
to Mr Jo. Newman	2	10	0
to Mrs Rose Newman	1	7	0
to accompte currant at Whitehaven	88	6	10
to Sir George Radcliffe	185	15	7

Totall to be deducted	365	7	$7\frac{1}{2}$

Page 23a

This day tooke bonde of Mr James Lowman.
Solde salte, boughte wheeles, bargayned horsse furniture, bargayned a payre
of great wheeles, drew mappes of Whitehaven, writte letters and considerations for[63] Lorde Deputy about our key at Whitehaven, and Mr Henry
John's case about the wayste peece of ground.

Oct. 22
23
24
25
26
27

[62] Error for 285.12.$10\frac{1}{2}$?
[63] Last 3 words crossed out.

I delivered Sir George Radcliffe my mapp & letter to give my Lorde Deputy & spoake to him about Sir Lancelot Lowther. I spoake allsoe with Cousin Richard Lowther.

This day I tooke out Richard Wibergh's oath againste 4 of our debtors signed by Paul Davis, Clearke of the Councill. The coppy followeth, 12^d for every name in it.

28 Oct. 1635:

Richard Wibergh made fayth that betweene the sixte of this instante October & the 23rd of the same or theireabouts he shewed the Right Hble. the Lorde Deputy's direction dated 2nd October 1635 to William Weston, Richard Balle, Richard Hatton and Edward Kellicke whereby they were required either to give Christopher Lowther the petitioner present satisfaction of his juste demaundes or otherwise to appeare forthwith to shew cause to the contrary, yet the parties aforesaid nor any of them have not hitherto given the said Lowther satisfaction of his juste demaundes.

Copia vera.   Paul Davys

Forenowne & after wayted to speacke with Sir George; packets hindred him & meeteinge Lord Chancelor but afternowne he tolde me he had not spoken with my lorde about my ballaste busines but would remember it.

The Yeelds[64] answer not ready; I delivered in the affidavet of the 28th to gett out an attachment by it & pd. for the attachment 6^s & de....[65] 6^d. I speacke with my lord's caterer who hath promised to buy salte on us, and lynge if from Newcastle can fynde to do good in it; about which talcke further.

The Jointe & severall answeres of the Maisters and Wardons of the Trinitye Yeald, defendts. to the bill of complaint of Christo. Lowther.

The said defendants saveing unto themselves all advantages of exceptions that may be taken to the uncertaintyes & insufficiences of the plt.'s Bill for Answere thereunto saith that they never bought or sould with the plt. and this Answere being retorned trewe with yor. saverall lordships favour they are not lyable to answere his demande; lett the plt. call to mynd to whome he delivred his goods, and them to question for his moneys due, and for as much that the plt. haith noe legall or just demand against the defts. they humbly pray Yr. Honr. they may be diss[charged] with good costs for the plt.'s unjust vexation.

Dublin Castle, 20 October 1635

Let this answer be shewed unto the pltf. that he may reply thereunto if he thinck fit.   Wentworth.

The Replication of Christopher Lowther, Complaynt. to the joynt and

[64] Yeald or yeeld, i.e. Guild.
[65] Smudged.

severall answeres of the Maisters, Wardens and Fraternitye of the Trinitye Guild.

This Complnt. for replication saith that the Maisters, Wardens, Clarks and Fraternitye of Trinity Guild, all or some of them, are due unto him the some of 50^l 0^s 6^d as in his peticion ys contayned, which said some is for certaine demandes uppon severall bargains of salt made with one Walter Fitzgaret, clerk to the said Guild who as ther servant made the said bargaines and see yt delivered to each severall brother who desired the same, not using anie part at anie tyme of yt for himself neither did this Complt. give the said clark anie power to collecte anie money due uppon anie the said bargaynes yet the clarke haith alwayes usuallye done and still doth the same for the merchants who doth allow him two pence in the pound for collection, as in the like case this petitioner haith done with there predicessors and haith had currant dealing from them but as it semeth the said Guild ar degenerated from the former integrity of those that preceded them, practising most dishonest and unmerchantable dealing with this complaynant, as he may trewlie say and with others alsoe as this complaynant is credibly informed, for the said Walter Fitzgaret haith collected all the *Page 24b* moneys due uppon the said bargaynes from the severall brothers, and of himself is insolvent and knowing his inability to pay he acknowledgeth the most pt. of this debte himself, and would free the Maisters & Wardens least he should be outed of his place and the Maisters & Wardens, they denye to pay it knowing they ar not like to recover it on Fitzgaret againe if they should pay it; haveing neclected, as this Complt. heareth, to take securitye of the said clark at ther entrance into there places for his honest cariedge in his place which was in there power to have done, er that they needed to have admitted him to the place, which dealing bringeth disgrace to the whole Citye and stoppeth the whole currant of tradeinge, wherefore beinge that the Mstrs. and Wardens & Fraternitye of the Guild are to make good the credit and bargaines of there clarke this complaynt. humblye prayeth Yor. Lordpps. gratious favour that the defendts. may be ordered to satisfie unto him his just debt of 50^l 0 6^d, the one half being a twelve month due, the other since before Easter togeather with his coste of suite alreadie expended or otherwise that he may have Yr. Lordpps. order for the examinacion of witnesses to the end he may obtaine with conveanient speed what is justlie due unto him, and the rather for that this Complt. and his servants stay heare in this Kingdome principallie for the prosecution of this cause, all which he humbly submitteth to Yr. Lordship direction and prayeth.

Dublin Castle the 12 November 1635

Wee referr this matter unto our verie good lord the Lord Chefe Justice of His Maties. Court of Common Pleas[66] whom we pray to examine and compose the difference, if he can by consent, otherwise to certify us what His Lordpp. finds with his opinion thereuppon.   Wentworth.

[66] I.e. Sir Gerrard Lowther!

[In the second half of the page are some roughly jotted calculations of the dimensions of a piece of land bought from Thomas Milburne "measured the firste of Aprill 1637". 7 yard pole or rod used for the acre. This continues onto *Page 25b*.]

Page 26a

Nov. 14

From the beginninge of November till now I have beene & all of us busie in our sayles & some buyinges as in our Journall.

And I have allmoste had a dayly travell[67] about my suite with the Guilde ere I gotte it soe farre as it is come to and am beholden to Sir Gerrard that would be pleased that I gotte the referrence to him, which without his consente I could not have had; for the forenownes he is at courte, Munday afternowne he heareth referrences, Tewsdays & Thursdays at Councell table, Wednesdayes & Friday sitt at Councell chamber upon concealments. I have in this tyme often vissited Great Uncle Lancelot who onely doth speacke me fayre.

Sir Gerr.

Sir Lanc.

One of my Lord Dep. men tolde me that he heard some tell my Lord Deputy at supper once that when my uncle was like to die that he intended to make my father his heyre. Sir Gerrard Lowther & Sir George Radcliffe tolde me that Sir Lancelot could not revoke the estate he had made to my cousen Lancelot[68] without Sir Gerrard's consent which I beleeve.

Page 26b

I have often vissited Sir George about our peere money & ballaste; his much busines preventeth him or otherwise he seemeth both willing & forward in it.

15

My cousen Richard Lowther tolde me as I remember this day that my Great Uncle and he was well agreed & that my uncle was to give him 100^l within 3 dayes & 2 statuts for 500^l more within a yeare.

16

I receaved severall letters from Will Burton as in the Journall besides 2 from my father to me & one to Sir George Radcliffe from him and a letter from brother William & Mr John Battie about 2,000 brlls. of wheate. The content of Sir George Radcliffe's letter from my father followeth, viz: thanckes for his favour to me; 2/ excuseinge me for the badde successe in the salte, cole and herreinges; about the hurte the peere hath receaved & for the reste of the peere money if com beforehand with promisse I shall allowe well for affecteinge it from the beginninge.

Sir John Melton looseth in his coleyerie yet. My father goeth for York the 24th of November instant; many reeles[69] loste about Sir John Melton's coleyerie of late.

Page 27a

17

Busie in entreinge, loadeinge & unloadinge our salte & coles.

18

Unloadeinge coles & makeinge & buyinge beefe. Directions given Mr Patrick White heere:

---

[67] Meaning travail?

[68] An error for Richard Lowther?

[69] [*Sic*] reels?

1. if Will Atkinson fraighte over 40 brrls. of salte & cole, the salte yow are to take yourselfe & make sayle of the cole as they will give.

2. and returne the hempe yow have ready for the salte & wheat if at 14^s per barrell & transportable, for the cole or ells the money they make; unless the barq be to have hir fraighte by agreement payd at Dundalk & then out of the coles money pay hir.   Chr. Lowther.

I sente George to Rafernam[70] to see the weighte of the iron for greate wheeles.   18

Receaved the wheeles & pd. him & solde 10 barrells of salte "shake" while   19
coulde & caske agayne at 7^s 6^d per brrll. The 10 brlls. toocke one barrell of them in caske unfilled up to fill the terme.

Sunday.   Spoake with Mr Balle, James Brown, Mr Lowman, Daniell   20
Hutchinson & Guilliams.

Mr Lewis Thompson,   21

I rec. yow letter of the 12th of October, thanc yow kindlely fr. your care. Yow write of the receipte of 1 6 4 in one parcell & 0 5^s 6^d in another parcell, but not of whom, soe that I cannot cleare the parties of whom it   *Page 27b* was receaved for soe much, soe I desire yow that hereafter yow will write the names & dwellinges of the parties of whom yow either receave or buy or bargayne with & to whom yow pay or sell anythinge. George telleth me that Will Postlethwayte is not dew to have anythinge of me at all save for three houres at moste, two of his men slitteinge one peece of tymber which if the tymber had beene of the scantelynge that I did bargaine with him yt had not needed soe that I doubte not but that he will pay you the marcke for the two barrells of salte that he oweth us for, without any such demande as [you] write he speaceth of. For the two butte scrowes at Four Myle Water I woulde have yow to get them fetched up to Belfast and then to get Andrew Crummey to make them up as they should be. He knoweth how to doe them for I was speakeinge to him to have done them when I was theire myselfe. Bargaine with him soe reasonably as yow can & pay him & when they are made, all the money that yow doe anyway receave for us bestowe it in hempe & putt it up & sende it to Whitehaven in the buttes when they are soe made up. Remember I pray yow to call on Ralph   *Page 28a* Osburne of Kirckistowne, John Porter of Newtowne for theire debtes;[71] Fowler & Kine for the iron, Gyb. for the hempe; John Hud of Knockfergus for his debte, Sellarie for his & of the reste of your townsmen for what they are oweinge & tell John Boyd I expecte that he will make the hempe ready that he wanted laste yeare of his bargayne. If yow buy any hempe with your owne money, I will take it of & give yow what reasonable profit yow shall demande, soe beinge bounde on Wednesday for England whence with each conveyance yow shall heare from me. And if in the Springe yow woulde have me to sende yow any salte write to me thither, or to Richard

[70] Rathfarnham, four miles from Dublin.
[71] Probably Kirkston Castle and Newtown-Ardes, Co. Down.

Wibergh & George Jackson & they will send me woorde & yow shall have what yow will sende for soe I reste your loveinge freinde,   C. L.

Page 28b blank
Page 29a

Dublin the 28 of November 1635

Mr Batty,

I receaved a letter from my brother William Lowther latelie dated in London in October last with another from yow to him to write to mee to furnish you with some 2,000 barrells of wheat touching which I spoke to Sir George Radcliffe who saith it is not prohibited nor will be at Dublin for aniethinge he knoweth of, soe if you will have 2,000 brlls. of wheat bought for you write over to Richard Wibergh and George Jackson my servants & let them be sure of money hear to performe what you shall give them commyssion for and soe farr I will undertake they shall honestlie performe for you. The price ys now about 14^s per barrell which is 28^s per quarter, about which rate I think it will continue.

This night I goe to sea intending by God's blessing for Whitehaven, whither you may write to mee of it farther if you please, onlie this I must tell you if it be thing that will not be done by our Ladie Day in Lent, neither can anie man then do this for you at all, for I intend that they shall then goe home for Whitehaven to mee, soe haveing not els, I rest,

Your ever loveing frend to his power,

Chr. Lowther.[72]

To his very loveing frend Mr John Batty, merchant in London at litle St Ellinsor upon the Royall Exchange.

Page 29b

Md. that I Chr. Lowther of St Bees in England have rcvd. at the hands of Robt. Bradley two letters of atturney for gathering upp of his debts, the one is to receave 12^l yearly due on midsomer daye of Ambrosse and Daniell Cockrage, the other is for all his debts in England, anie way due unto him and for receipt thereof or anie pte. thereof I the said Christ. Lowther doe consent to allowe in pte. of his bond to mee of one hundereth pounds untill the foresaid debt to me be fully paid and satisfyed as witness my hand the 28 day of November 1635.

Witnesses: Richard Wibergh; Geo. Jackson.

Dublin 28 November 1635

John Illingworth and Henry Schedill[73],

I thinck neither of yow that it [is] either England or Ireland that can shelter yow out of my finding of yow. Both of yow are debtors unto mee for woolle that my carelesse servants trusted yow withall. Yow John Illingworth owe mee 13^l 11^s 0, and yow Henry Schedill owe me 4^l 1^s. I desire

---

[72] This copy does not appear to be Christopher's handwriting.
[73] Sometimes appears as Scedill but more often as Scedule, or Schedule.

both of yow in love before I further proceed against yow which will be to your great cost and charges, if yow doe, that yow will pay mee my owne which is justly due unto me—otherwise I will make yow lye by yt, if yow either continue in this kingdome or fly to England, assure yourselfes neither will I be baffled out of my owne. Yow shall well knowe Roger Bateman of Athye ought some money to me and he bouldly would not care both to denay and forswere it, but as I have made him satisfye me for all his boasts, soe will I yow if yow doe not satisfye the bearer man, whom I have and doe authorize to give yow acquittance and discharge for any thinge that yow and he shall agree upon, soe etc   Yr. lovg. frend if yow so use him, Ch. Lowther

Nota: all those goods per contra are entred in shoppe leager ii.

Page 30b

5ˡ 0 0 my salte dr. to cash at Dublin.				Novembr. 28
I lefte Dublin at 10.0 of the clocke.				Novembr. 29
Gave Richard Wibergh to buy mutton	0	2	6	29
On Munday at 10 of the clocke arrived at Douglas, that nighte the wynde easterly & did ride all nighte in the roade.				30
Boughte of Mary Corckie 4 pottes of honey at 14ᵈ per quarte, viz:				30

1	potte cont.	24	qrts.		
1	white pipkin	4	qrts.		
1	black pipkin	3	qrtes.		
1	water tankred	2½	qrtes.		
4	potts cont.	33½	qrts.	1 19 0	

The 4 pottes coste	0	1	11	
Spente in buyinge it 1ˢ 6ᵈ and to lighte us downe 2ᵈ	0	1	8	
Voiage to Whitehaven dr.: spente at Edmond Christian wines 1ˢ 6ᵈ and to William Curlew anchorage 1ˢ 6ᵈ	0	3	0	
We came into the harbour,[74] wynde north easte. Voyage to Whitehaven dr.: spente at Nich. Walker's 6ᵈ; at Mary Corckie's 12ᵈ	0	1	6	Decembr. 1
I boughte of Edmond Christian's widdowe 2 flitches of bakon which weyed 64 at 1½ᵈ per lb	0	8	0	Wednes. 2
Spente to get it for twise	0	1	0	2
Bough[t] 60 quarters of mutton at 2ˢ 10ᵈ per peece	2	2	6	Thurs. 3
Spente to get it for	0	1	6	Henry Vinch 3
Boughte of Mary Corckie's house 15½ qrtes at 13½ per qrte	0	17	10	3
	6	0	5	

[74] I.e. of Douglas, I. of Man.

Page 31a

Decr. 3	Broughte per contra recd.:			
	5 0 0 and disburssed	6	0	5
Cordige	4 9 4 recd. of Robert Joyne [r?[75]] for two hund [wt.] & 26 lb wt. of cordidge			
Thurs. 3	Spente at receaveinge of it	0	0	10
shop 3	A potte to put honey in	0	1	0
	Spente at buyeinge the honey	0	0	6
3	For hens, breade, egs	0	0	7
Fri. 4	At one of the clock we arrived at Whitehaven, wee all well.			
4	Gyven Fidlers 4^d that came to the down	0	4	0
5	I vewed the driftes & sees howe thinges wente. 40^l remayninge cash with Will. Atkinson.			
Sunday 6	Set out tanne pit and tanne h[ouse] & bargained ½ making of walls with James Willan at 30^s & Richd. Pruddey to wall thother halfe and gave James 6^d in earneste to drincke betweene them	0	0	6
Munday 7	Came to Lowther, all well theire.			
Tews. 8	10 0 0 of my mother to pay my brother Will Lowther.			
Wed. 9	To Middleton to Gyles Moore's	0	2	1
Thurs. 10	To Skipton to Richard Squires	0	3	0
Friday 11	To Leeds at nighte, gave my brother	10	0	0
12	Brige fayre day, see cloath boughte			
Sunday 13	Dyned at Mr Hopton's & gave cloath dresser	0	0	6

Page 31b

Mund. 14	Helped to tufte 21 fyne dozens & to pack 24 ordinaries
14	Dyned at Mr Busfield's.
14	I writte for London to Mr John Batty the effecte of what I writte from Dublin the 28th November & to advise what he hearde at any tyme to me or Mr George Gylle of our Canary busines, or what he did touchinge Mr Will Halle.
Tewsd. 15	I wente with my brother to York to my father, Mr W. Busfield with us, on which day spente a shew settinge on at Tadcaster 1^d; for hay to the horsses, etc, there 4^d. This day see the buyinge of about 20 dozens where note for ordinaryes they buy grayes about 40^s, 41^s, 42^s, 43^s, 44^s per peece, dressed drye, 3^s per peece more. This day we packed a packe of ordinaries; grayes about 20; skyes 1; reads 2; burnets 3; to sorte out the packe and we tuffted with silcke a packe of fyne, about 24 in a packe, leade and poyntze coloured moste and some few muskes for musckes are not now soe much in requeste.
Wednesday 16	My brother Will haveinge receaved of my father & brother

[75] Smudged.

the nighte before 80^l he wente to Leeds and I and Mr
W. Busfield stayed & that nighte receaved of my Lord
Mayor, Mr Hodgeson 100^l each of [us] for which gave him
6^s 8^d for the hundred payable 15 January nexte.

19 9 4   16 10 2   December 16
Mr Busfield gave his bill of exchange for both the hundreds,   *Page 32a*
but my brother Will is to have the one and pay the one
noble.

We dyned this day at Lord Mayors.

We receaved likewise each of us of Sir John Hotham, High
Sheriffe 200^l a peece for which gave each of us our notes to
him payable to Sir William Russell, Treasurer of the Navie
at London the firste of February nexte.

I receaved out of this 200^l of my brother 10^l 0 0 which I   Thurs. 17
lefte with Thomas Hammon pewter[er] in York in Thurs-
day market to buy hempe for me with, which he is to sende
by the Barnard Castle carrier to James Bland's of Penrith   10 0 0
Spente in bargayninge with him   0 0 6   Posted
My expences at my hoste's Scarres, viz   greatest
                                                                         ledger

	£	s	d	
my brother's supper & my diet & one drincke	0	2	6	
girthe 3^d; shew 3^d	0	0	6	
mayle pillion	0	0	4	
hay, myne & brother's horsse	0	0	6	0 7 4
oates	0	2	0	
oastler, house, etc	0	0	6	

At Tadcaster Mr Busfield and myselfe   0 1 2   17
To Wakefield, my brother boughte 8 fyne dozens. Spente   Friday 18
   our horsses   0 0 4
My brother boughte about 24 dozens.   Saturd. 19
Dyned at Mr Tom Metcalfe's.   Sunday 20

Munday my brother and I ordered all busines.   *Page 32b*^{76}
Boughte about 20ty dozens. I gave the woorckemen at my   December 21
   comeinge away at Matthew Foster's to drincke   0 1 0   Tews. 22
Henry Gybbins & Thomas Keemes   0 1 0
the boye which looked at our horsses   0 0 6
the little mayde at Matthewes   0 1 0
We wente that nighte to Kippax.^{77}
We wente by Speacke.   Spoake with Mr Thorpe about my   Wednesday 23
Lord of Exeter's money and came that nighte to Egleston.^{78}

---

^{76} At the top of the page is a heading dated 1634 and the title of an account between himself
and his brother Will but this is crossed out.

^{77} A village seven miles south east of Leeds.

^{78} Probably Egglestone Abbey near Barnard Castle.

Thursday 24	Came by Appleby and coste me on Mr Edward Guye his sonne & ourselves	0	1	8
Friday 25	We rested, beinge Christmas this day.			
Saturday 26	And this day wente to Ackornebancke.[79]			
Sunday 27	Wente to envite Uncle William Lowther.			
Munday 28	Uncle William & Sir Christopher Dalston dined at ours.			
Tews. 29	We dined at brother John's at Hackthorpe.[80]			
Wed. 30	I gave piper 6^d and coocke 6^d and came to Whitehaven.	0	1	0
Thurs. 31	At Whitehaven and soe on.			
January 2	Spente with William Fletcher & others	0	2	4
6	My partner Rowland Jackson came hither the sixthe & stayd till 8th. I gave aplemen	0	0	6
January 8	29 9 4 recvd. disburssed.	27	8	6

1634/5 my brthr. C. Low.[81] dr

Page 33a

March 20	To cash as per an accompte given him the 5 of December 1634	140	3	10
	To cash pd. Mr Dickins for his wyne lycence	0	10	0
	To cash loste per exchange, & for brock[erage] & factorage of 170^l till 17 December	4	11	5
	To cash pd. Mr George Gyll for his still	5	7	8
1635 June 27	To accompte in the handes of George Gyll pd. Mr Batty in pt. of Canary's fraighte	40	0	0
	To cash as by particulars hereafter:			

Woolle	to Foxe the smith about gray horsse	2	6
Woolle	to Muncaster for the horsse to Lowther	2	4
	for tayleringe my white suite	18	9
	loste per exchange of 170^l to Hamburg at $36^s\ 7^d$ and recharged at $35^s\ 6^d$ is	5	2	0
	for factor[age] & brokerage of it	0	8	8
Woolle	for Tho. Reames charges to Halifax about woolle debtors	11	0

The above bracketed group totals: 7 5 3

1635 Dec. 17	To cloath acc. for a gray doz. at Whitehaven	4	0	0
	To cash for factoridge of wynes selleinge to Mr George Gylle	0	10	0
18	To cash that I toocke to pay Thomas Hammon. to buy hempe	10	0	0
March		212	8	2

---

[79] Acornbank, home of Sir Christopher Dalston.

[80] Hackthorpe Hall, Westmorland, a few miles from Lowther Hall and probably the childhood home of Christopher and his brothers.

[81] The two following accounts were presumably copied from William's own book.

My broth. C. Lowther is Credr.

Of Michell Robinson per cash recd.		2	0	0	Feb. 5
Per cash received at London resteing dew betweene my brother aboute his suite make		1	7	5
Per cash recd. of severall men viz:				

of Mychall Robinson	1	8	4			
of Tho Dickson	0	10	0			
of John Howker	1	0	0	}	8	11	8
of Gylbert Walker	3	0	0			
of Atkinson the butcher	2	13	4			

By cash rcd. of Mr John Batty in pt. of the Barrillio accompte	20	4	2	Canary
By cash rcd. by George Gylle for the 11½ pypes of wyne, wanteing 15 gallons at 11^l 10^s per pype solde for ½ money recd. the 6th of June & the reste at 20th of September	130	15	0
By cash recd. in accompte of William Wickliffe for my brother	4	0	0
By cash rcd. of Atkinson the butcher in full	1	0	8
By cash rcd. of Will Atkinson at Lowther in lew of the hempe	10	0	0	Dec. 2
Restes to balance yet dew	34	9	3
	212	8	2

Shewmakeinge Dr

For upper lether: a dicker	5	0	0
for 10 bendes for sole lether	3	6	8
for ½ of a dicker middle sole	2	10	0
for 10 lb wt. of rozin	0	1	8
for a pynte of oyle	0	0	3
for 10 lb wt. beaten hempe	0	6	0
for spinninge it 2^d per pounde	0	1	8
Totall	11	6	3
Curryinge at 14^d per hyde	0	11	8
House rente for him[82]		2	1
Makeinge at 4^s per dozen, makeinge a dozen payre for every upper hyde with all appurtenances	2	0	0
Totall	14	0	0

---

[82] Badly overwritten. Appears to have "d^o 2^d per dozen" after "for him".

Curryinge

A quarte of oyle & $\frac{1}{3}$	0	0	8
$\frac{1}{2}$ of a pounde of tallowe	0	0	2
labour of shaveinge & curreinge	0	0	4
Totall	0	1	2

At Penrith theire oyle & tallow is 2^d dearer. And note drie lether is litle lesse because the labour is more & a litle liquor theire must be nevertheless.

Page 34b

Shewmakeinge Cr

Per accompte of sayles of 120 payre out of the provision per contra which is:

- 12 payre of upper lether in a hyde
- 12 payre of soales in a bende
- 24 payre of in soles in a course hyde

Beinge solde at 24^s per dozen is in all for the 10 dozen of theise syzes viz:

24^{ss}
- 2 of the sixes
- 2 of the 7
- 2 of the 8
- 2 of the 9
- 2 of the 10
- 2 of the 11

	12	0	0^{83}
Besides children shewes, bootes & speckes	3	0	0
Sayles totall	15	0	0
Charges totall per contra	14	0	0
Gaynes to ballance	1	0	0
	15	0	0

This stocke may be returned each 5 weeckes, in anno, teme which if it soe may be then out of 14^l get in anno — 10 0 0

And two men will doe this. Informed per Thom. Harrison of Lowther.

Page 35a
Janu. 8
Linge 8
C: Profitt
& losse

29 9 4 broughte from follio 32^{84}	27	8	6
Gave my partner toward payment of Myles Dickson of Bristol's 10^l 10^s, and Will Atkinson gave him 3^l 8^s besides, which was in all 4^l 10^s	1	2	0

---

[83] I.e. 120 pair sold at 2^s per pair.
[84] See above p. 168.

John Lowther came to skoole, stayed all nighte,				9
nexte day wente with him to skoole mstr.				10
Spente with John Williamson at Anth. Hyndes	0	0	6	11
This nighte Thomas Hambleton, Will Hodgson, Anthony Hynde & I concluded buildeing of a shippe of 80 tunnes or upwardes & notes of it from each to other.				
Cut. the becke at Whitehaven.[85]				12
Gave Patrick Maxwell for mendeinge, the watch & golde weightes, etc	0	2	6	13
Solde Will Burton & Will Atkinson two thirds of the *George* after this voyage ended at 140^l: each of them 20^l in hande & the reste: 12 moneths day; recvd. in earneste 0 11 0 of Will Burton, Patrick Maxwell beinge presente upon which spente then	0	1	0	13
Gave pipers at house	0	0	4	14
Spente laste Sunday at Sir William Cotes	0	0	4	15
Came into the harbour a Devonshire shippe which was fraighted from London to Chester & overrune her coursse.				
Fellowes about putteing coles in John Fletcher.				16
I receaved a letter from my father per Ecleston boy[86] in the morneinge, the afternowne a letter from John Musgrave & coppy of Will Fletcher's order as my father desired.				Sunday 17
30 0 4 totall recd. & disbursed	28	15	2	20

Page 35b

Spente with Christopher Grayson, Anth. Crost[hwaite], Henry Tubman, etc about ballast	0	0	6	21
Given James Willan Tannehous founde	0	0	3	22
In expences p[ro]p[rio] on Chr. Hayre, etc	0	0	6	23
I have beene this while in perfecteing some accomptes,				24
viz: barq *George*, Canaries, Mr John Batty's				25, 26
Sir Robert Mansfield's & my brother				27
Will's & hempe, etc				28
have agreed this 30th of January with Christopher Grayson, Anthony Crosthwayte, Thomas Hambleton, John Hambleton, Henry Tubman for theire ballaste.				29 30
Sunday.				31
30 0 4 recd. disb.	28	16	5	

carried to follio 38.[87]

Richard Myles Mstr. of the *Margaret of the Forreste* enquire at the Redde Bulle upon the key at Bristol, Richard Raford the housekeeper; he offereth

Page 36a

[85] See above p. 149.
[86] Probably Eglestone, near Barnard Castle.
[87] See below p. 173.

to take 10^s per tunne fraight from Whitehaven to Bristol.

Witness: Henry Boyland the 28th January '35/6

Hull 1635.   The modelle of a shippe of a 100 tunne per Mr Robert Drew of Hull, Febr. 16th.

1. hir keele longe 50 foote.
2. hir breadth of forebeame or loase 21 foote sixe inches.
3. hir breadth of mayne beame 21 foote.
4. hir transome beame 14 foote longe.
5. hir deapth in holde betweene the bounde beames and hir keele 8 foote, and betweene hir bounde beames and upper beames 4 foote more which is 12 & better in all.
6. have 5 bounde beames in midle to strengthen.
7. let the scarfe[88] be five foote.
8. let your flower[89] beames be a foote thicke, your other in tymbers about 10 inches.

Page 36b

1.   1633 May the 30th in George Jackson's accompte of John Pennington & Mr Rawson recd. 2 4 0 but not accompted   George J. dr.

2.   1633 Sept. 8th in G. Jackson's accompte of Quinton & Henry Baldin for mohayre 2^l 10^s; 2^l 5^s onely sette downe recd. soe error 5^s.

3.   1633 Sept. 31st in ditto's accompte recd. of Tho. Dunninge for kersie & salte: 1 16 0 for which George is dr.

4.   1633 9ber 16th in George his accomptes for money recd. unset downe of Arthur Freeman by his father for a greene dozen 5^l 13^s 6^d, and of John Pennington 6^s 3^d for which he or Rowland is to be debtor.

1633 October 13th, 25 17 4 recd. for hydes & 22 2 0 onely sett downe soe is dewe 3 15 4. George is dr. for it.

Page 37a

Per ma soer Jane Lr.[90] about October 1636

Malte 8 sackes	7	0	0
Rie 6 loade	4	10	0
Wheate 3 loade	3	0	0
Eggs, butter & soape 1^s 6^d per weeke	3	18	0
Hopps	0	14	0
Salte	1	0	0
Pepper, sugar, ginger & other spices	2	10	0
fresh meate 10^s per weecke	26	0	0
A cowe wyntering & summeringe	3	10	0
	52	2	0

---

[88] Overlap where timbers join together.

[89] Floor beams which abut on the keel and separate the ribs.

[90] Perhaps his sister-in-law to be, Jane Busfield. The account is written later than its date.

2 horsses sommeringe & wynteringe:

3½ loades of hay	9	0	0	⎫			
sommer grasse	3	10	0	⎬	15	0	0
oates	2	10	0	⎭			

servantes wages

2 mades' wages	3	0	0	⎱			
1 man	2	10	0	⎰	5	10	0
Extraordinarie expences					3	0	0
Sessements & layes					5	0	0
House rente					13	6	8
Apparrell					26	0	0
					119	18	8
Coales					2	10	0
Totall					122	8	8

February 1

Page 37b blank
Page 38a

30 0 4 broughte over recd. & disbursed	28	16	5

Jan. 31
Feb. 1
Munday

I departed Whitehaven, came by copper woorckes at Keswicke, see theire vitrioll, of both sorts, Hungarie and Danice[91] vitrioll and the Hungarie vitrioll he holdeth at 30^l a tunne & the Dance at 15^l & samples of both I broughte.

I came from Tho. Gaytsgarth's were I lay and gave in the house to Lowther were stayd till the nexte day.   0 0 10

2

2 0 0 receaved of my mother.

At nowne thence I wente to Middleton to young Gyles Moore's whence came next day, where I gave in the house   0 0 10

3
4

soe by Ingleton where dyned,[92] and at Clapham had a shew set on   0 0 4

and laid at Gargrave where it coste me that nighte and morneinge   0 2 6

I got to Leeds beinge Friday in the afternowne where staid that nighte & soe came nexte morn thence to Sandholme where coste me   0 2 8

5
6

haveinge passed Selby & Barneby ferries.

I gotte immediately afternowne to Hulle to the *George* to Mr ......[93] Mann's to my brother.

7

[91] So written but means probably Danzig not Danish, a point I owe to the expertise in Baltic economic history of Dr Heinz Kent.

[92] Probably with the Ingleton branch of the Lowther Family since no cost is stated.

[93] Blank.

8	We entred 18 packes cont. moste of them about 26 peeces in a packe but entred at 25 and in one packe had a bill of store for 10 dozen.	
9	This day all the reste of the packes were shipte aboard of my brother's.	

I gave the packers yesterday   0   0   4
and for tabacko to the meare[94]   0   0   3

10   I see the roapemakers, toocke modell of a shipp from Mr Drew as in follio 35[95]. My brother's letter maketh mention of 476 dozens shipte in Robert Drew this tyme & Mr Busfield about 700 dozens shipped then allsoe.

Feb. 11   Robert Drew hade entred in him 2,891 dozens and 55 kersies
Thurs.   { 800 yrds & goades[96] of baze and cottens
               { and 5 fothers of lead

     iii dozens, at i in a packe of 26 dozens unentred, viz:

139	Henry Thompson	5 kersies	5 fothers leade	
653	William Busfield)			
10	allowed him for store)			
141	Henry Watkinson			
121	John Thompson			
45	Leonard Thompson	30 kersies		
305	William Scotte			
38	William Dobson			
439	William Lowther			
169	John Metcalfe)	10 [kersies]	800 yrds)	Bayze
5	allowed him)		goades)	cottens
178	John Ramsden			
420	Robert Lowther	20 kersies		
216	Thomas Hoyle			
12	allowed the mstr. for portage			

2,891   doz. totall: 55 k[ersies]   800 bayzes   5:lead

    iii every 26th dozen unentred.
    i0 allowed my brother unset downe

3,012   dozens 55 kersies 800 yrds. bayze 5 foth. lead

Custome house officers

1. Colector Mr William Sommerfeilde—I feaed his man.

[94] I.e. mare.
[95] See above p. 172.
[96] A goad = $4\frac{1}{2}$ feet.

2. Customer Mr ....[97] Murton.
3. King's Searcher Mr .....[97] Fenton.
4. Farmer's Searcher Mr William Thortonn.
5. Collector of the pretermitted customes, Anthony Kirke.

Wayters

Tymmothy Mosse; Tymmothy Jimsonn.

				Page 39a
32 0 4 recd. broughte over & disburssed	29	4	2	Feb. 11
Pd. for a boocke of husbandrie rules & one other	0	1	2	
Spente yeaster nighte with Mr Hyllarie, etc	0	1	0	
Our ferryinge over at Barneby Ferry	0	0	4	
We came to Selby & stayd theire all nighte	0	0	0	11
We came to Leeds by Parson Thoneton's.				12
Pd. for brimston powder & quicksilver for meare	0	1	0	Satur. 13
We visited Mr Medcalfe.				Sund. 14
Stayd within readeinge & compteinge.				Mund. 15
Mr Busfield supped with us, spente	0	1	0	16
I writte to Thomas Hammond about sendeing away my hempe per Mr Sawer.				17
Visited Mr Medcalfe & Sir Richard Hutton.				18
I writte to Mr John Batty & Mr Gill by my brother.				19
I writte to Mr Alexander Shephard by my brother Will & to Mrs Jane Busfield.				20
I receaved answer of Thomas Hammond for which hempe dr. to hym for more boughte than the money I gave him in December laste with factoridge	4	2	0	
My brother William sett forward to London.				Mund. 22
Tho. Guy went to Selby to packe & I ordered my brother's letters and other papers, & redd all my father's letters over allmoste, & many others & a bunch of notes & letters more.				23
Was likewise busie in over-vewinge his accomptes				24
and papers				25
I ordered the cloath straighted: Tho. Guye.				26
I went to Halifax per John Houcker whose debte of 5 19 0 I accompte but promiseth 20^s out Our Lady Day, soe on to Halifax to Thomas Bynns.				27
				Page 39b
Thence in the afternowne to William Armitage's, a poore				Feby. 27

man yet gotte 2 waynescotte chistes, one bedsteede, one cubboarde, one litle clapboarde chiste, which are debitor to ditto William, taken at 3^l though not woorth 50^s soe profitte & losse debitor to ditto wares 10^s; and William Armitage

[97] Blank.

is dr. to stocke still as before 8^l per bonde dew Candlemas 1642.

28   Beinge Sunday stayd at Halifax till after the afternowne sermon & then wente to Warely[98] to Ambrosse and Daniell Gawckroger about Bradley; 12^l assigned to me which they will take care to see me payd.

29   I solde the bedde & thone[99] of chists I had of Armitage for 1 9 0; for which cash debitor to ditto wares 1 9 0. The reste of the goods lefte at Mr Thomas Binns in John Wilkinson's keeping to sell, which I hope will give 24^s.

29   Spente in travell about the Armitage wares debr. to cash 0 14 3. Yeasterday I served a King's letter and a decree on Gylbert Walker who saith he will pay at our Lady Day. 33 9 4 recd. & disb.   30   2   11

Page 40a

Feby. 29   Returned to Leeds, Thos. Reame with me, per Samuel Barrowclough, John Howcker's sonne-in-law who refused to be bound for his father.

Mar. 1   Boughte 13 peeces in all for 39^l odde money. After writte to
Tews.   London to Brother William and sente my father's etc, & Mr Sommerfeilde's letter alonge with them per George Sawers.

Wed. 2   Sett Thomas Guy's boockes in better order and ordered the cloath in the upper warehouse & loocked amongste the woorckmen.

Thurs. 3   Stayd within; I writt to my brother William Lowther per poste.

Fri. 4   Dined at Mr Metcalfe's; after wente Leeds.

5   3 0 0 cash dr. to Brother William at Leeds.

5   Bought 24 peeces at 81 18 0 of which 7 ordinary & 17 fyne. Mr Busfield breakefasted with me; after wente to York.

6   Sunday after nowne came from York to Leeds; receaved 3 letters from my father, one to Sir George Radcliffe, one to Mr Eden, another to Mrs Ramsay.

6   I spente at York Saturday, Sunday, for which hempe dr. posted,   0   4   0

6   Thomas Hammond dr. to cash payd him in full posted,   4   2   0

7   Ordered cloath at Matthew's; sente chayres to mende; supped at Mr Busfield's.

8   We boughte 12 peeces, 9 ord., 3 fyne, which coste 32–3^s & I writt to my brother Will per George Sawer's conveyance.

[98] I.e. Warley, township 2m. W. of Halifax.
[99] I.e. "the one".

Page 40b
I ordered the boockes of dresseinge & the petty charge   March 9
boocke & writte to York by Tho[mas] Hollingwoorth.

An Inventory of my brother Will's stocke the 16th February laste

Dr.				Cr.			
Cloath dr.	384	15	7	Stocke	1,369	6	3
Cash	205	19	5	My father	1,509	8	6
Per losse	15	16	0	My mother	20	0	0
John Phips	671	3	2	Uncle Richard	150	0	0
My bro. C. Lowther	82	14	3	Mr Gill	190	0	0
Robert Bradeley	163	9	1	Matthew Foster	100	0	0
Debts	172	11	10	Will Sommerfielde	73	3	4
Voyage Hamb[urg]	1,715	8	9				
	3,411	18	1		3,411	18	1

This day Galles[1] came from Turnebridge   12 0 0   9
and writte to London to brother Will.
I deptd. Leeds, breakfasted at Mr Busfield's before I came,   10
    and gave Matthew's mayde   0 0 6
and that nighte gotte to Gygleswicke in charges
proprio there then   0 2 7   11
then wente on [to] Mr Lancaster's were laid. I gave
theire   0 1 6   12
& soe came to Lowther.
weere staid Sunday, walked downe to Buckholme, etc. Sente   13
the letter to Ask[h]am[2] by the boy Lancelot Wilkinson &
the letter to Mr Eden by Rich. Cragg.
36 9 4 recvd.   & disb.   34 13 6   Sund. 13

A note of my father's stocke 22nd June 1635   Page 41a

My cousen Wibergh upon Clifton K 1639		510	0	0
Tho. Wibergh for Cleaseby Crofts then		20	0	0
Rowland Jackson 30th Aug. 1639		300	0	0
	Totall	830	0	0
Atkins of Bolrons lease & wardship		60	0	0
Mr Washington's tythes for 2 yeares		60	0	0
Idem 20^l per annum for 2 yeares		40	0	0
John Cowper 7^l per annum for 3 yeares		15	0	0

[1] Substance used in dyeing.
[2] Village next to Lowther.

Will Fletcher's lease to Christopher	20	0	0
20^l per annum for Mr Conyer's life	110	0	0
Totall	225	0	0[3]

My sonne Christopher hath now	2,130	0	0
My sonne William, March 1635	2,988	14	9
William Ion & Michael Mownsey	324	5	0
Sheepe, Lowther, Asby & Thwaytes	200	0	0
Catle & horsses at Lowther	340	0	0
Householde stuffe at Lowther, Meaburne, etc	500	0	0
Whereof is desperate 1,000^l Totall	6,482	19	9

14	Stayd at Lowther; writt to my father, boughte 11½ yrds. of Scotch cloath	11	6
15	Wente to Whitehaven.		
May 15	12^s 4^d was before made lesse disburssed then was with which the diference of the somes recieved over the…[4]		

Page 41b
May 16
1636 25

From that tyme stayd at Whitehaven to the 25th March 1636.
[March] Cash dr. to shippe *George* recd. of Will Burton in full of his 20^l beinge his firste payment, 11^l before given me in earneste. Debt C follio 6.
19 19 0.
5 10 8 Cashe dr. to coles recd. of our barq.
Cash dr. to shippe *George* receaved of Nicholas Burton for Will Atkinson his part. Dr C foll. 6.
20 0 0, viz: 6^l in money and 14^l by John Willan to my father the 20th November laste.

My father dr. theirefore for the 14^l allready entred on the 20th November laste		14	0	0

Cash dr. to shippe *George* gained, God be praysed, by this voyage ended this day—

3 1 8 and disb. to Will Burton for by rentes [?][5]		3	2
Shoppe dr to cash for 10 lb wt. of tabaco	0	16	8
Profit & losse dr. to Will Burton for shop chapmen [?]	0	14	0
April 18	83 15 0 Recd. of my father's rente			
22	My father dr. for Seacote Inge rente	0	3	0
22	For the Bpps.[6] rente: my father: 12	22	12	4

---

[3] Error for £305?
[4] Ends thus.
[5] This and the two following lines so cramped and illegible the words can only be guessed at.
[6] I.e. Bishop of Chester's.

5 12 0 cash dr. to my father recd. for him by me.				27
My father dr. to cash pd. my mother	80	0	0	29
Shoppe dr. to cash for 15 brlls. of heareinges at 18ˢ per brll.	13	10	0	
Mr Chamley dr. to cash paid to him what we oughte him ...				
Aprill	7	3	0	
My father dr. to cash given schoolemaster at St Bees at				
Easter laste	1	0	0	
73 12 4 recd. & disb.:	175	1	4[7]	

Page 42a

1 0 0 recd. of Michael Crostat[8] of Gilgarron in full of his bonde at York				
In expences proprio to Kendayle that had his house burnte	0	2	6	
To the poore on Easter Sonday	0	1	0	
My journey to Leeds	0	2	4	3
In expences pprio. for 2 payre of knitt stockings	0	4	0	
My father dr. to cash for Seacote Inge rentes	0	3	0	
Sunday now beinge at Leeds I supped at Mr Busfield's.				May 1
On Munday cleered the peere accompte.				2
On Tewsday cleered house and salte pannes bewildringe accompte.				3
On Wednesday, St Christopher's day, my christeninge day, I cleered housekeepeinge accompte and did keepe it more holy then ordinarie, the Lord blesse me with his spiritte:				4
and spente at dinner in wine with them	0	1	0	
and gave Matthew's woorckemen to drincke	0	1	0	

On Thursday drew a guessinge inventory of my estate; after
wente to York to my father where conferred that nighte
about my brother Will's marriage, my brother then with
me, with my father, and from him receaved these considerations following:

                              5

May 5 1636

1.   William Lowther to stay at Hamburg 2 y[ea]rs and after first year
     Thomas Guy to goe over to him.
2.   At William Lowther's comeinge over, then Christopher Lowther to   *Page 42b*
     goe over to Hamburg to stay theire untill 1640.[9]
3.   Then I[10] am content to give way [to what] yow thinke of marriage.
4.   For returnes of money may have 100ˡ per weecke at Hull, at Christ-

---

[7] £174.10 written on *Page 42a*.

[8] I.e. Crosthwaite.

[9] Probably due to the death of Sir John in 1637 this was changed, and Christopher went in 1637, William being away probably less than a year. William married Busfield's daughter Jane.

[10] I.e. Sir John.

mas, Easter, Midsommer, Mich[aelmas]. Mr Elmehirste Lady Day & Michaelmas the Auditt; May, Beverley Fayre, the Archbishop's receaver or Mr Thorpe, or of Mr Hodgeson of York at 6^s 8^d per 100^l at woorste.

5.   Then Christopher returneth from Hamburg, he and Will both at London and sometymes Leeds.

6.   Cast[11] soe as to doe your busines with care and ease.

7.   To provide a servante or an aprentice a yeare hence.

8.   Christopher hence to be at Leeds the 23rd June till 23rd July after, to come the 10th of September to stay till 10th of October and after to goe to London if occasion require till Martinmas.[12]

9.   If advised, to sende some cloath for London.

10.   To consider whether better 3 adventures and greater to prevent wynter voyages.

May 5	181 2 8 recd. & disb.	175	5	5

Page 43a   The considerations followe, viz:

11.   To provide parteners at Hamburg & London; a man of creditte at London for returnes for 5 yeares.

12.   To consider for the shippe to provide parte of this or the other.

13.   To advise from Hamburg whether to live at Hamburg or Rotterdam.

14.   To pay by Mr Elmhyrste or others to Mr Wilden at Martinmas what moneyes yow have of myne this somer.

15.   To send to Mr Jo. Emmerson to Newcastle the powder and match before Midsommer.

16.   To sell if cann sell at 5 per cent at Leeds, soe hinder not shippeinge.

17.   To consider for returnes if sicknes be in London, for Amsterdam or otherwise.

18.   Chr[istopher] & Tho. Guy to learne Dutch.

19.   Christopher to gett allowance of the Trinity House for the peere, theire orders and power.

20.   To advise for 500^l of Sir Richard Graham.[13]

21.   To loocke amongste Leeds debtors.

Page 44a

181 2 8 rcd. & disb.   175   5   5

May 6   My father lente me his stoned horsse to ride to Hull. I
        bayted at Wighton, a marcket towne in the Wouldes,
        where much hempe solde at Martinmas tyme & theire
        about.   Spent   0   0   6

---

[11] I.e. keep account.
[12] I.e. about November 12.
[13] Probably Sir Richard Graham of Netherby, Bart.

To fore newne gotte to Hull. Made out the 5 entries the forme followeth:

In Hull the 6th of May 1636

In the *Merchant of Hull*, Rob. Drew master { usq. Hamburg
{ William Lowther, mercht.

21	qts.	25 ps.[14]
23	qts.	25 ps.
25	qts.	26 ps.
26	qts.	25 ps.
27	qts.	25 ps.
28	qts.	24 ps.
29	qts.	25 ps.
30	qts.	24 ps.
31	qts.	24 ps.
32	qts.	25 ps.
33	qts.	22 ps.

                                    William Lowther[15]

Note that of theise theire muste be fower, and one other in woordes given the officers of the custome house.
& gave Mr Sommerfielde them, he signed one of them, would by them enter them on Saturd[ay] at Custome House.
This day beinge Saturday I shippte sixe truss[16] as the   7
porters saide theire were, but I beleve but 5 for Richard
Robinson should have had 3.
and 8 is all should be come downe.

	£	s	d	
My charges at Hull myselfe & horsse	0	5	8	*Page 44b*
Gave porters	0	0	3	
At Wighton in comeinge backe	0	0	6	
At York my charges and boateinge	0	2	11	May 8

Came in the afternowne to Leeds with Mr Sergeant Beaston.
I made oath of serveinge a King's letter & decree on
Gylbert Walker before my father.
0 9 4 recd. of Thomas Guy the 9^s 4^d which I disburssed   9
above at Hull, York, etc.
Recd. a letter from my father to me and my brother Will,   10
    and an Attachment againste Gylbert Walker for 7^l 10^s
    debte & 20^s costes decreed the 6th day of October laste
    from Sir Will Denman, Sheriffe, dated the 9th day of

---

[14] Pieces?

[15] Above "William Lowther" is drawn a doodle of wheels and cogs. In the margin to the left is a symbol formed of C and L which probably was marked on the packages.

[16] Doubtful. Could just be "tru. as" (i.e. truncks as).

	May 1636 to the bayliffes of Aybrigge or any other his bayliffs. Mrs Jane Busfield came from London, supped, theire cost me in wyne on them	0	0	7

11   I see the redwood milnes coste me   0   0   4

the forme partely per contra[17]: one mylne stone for the lyer & 2 mylstones goeinge about an iron axeltree on the other mylstone. They will grinde 8 milne fulles in 24 houres which will be 4 hundred weyghte & they have 2^s 6^d per hundred weighte besides beinge d[elivere]d moyste & recd. drie; one mighte grinde barque or aples or the like with it.

181 12 0 recd. & disb.:   175 16 2

Page 45a

27 December 1635 my brother Christo. Lowther[18]   Dr.

March 12

To cash paid out in charges for 5 pypes of wyne for his proprio accompte for customes	10	14	0
To cash pd. Mr Jo. Batty as per his accompte in pt. of 8 pypes in $\frac{6}{6}$ and $\frac{1}{4}$ in $\frac{8}{8}$	40	0	0
To cash paid Mr Dickins for his wyne lycence rente & acquittance	1	1	0
To cash for the losse of exchange of 60^l taken up to pay the same	1	10	5
To cash pd. Mr Cheslin the cowper	0	17	10
Pd. per George Gill	0	8	0
To cash pd. my brother himselfe per Thomas Guy the 5th of March laste when he wente to York	3	0	0

Page 45b

Dec. 27 1635 My brother Christ. Lowther is   Cr.[19]

Per George Gill for accompte of wynes solde by him viz:

7 pypes and $\frac{1}{4}$	87	0	0
More for $\frac{1}{2}$ of the 4 pypes $\frac{1}{3}$	30	6	8
Per cash of Michael Storie in full	1	15	0
Per Robert Chester of London dew for the other $\frac{1}{2}$ of the $4\frac{1}{3}$ pypes dew the 16th of September nexte	30	6	8

Rest of page blank.

Page 46a

May ii

181 12 0 rcvd. & disb. broughte over from follio 44 a leafe overrunne   175 16 2

I made an experiment with corcklette woolle[20] with Richard

[17] I.e. the doodle referred to in footnote 15, p. 181 above.

[18] Since the account is in Christopher's handwriting it must have been copied from an account of his brother William's.

[19] This account, the only item on *Page 45b*, faces the previous account on *Page 45a*, as in ordinary book-keeping.

[20] "Woolle" probably written in error for "woode", i.e. wood for dying.

Sharpe one of our beste cloathiers who liketh it & thincketh
it will serve in lew of red or sweete woode, which costeth
them $7\frac{1}{2}^d$ per pounde, and note that an ounce of Galles &
halfe of a pounde of reede woode will but die one pounde of
woolle, and 2 pounde of copperas will but serve to make a
cloath of 30 yrdes. longe a sad burnet.

Recd. Mr Batty's Canarie accompte of my brother &   12
coppieth the inventorie he hath laste taken beinge about the
4th of May instant, viz:

Cloth	215	15	0	Stocke	1,369	6	3
Cash	306	11	10	Father	1,830	17	8
Per losse	33	14	11	Mother	20	0	0
Hen. Crispe	1,386	11	11	Uncle Rich. Lowther[21]	150	0	0
Robert Bradeley	163	9	1	Matthew Foster	100	0	0
Debtes	170	7	10	Wm. Summerfield	123	19	0
Hamburg voyage	1,159	1	1	Henry Crispe	270	0	0
Rotterdam voyage	307	19	5	Magasigne	50	0	0
John Pollard	119	8	11	Christ. Lowther	9	2	10
Cheslin	30	6	8	George Gill	1	14	1
Wares	31	13	6				
	3,925	**0**	**2**		**3,925**	**0**	**2**

Page 46b
May 13

Friday sett forwards towards Halifax. Howcker of Wike[22]
not at home, in Lancashire, soe through Halifax to Gawk-
rogers of Warely[23]. Bradeley's wife come over, meaneth to
have the 6^l dew at Midsommer soe I returned to Halifax,
lay at Thomas Binns the nighte.

I received for the cupboarde & chiste of Armitage 0 19 6   14
for which cash dr. to ditto wares. 1 6 0 cash dr. to Gilbert
Walker for soe much rcd. for costs of suite & charges,
theire beinge 40^s behinde still.

That nighte I gotte to Clitheroe[24] in Lancashire.

I gotte from Clitheroe to Lancaster where I stayed all nighte   15
beinge Sunday.

I vewed in the morneinge our wynes at Lancaster & gotte   16
Mr Atkinson the vintener to see them & till he spoacke to
Mr Bradshawe could not buy them. Theire is one full hgshd.
of white & in 2 other hgshds. $\frac{1}{2}$ a hoghd. of claret turned

---

[21] Probably Richard Lowther, J.P., barrister of Gray's Inn, and brother of Sir John.
[22] Township $6\frac{1}{4}$ miles NNE of Leeds.
[23] I.e. Warley, township 2 miles W. of Halifax.
[24] Clitheroe, market town 26 miles S.E. of Lancaster.

eager[25], and a remnant of white turned eager all worth 50ˢ.
I wente thence to Kentdayle, stayed a while and after I
wente to Lowther and this journey coste me 20ˢ for which:

Robert Bradeley dr. for his busines	0	6	8
Our woolle drs. of Halifax dr.	0	6	8
And our wynes at Lancaster	0	6	8

17   My brother sent my father a ballance which doth followe
over the leafe.

183 7 6 recvd. & disburssed	176	16	2

Page 47a

Balance is debitor

May 12

To cloath remayninge	232	6	4
To cash resteinge	71	18	10
To Henry Crispe factor at Hamburg	1,520	6	10
To John Pollard factor, Rotterdam	119	8	11
To voyage to Hamburg	1,159	1	1
To voyage to Rotterdam	307	19	5
To Wards accompt	31	13	6
To Galle's accompt	46	0	0
To Mr Cheslin the wyne cowper	30	6	8
To Matthew Foster	42	0	0
To Robert Bradeley	163	9	1
To olde woolle debtes	173	2	10
Some is	3,897	13	6

Christopher Brooke[26]	9	0	8
Samuel Bucktroutt	5	15	0
John Ellingworth	13	11	1
Medcalfe Ferra	22	13	0
Matthew Glover	2	6	8
Robert Glover	5	19	6
Addam Hebdan	15	5	0
Simonde Hacksworth	0	5	0
Richard Helme	15	13	0
Francis Horssman	2	3	4
James Lambert	10	10	8
John Lambert	13	5	5
John Parker	12	2	0
Christopher Robinson	0	10	0

[25] [Sic] vinegar?

[26] This account is written in a very cramped hand at the lower third of the page. The account is not totalled but amounts to £136 16 10.

Henry Schedule	4	1	0
Matthew Thompson	4	15	4

Ballance is creditor[27]

By stocke	3,172	17	3
By our mother	20	0	0
By our Uncle Richard Lowther	150	0	0
By Matthew Foster	100	0	0
By Mr William Sommerfielde	123	19	4
By Henry Crispe	270	0	0
By Magasigne	50	0	0
By Christopher Lowther	91	2	10
By George Gill	1	14	1
Some is	3,897	13	6

Oliver Wray	1	12	0
Thomas Langstarre	0	3	0
Leonard Altman	3	9	6
Marmaduke Winterskill	5	1	6
Richard Whitehead	4	12	6
John Theackston	0	8	0
Thomas Warde	2	14	6
Richard Leath	3	16	0
John Coates	0	3	11
Abraham Burnell	3	8	4
Arthur Doners	7	0	0
William Wicliffe	2	15	0
James Michell	0	1	9
	173	2	10[28]

183 7 6 broughte over from follio 46	176	16	2

I wente to Whitehaven where stayd till 26th of May directinge, etc on which day my father and mother came & stayed till 3rd June.

This nighte wente Will Atkinson to Newry[29] in Mackwilliam's, carried 719 bushells valued at 54 16 6 besides fraighte & cust[om].

[27] This account faces the debit account on the previous page.

[28] This total shows that this is a detailed account of the total of old wool debts on the previous page.

[29] Seaport 30 miles from Belfast.

June 1	This day Will Atkinson gott to Carlingford, his 719 bushells made out at Newry 185 brlls.			
5	Whitsonday Will Burton returned from Wexford.			
8	Dublin. George Jackson's letter to me.			
17	Timber accompte of the Wexford's man.			
20	Accompte proprio dr. to cash for 2 doz. of poyntes silke & buttons boughte 6^s 0^d.			
28	Will Burton's accompte of the Wexford voyage.			
29	St Peter's Day, Wednesday. I came from Whitehaven & gave James Willan	0	0	6
	and laid at Threlket[30] coste	0	1	0
30	Came to Lowther and stayd there			
	20 0 0 cash to accompte in the hands of Richard Powley recd. of him the 25th day of June instante as in his cash: 56.[31]			
	My father Sir Jo. Lowther is dr. to cash pd. him for his salt-panne, 2 laste rentes in salte 27 10 0.			
	Posted Braystones & Eyneside[32] rents 7 10 0			
30	50 0 0 cash dr. to my father lente unto us.			
	6 11 0 cash dr. more in prte. of other 50^l lente.			
July 1	Beinge Friday I wente to Ingleton and staid all nighte, given theire	0	2	6

Page 48b

July 1	A horsse shew this day	0	0	3
2	I went to Skipton, bayted at G.....[33]	0	1	6
3	and at Skipton, were dined at Castle & afternowne wente to Leeds cost me	0	3	6
4	Tho. Guy wente to York toocke up a hundred poundes of Mr Elmhirste for which Mr Busfield is to pay it to Mr Raylton the 4th of Auguste & we to lett him have another 100^l for it upon our exchange.			
5	I wente through all my brother's letters.			
6	I loocked how all thinges had passed since my laste beinge here.			
7	Followed on our busines.			
8	And soe the like then and receaved letters per poste from George Gill & my brother William & one to my father.			
8	Accompte currante at Leeds in the order of Thomas Guy dr. to cash pd. to him 48 11 6.			
9	I and Mr Busfield wente to York and toocke up of Mr Richard Elmhirste 170^l for which he and I bounde & likewise for the 100^l Thomas Guy toocke the 4th July payable			

[30] Probably Threlkeld, Cumberland.
[31] I.e. Cash book *Page 56.*
[32] This is a conjectural reconstruction of a badly smudged name.
[33] Abbreviated and smudged. Either Gargrave or Giggleswick.

viz: 100^l the 4th of Auguste & 170^l the 8th Auguste which
Mr Busfield is to pay onely though had but onely 170^l &
for the other 100^l we are to let him have another hundred
for it.

Spent at York in all	0	2	0

261 19 0	261	14	11

Page 49a

25th June 1636   Ballance of my estate   Cr

In Canaries in $\frac{8}{8}$	{ 10	6	3	
	{ 531	8	6	
In Canaries in $\frac{6}{6}$	76	8	5	
In Dublin to Belfast	210	0	0	110
In Belfast & theireabouts	159^{34} 5	10$\frac{1}{2}$		50
In Yorkshire woolle debters	20	0	0	
My brother William Lowther	9	2	10	
My cousin John Senhouse	155	10	0	
William Burton & William Atkinson	53	6	8	Barqs
My $\frac{1}{3}$ parte of the *George*	46	13	4	
Peere about	303	0	0	
Whitehaven house, land and householde stuffe	250	0	0	
Salte pannes	467	7	4	
Shoppe goodes	100	0	0	
Cordige	100	0	0	
Sundrie wares	100	0	0	
Debters	100	0	0	

Ballance   Dr   *Page 49b*

Per Mr John Batty supposed	14	4	3
Per Mr Richard Morris expences[35] for theire pt. in salte pannes	153	0	0[36]

Dr   *Page 50a*

In cash	626	13	8
Henry Crispe, factor	2,014	7	2
John Pollard	27	8	8
George Gill	26	5	11
Father	323	16	8
Richard Sharpe	16	0	0
Tho. Reame	4	6	8
Henry Gibbins	5	12	8
Accompte at Whitehaven	41	3	5

[34] The figure 9 is uncertain.
[35] A doubtful reconstruction of an abbreviated and badly smudged word.
[36] This account is left incomplete. It faces the account on *Page 49a*.

Tho. Simpson	15	15	0
Galles	26	6	0
Wares Math[ew?]	33	18	10
Cheslin, cowper	30	6	8
Robert Thompson	1	5	0
Henry Pawson	7	0	0
Robert Bradeley	123	9	1
Woolle debts	163	12	10
Cloath	1,135	8	6

October the 4th	4,635	14	9

Page 50b   Creditor

Stocke remaininge	3,172	17	3
Henry Crispe, dr.	470	0	0
Wm. Lowther	40	0	0
Our mother	20	0	0
In brother John Lowther	408	11	6
Wm. Summerfield	64	2	8
John Butterfield	64	16	0
Hugh Currer	50	0	0
Matthew Foster	56	15	0
Richard Lowther	150	0	0
Magasigne	35	0	0
William Busfield	100	0	0
Profitt & losse	3	12	0

	4,635	14	9

466^l od monies gained with 2,450^l stock, 250^l more recd. since March, which makes above 20 p[er] c[ent] interest to be deducted for my uncle R. Lowther and Mr Foster & my mother; the gains of the *Matthew*[37] not yet broughte to accompte and whether losse or profitt cannot tell.

Stock now in good monie, besides proffitt	2,744	11	11

Page 51a
July 9

261 19 0 brought from 48 follio	261	14	11
Disburssed given Tho. Boocke, joyner, 29th May	0	5	0
Given To Richard Pruddey 24 June	0	2	6

July 9   3 bills of exchange given this day by me and Mr W. Busfield recd. of Mr Elias Edwardes payable viz: the 20th of Auguste:

[37] Presumably a ship, so italicised.

To Mr Robert Foote, Ironmonger, at Dice Key in London   36 0 0
To Mr Robert Thurkelle at the White Harte in Thames
  Streete   49 14 0
To Mr Edmond Wrighte, Alderman, in London   44 6 0
Pd. for 11 dayes use from the nineth of Auguste till 20th   [blank]

I wente to Halifax, receaved of Mr Ralph Strudwicke   July 13
charged on Mr Gill payable the 14th Auguste to himselfe
38^l signed by me & Mr Busfield ... 19 0 cash dr. to 3 Irish
woolle debtors recd. of Gilbert Walker given him a generall
acquittance. 0 2 0 cash dr. to wares from a litle chiste of
Armitage's solde for 2^s.
In expenses at Halifax to take up money, 2^s
Bargayned with Mr Hugh Currer for 60 kersies of 18 & 19
longe to be dd. on Tewseday the 26th of July nexte in Leeds.
I writte by Matthew to my father & Mr Elmhirste; Thomas   14
Guy went to the spaw[38] to his mother.

I writte to my brother Will per poste & receaved allsoe 2   *Page 51b*
letters from him and one from Mr George Gill, and writte   15
to him likewise & gave him notise of 130^l charged on him
the 20th August & 38^l the 14th Auguste. He writeth me of
320^l remitted to him from my brother dew the 22nd of
Auguste 1636. R. Lowther bound Ju[s]tis.[39]
Matthew Foster came this day from York and broughte us   15
300^l in 22^s peeces all good from my brother John borrowed
of him by me for which I thanke him.
Beinge Saturdaye we boughte 122 pounds worth of cloathe   16
& above 26 fyne & 3 ordinaries.
Beinge the Sabbath I receaved the Communion at New   17
Church, about 1,000 communicants; afternowne receaved
of Mr Ralph Strudwicke 44^l which made the somme 38^l
recd. at Halifax the 13th 82^l for which I gave him my bill
payable the 14th of Auguste by Mr George Gill signed like-
wise per Mr Busfield.
Stayed within; silked and ordered about 25 peeces.   18
Teusday boughte 14 peeces fine & 5 ordinaries.   19
Lente Richard Sharpe 20^l to buy woolle with. Writte to   19
Robert Drew by William Lodge. Writte to my brother
William Lowther and George Gill giveinge him notice of
Ralph Strudwicke's 82^l charged on him the 14th of
Auguste.[40]

[38] Probably Knaresborough.
[39] Too cramped to be legible.
[40] Entry in margin: "missed of sending it".

20   Sorted out a trusse of fyne cloth for packeinge. I recd. 35^l,
      the gunpowder & match money of Wm. Thompson charged
      on my mother & 47^l more of Anthony Bindlosse charged
      on her likewise.

      264 0 0 recd. ———————— Disb. ——————— 262 4 7

Page 52a   We receaved of Edward Birckbecke which I charged on my
July 27   sister Mary Lowther 40^l pble. at sighte.

Aug. 4   Taken up at York of Mr Thomas Hawley charged on
          George Gill 120^l pble. 30th instante.

9   Recd. of James Webster 40^l charged on my sister Mary
     Lowther to pay in the country.

9   Recd. then 20^l of Arthur Bindlosse charged likewise of his
     which makes 100^l taken up. This day I set forward to Hull
     to cleare away Robert Drew.

12   Taken of Mr Wm. Sommerfield 100^l charged on George
      Gill the 8th September, out of which cleared all with Mr
      Sommerfield, save this custome 401 doz. & 60 kersies pre-
      termitted & fees of this payd allsoe.

13   Taken up of Mr Elmhirste by me & Mr Busfielde each of us
      $\frac{1}{2}$, 300^l pble. the laste of October, each of us 300^l & Mr
      Elmhirste is to pay us 300^l the laste of November.

14   I spoacke to Sir George Radcliffe who tolde me that the
      Lord Baltinglasse hath now a letter from the K. & that the
      65^l will be payd.

      Mr Bower & Mr Burrus say we shall have the returneinge
      of my lord's rendering.

      0 7 8 cash dr. to Leeds accompte recd. of Thomas Guy that
      I spente in my comeinge from Whitehaven.

Page 52b   Accompte at Leeds is dr. to me for 1 8 6, makeinge the
August 16   48 11 6 which I pd. in to Thomas Guy July 7: 50^l, parte of
              the 100^l lente us by my father.

18   I gave Mr Busfield a bill of exchange for 50^l payable to
      Mr Robert Edwards & Mr No[r?]the by George Gill.

19   I writte to George Gill, gave him notific[ation] of it, and of
      250^l I receaved of Mr Elmhirste for which he was to pay
      him 500^l the laste of October & for the other 250^l we to
      have it the laste November.

21   Gotte to Lowther, spente in travell   0 3 2

Sun. 21   I entred in bonde to my brother John for 800^l principall
           and 42 13 4 use for 8 monethes in all 842 13 4 to be paid
           in the Royal Exch[ange] at London the firste of May of
           which have yet onely recd, 190^l, witness John Teasdayle,
           Matthew Richardson.

Remember to desire a monethes tyme for the returninge it.

I sett forward to Whitehaven   22

264 7 8   263 16 3   Aug. 22

Aug. 22 Whitehaven Considerations
Salte Pannes

In 40 weeckes coles 50 tunns per weecke, is 2,000 tunnes at 2^s per tunne		200	0 0
Wages 50[41] weeckes at 24^s		60	0 0
Yearely mayntenance of pannes		40	0 0
	Total	300	0 0
6,000 bushell of salte at 1^s 6^d per bush.		450	0 0
	Gaynes	150	0 0

The reason why we have not gayned soe much is 732 tunnes of coles is spente, beinge lesse in measure then really they ought, or that farmers will be content with, which is:		73	4 0
parte house rent, house keepeinge & wages is		20	0 0
& theire is gayned by us this year			
againe our sayles are under 18^d per bush.		14	16 0
Our sumpe I am veryly perswaded in wynter hindreth us with dirte & drainyng[42].		22	0 0
	Totall	150	0 0

and if we keepe them in our owne hande we must commpte
lesse of the housekeepinge & under sayles sett downe
above 34^l 16^s 0 admitt   40 0 0

Then will remayne 110^l which weere gayne sufficient for
them soe if they give but 80^l & 22^d per tunne for cole we
lose 46^l 13^s 8^d.

Collyerie

1. I thincke it suffereth much especially in summer for wante of sufficient stewarding, theirefore may imploye Addam & Jackson in the oversighte which they may doe besides theire tanneinge I thincke & may theirfore parte with Hugh, & to them if can agree to lett the tanneinge busines; if it goe not well on to adde up the reste of the malte house, which will be beneficiall to the mill, & that may the Banckemen follow in lew of tanneinge.

---

[41] Originally 40, crossed out and 50 substituted.
[42] Smudged and illegible.

2. And other two fellowes to attend the horsses about coles leadeinge, peere & the like.

3. When mill builte a milner till have triall & then let her.

4. A maide to keepe house.

Page 54 a

5. Soe shall lett of shoppe & Dick Powley, and if lett of saltpannes, Richard & Will Atkinson; and James onely take when needeth him.

6. In the meanetyme to secure the peere & ballaste wharfe.

7. If Thomas Varay come, to follow the mill or remove Alexander's bulwarcke or at the peare as my father pleaseth, or at the sumpe mendeinge.

8. To lett Will, Atkinson the wine licence & shoppe howsoever & to let Henry Boyland the roapemakeinge or Will A[tkinson].

9. To cause olde rootes to be cloven & gotte presently for pinninge the peere.

10. To overpitch all the smalle cobles with greate sledge stones.

11. To cause drifte at Woodagreene to goe forwarde with what haste that may be & consider where may gett coles theire for this wynter.

12. To cause a pitte to be sett on in Davies feilde beyonde dike or in the Lowe Bande.

Page 54b

March 6 1636.   The King's Wyndmilne at Pomphrett[43], anncient without memorie of man.   John Fentiman, milner.

He keepeth hir to $\frac{1}{2}$ parte of corne & valueth hir to 20^l per ann. both halfes. The milne is high 16 foote, broade 20 foote; the walle thicke 33 inches. It is all hewen stone; the lower roome it is high $10\frac{1}{2}$ foote; the higher is $5\frac{1}{2}$ high; a woodden stayre above all. The frayme of woode upon the toppe of the walle is a foote thicke in which is a distance of a foote for 24 rowlers of woode of a foote longe & 9 inches over at the out ende & 8 inches at the in ende over, & iron pinns through them; then hath she a frame of woode goeinge 2 thirds about the inside of the mylne with 12 longe smalle rowles ende way sett in the frame which is 2 foote deepe from toppe[44] to the bottome & this holdeth the toppe from blowinge over.

44 cogges & 8 spindles in the trundle. The stones thick at side 9 inches, at the eye 18 inches, 9^l a payre broughte to the mylne. A seller 8 foote deepe under the mylne in the earth; 2 doorres the one 3 foote wyde the other 6 foote wyde; covered with thatch. The sayle cloathes 15 foote longe & 4 foote broade, each of the 8 sayles.

Page 55a
Aug. 22
Sep.   1
     2

264 7 8 broughte from foll. 52   263 16   3
Wednesday, my mother came to Whitehaven.
My father, Uncle Richard[45] & his wife, Mr David Ramsay & his wife came & all layd at our house.

---

[43] I.e. Pontefract. W. Riding of Yorkshire.   [44] "outside" crossed out.
[45] Possibly Richard Lowther, London barrister.

My father wente home, Uncle Richard, wife & my mother to Kirckby.   6

1 0 0 cash dr. to my father recd. of R. Mich. for his fine of lycence for   10
2 acres for 7 yeares.

1 2 0 cash dr. to ditto recd. of Parson Antrobus for his pension given him a   13
generall discharge for all arreares from my hande & seale witness Mr Radcliffe & Lancelot Ayray.

50 11 2½ cash dr. to accompte curr[ant] at Whitehaven recd. from Richard   13
Powley as in cash 63.

15 0 0 cash dr. to ditto accompte recd. of William Atkinson in pte. of the
wyne accompte D:C: 81.

Came to Egleston, see the paper mylne in buildeinge.   14

To Ripon where laide all nighte.   15

I came by the thre spawes in Knaresborough foreste & druncke at them all   16
but none did woorcke with me & that nighte to Leeds.

I went to Howden;[46] 18th to York; 19th to Leeds.   17

& I recd. 90¹ of my brother John pd. to Thom. Guy as in his.   19

boughte 43 peeces of cloath amountinge to 164 4 0 & after wente to York.   W.L. 20

I stayd at York recd. 200¹ of Mr George Hadley repd. to Tho. Guy.   21

I came to Howden, recd. of Christopher Rayner 50¹.   22

I came to Leeds where founde my brother William who came hither   *Page 55b*
the 20th.   Sept. 23

Saturday.   After Brigge faire we wente to York to my father.   24

Sunday I receaved of my father 100¹ repaid to Thom. Guy and I gave my   25
father my note for 250¹ recd. of him in pte. of 440¹—soe is yet to take
up of him 190¹.

I gave my bille to Mr Rich. Elmhirste for 200¹ payable in Middle Temple   26
Halle the laste of October and he gave us his bill for 200¹ payable to my
father the laste of November.

I visited Sir George Radcliffe with a qrte. of Muscadine.   27

Recd. from Thomas Dickson in pte. of his 22ˢ woolle debte 0 5 4 by   28
Thomas Guy, repaid it to me.

Pd. to my mother by my sister Mary Lowther[47] 36 11 6 for which I pd.
Tho. Guy as much at Leeds.

My father Sir John Lowther dr. to cash pd. at Leeds for him in pte. of the
290¹ he is yet to pay, 30 0 0.

Beinge Friday I, my brother & Mr Busfield agreed with Mr Symmonde   30
Leach to returne him 100¹ a weecke the yeare through & soe on.

Being Saturday   Octo. 1

I made a ballance of our estate at Leeds which is in follio   4
50[48]. Payd for my sadle trimeinge 0 12 6 & departed Leeds

---

[46] Market town 21 miles S.E. by E. of York and about 18 miles west of Hull.

[47] The former Mary Fletcher of Hutton-in-the-Forest, his brother John's wife.

[48] See p. 188 above.

to Pomfreit where I mett my father that nighte.

232 6 2½ recd. and disb.:   331   0   3

Page 56a

Octo. 6   To Wentworth[49] where my father & I dyned with Lord
Deputy & see theire cole woorckes & gave them   0   1   0

7   At Gargrave.

8   At Kentdalle[50] at Mr Sleddall's.

9   Mr Sleddall was made Mayor & my father Recorder.

10   Sunday wente to church in State and afterwards came to
Lowther.

12   Wente to Whitehaven.

13   Kepte courte at Whitehaven which lasted 3 days. In dis-
burssement proprio not particulated   1   7   0

And lente John Varay of Clifton   0   5   0

Recd. of Tho. Hambleton for his fine of Nuncie[51] 1 8 0
house of 6^d rente. Recd. of cousen Senhouse dew upon his
bill at St Andrew Day insste. for his by debtes 37 9 0.

Given to my Goddaughter & servantes at Kirckby; &
Thwaytes about Thwaytes courte, 0 7 0.

Disburssed by me in pte. of the 70^l sente to Dub[lin] to buy

Dec. 5   ... to George Jackson 38 13 0 ... in Rowland's cash [or
cask?] 5 December last yeare [?][52].

November. Recd. of my father's lande rentes at St Bees dew
73^l at Martinmasse laste. My father dr. for the same sente
by my brother W. 73 0 0.

Dec. 3   To colections at church severall tymes   0   2   0

8   To my father in earnest of Lowedemayne lease to Henry
Benne & George Millikin   0   2   0

Recd. my Receavers pay for schoole   3   0   0

Page 56b

1.   Crayne up the caske stones for the inside of the Fanie[53] and the end
of the Peere.

2.   Wynde up stones and shillie[54] at the Peere side to pave & levell from
the new woorcke with breaste up tenne yardes broade with the walle as
yow quarry to the side of it; apply the horsses to the peere.

3.   If cannot be otherwise doe with the milner or woorckeman follow
the milne.

4.   If money can be made at Whitehaven or Dublin or north George to
to buy a barq loade of woolle & some corne if cheape for Whitehaven,

[49] Wentworth Woodhouse, Lord Wentworth's home.

[50] I.e. Kendal.

[51] Cramped and illegible.

[52] This is a badly blotted entry with a very poor quill, much of it conjectural.

[53] Conjectural.

[54] Dialect for shale.

but if George be come home or that it cannot conveniently be done then to thincke of an adventure to France from Whitehaven & Ile of Man.

5.   Each nighte sett each to finish his owne accomptes & see them at it.
6.   Try with the wymble[55] in the drifte.
7.   Distrayne of the Constables for the generall amercements for he may levie them againe.

---

1.   Remember to calle on Francis for Mrs Birckbecke.

---

447 5 2½ recd.	Disb.	444	15	8

Oct. 18
Page 57a

Feb. 22 1636/37   A supposition of our stocke in the order of me
                     C. Lowther at Egleston Abbey the 22nd February

In Canaries olde adventure $\frac{8}{8}$	541	14	9
,, new adventure in $\frac{6}{6}$	76	8	5
In Ireland in all about	304	0	
In Yorkshire woolle debtes about	18	0	
My cousen John Senhouse with us	112	0	
Other debtes about Whitehaven about	150	0	
My thirde parte of the barq George	46	13	
Peere about	310	0	
Whitehaven house, lande & householde stuffe	300	0	
Salte pannes	467	7	
Shoppe goodes aboute	200	0	
Sundrie wares of timber barrells, planckes	80	0	
Cordige about	80	0	
	2,686	3	1

Mr Marris deducted 138 10 0
Leeds drs. for Bradeley 40 0 0 }   250 0 0[56]
Salte & coles & 100^l to answer my father 100 0 0 }

Page 57b
The firste
of Decembr.
1636

Three Cockermouth or nine Winchester bushells of barlie weighed 23 stone (of 14lb to the stone) & 7 pounde wt. over from the mylne it weyed   21st 10^{lb}½
it had seedes   3 3 ½
it had 8 Winchester measures lighte hande measure (as they measure oatemeale) three gallons & a quarte strictley, all which meale weyed 18 st. & 11 pound[57] the Winchester

---

[55] An instrument for boring in soft ground, or for extracting rubbish from a bore hole in mining (O.E.D.).

[56] If totalled comes to £278 10s but so written.

[57] Conjectural, badly blotted.

bushell weyed of thicker meale light measure 2 stone 3 pound.

{ 7[lb] the tare of the sacke deducted already.
{ 12[lb] the tare of the Winchester bushell deducted.

Page 58a   the 20th January 1636/7

10 peckes of bigge[58] of 6 gallons the peck weiged 21 stone
7 poundes from mille. And it made 9 upmett. peckes of
mealle & 4[lb] weighte in all: 18 stone 4 pounds soe was
seedes 3 stone 3 pounde upmett. peckes of meale to leven
& ....[59] 4 upmett peckes of bigge mealle (of 2 stone, 14
pound to the stone, each pecke) and 4 upmett. gallons of
5[lb] neere per gallon.[60] 4 upmett peckes 4 upmett gallons
weighte 9 stone and 4 pounde of which 6.4 sett Leiche and
3.0 to pay Stew:

6 stone and 4 lb. toocke Barme and water. 4 stone 10 lb.
54: and 10 water and barme and 3–3–0 meale to kneade it
up which is 14–0 of payste which at 16 ounces of payste
each loafe made 195 loaves which we got in breade 12 oz.
each loaf 10 st. 6 lb. 4: Totall breade weight 3–7–12 Baked
in a 10th more breade.

Page 58b   26 pounde of Meale tempsed in a hayre tempse for pies
made 22 lb. of flower reste 6 lb. course.

Page 59a

Feb. 18   447 5 2½ (broughte from foll. 56)   444 15 8
          1 0 0 cash dr. to cash in the order of Richard Powl[ey].

20   Being Munday I wente to Lowther towards Leeds.

22   At Egleston drew a supposition of an inventory of our
          Whitehaven estate.[61]
          For a payre of stockings   0 2 0
          Given the paper milne boyes   0 0 4

Mar. 1.   A Ballance of our Leed's Estate the 22 February 1636/7

To cash remayninge then   394 0 6
Clothe   15 1 6
Voyage to Hamb[urg] 2nd November   2,352 9 10
more thither the 21 February   1,622 12 10
Voyage to Rotterd[am] till 21st February   1,340 3 1
Henry Crispe   47 0 6

[58] Bigg, a poorer but hardier variety of barley.
[59] Left incomplete.
[60] The rest of *Pages 58a* and *58b* appear to be rough costings of breadmaking, written
with a bad quill, much smudged, and one quarter crossed out.
[61] See page 195 above.

Richard Sharpe	5	0	0
Tho. Roame	4	6	8
Henry Gibbins	5	12	8
The accompte at Whitehaven	41	3	5
Thomas Simpson	15	15	0
Richard Atkinson	34	17	6
James Procter	39	1	0
Galle's accompte	26	6	0
Wares	24	11	0
Horsses	12	18	4
Robert Towenson	1	5	0
Rober[t] Bradeley	123	9	1
To accompte of debtes	162	16	10
	6,268	10	9

Ballance of the accompte at Leeds[62]

Page 59b

By stocke the 12th May 1636	3,172	17	3
by John Pollard	29	0	0
by George Gill at London	569	14	9
by my brother William Lowther	40	0	0
by my father oweinge to him	150	0	0
by my brother John Lowther	543	2	7
by my mother	20	0	0
by Mr Summerfielde collector[63]	9	7	0
by John Butterfeilde	51	0	0
by Heugh Currer	15	0	0
by Matthew Foster	57	18	4
by magasin for Westm'land	36	0	0
by James Taylor of Rochdale	44	18	0
by Thomas Blande	200	0	0
by profitte & losse	449	11	2
by Abraham Burnell	22	10	0
by Thomas Gibson, kersieman	20	0	0
by Abraham Smith, kersieman	9	2	6
by Matthew Hollinges, kersieman	15	0	0
by Richard Kershaw, kersieman	15	2	0
by James Gibson, kersieman	6	17	0
by Sir Richard Graham	520	0	0
by Kitchman Matthewsman	31	4	0
by Richard Greene for reedes[64]	27	8	6

[62] This account faces the account preceding in the original.
[63] At Hull.
[64] I.e. reds.

by William Fletcher for whites	14	14	0
by Thomas Cordley, kersieman	20	0	0
by Joseph Bower, kersieman	20	0	0
by Richard Dentie, kersieman	10	0	0
by Widdow Hyrd, kersiewoman	39	9	2
by Samuel Hollis, bayzeman	32	0	0
by Nicholas Burch, bayzeman	17	17	6
by Ellis Haslem, bayzeman	10	12	0
by John Haslam, bayzeman	10	13	0
by John Hamer, bayzeman	36	15	0
	6,268	10	9

448 5 2½ rcvd & disburssed: 444 18 0

Page 60a
March 1

I wente to York stayed all nighte & gave my father the ballance on the other side. He assented that wee take a partener at London as wee like beste.

2 I receaved 48ˢ sente by John Woodhead from Halifax from Abraham & John Briggs for use money in pte. of Bradeley's debts dd. over to Tho. Guy.

2 I gave Oxeley order for a bill against Sir Richard Fletcher[65] & directions for a letter against Tho. Wood.

3 I phissicked; it coste me two shillings in aloes, rosada 2 drams 1ˢ & 3 drams rhubarbe 1ˢ.

3 This day hath our deputy Mr Bennett of Hamburg to calle me over for an assistance in Saxon marte which is midsommer.

Directions for my brother William goinge to London on Munday nexte.

1. To knowe of Mr Batty, Mr Manne, etc, whether they will proceed to sew out a commission of bancrupte against Hall; if they refuse then yow to sew out one for us & make acquainte Mr Lonegan if he will joyne; he I beleeve can beste informe yow how the case standeth with him though he have made conveyance of his lande to the use of his wife etc; if it was not before marriage it will doe him noe good to avoide us as I beleeve & am tolde.

2. Goe to the Rowls which is over against the Six Clarckes Office in Chancerie Lane & theire search for the pattent made to the Abbot of Sᵗ Marie's by York by King Henry the Eighte of privilige and gett it exemplified under seale if 5ˡ or 20 nobles will gett it at the entreaty of Sir John Lowther for the Manner of St Bees parcell of that monastery.

Page 60b
He did it

3. Pay in the rente of my wyne lycence beinge 20ˢ for one yeare ended at Christmasse laste and gett acquittance.

He did not.... Yow may entertayne Mr George Clearcke or some other honeste, able &

[65] Of Hutton-in-the-Forest, father-in-law to Christopher's brother, John.

substantiall reputifull man to partener, to begin of midsommer nexte, if dislike of neither party be founde within one moneth before then upon such tearmes as may be beste for us both, in your judgement, and I shall make goode the same for what is in my power & for cash what allowance myne, yours or anssering shall be while beyond sea or heere, I thincke if he would conclude 2 percentum for factorie beyonde sea both at Hamburg and Rotterdam, towards the charges of either me or an aprentice alwayes bringeinge up theire it weere well, and $1\frac{1}{2}$ per centum for all shippeinges hence & alle thinges to be managed by us principalles.

My brother and Mr Busfield at Hatfield[66] at Mr Postinglea.				May 6
By Thone, Turnebrig[67] & Selby to York.				7
Girdle mendeinge 2^d, 2 debtors books 1^s	0	1	2	8
With Mr Metcalfe per wager loste	0	0	6	12
At Pomphreistoe [Pontefract] mylne to millners	0	0	4	
the 6th presente.				

At Brigge fayre in the morneinge to Holme 18 myle of[f]   14
to lett a lease to Abraham Swallowe & John Hadfield for
house & lande theire; laid at Milnebridge[68].

At Halifax where see Mr Busfield buy some kersies, and I   15
lefte orders with John Wilkinson at Thomas Binns touchinge my woolle and a letter to Liverpoole.

---

448 5 $2\frac{1}{2}$ recd. & disburssed:	445	0	0

Page 61a

Spente at the oylemylne & with my sister etc	0	0	10	March 18
0 12 0 recd. of Matthew Foster for Richard [?] Dixson of				18
Calfe Layne in pte of his debte.				
I went to Midlam[69], mett my brother John	0	1	[?]	22
We wente to Wenseladayle to Hardraw[70] where stayed all				23
nighte, coste me my horsse onely	0	1	0	
Gotte to Hackthorpe[71] stayed theire all nighte.				24
Wente rounde about all groundes at Hackthorpe and Lowther.				25
I went to Meaburne[72]; see Mr Lancaster etc, all well.				26
Beinge Munday wente to Whitehaven & writte to my father				27
the day before, and that day from thence.				
I gave James Willan walleinge at Plumlandes	0	0	3	˙29
Beinge Good Friday my mother & I wente to St Bees,				Aprill 7

---

[66] A town some 20 miles south of Selby.
[67] Thorne is 3 miles north of Hatfield and Turnbridge is a few miles north of Thorne.
[68] Township near Huddersfield.
[69] Middleham, Wensleydale.
[70] Chapelry near Ayesgarth $18\frac{1}{2}$ miles W. by N. of Middleham.
[71] Hackthorpe Hall, the home of his brother John.
[72] Maudes Meaburn, another Lowther manor west of Hackthorpe.

receaved the Communion, spente at Henry Ayray's with
Mr Polwheele   0 0 6

11   Beinge Easter Tewsday the Bpp. of Carlisle, the High
Sheriffe, Barronet Curwen[73] & the moste of the divines
theire abouts weere at the Schoole of St Bees where my
nephew Richard Kirckby[74] beinge not 12 yeares olde made
an oration to the Bpp. & the reste to content [?]. We [?]
concluded that Sandwath shall have such interest in the
sheepgayte[75] for three hundred sheepe as the schoole hath
payeinge 4^s yearley and 15^l besydes.

13   We keeped our courte. I gave John Musgrave for his paynes
11^s & jurie 2^s 6^d, 0 13 6.

14   I sente my god-daughter Agnes Kirckby by John Musgrave
then   0 2 0

15   I received for 6 draughte peeces of Matthew Gragge of the
Abbay of St Bees   0 16 0
I lefte with Will Atkinson all the schoole papers and 7^l$\frac{1}{2}$ of
money.

17   1 0 0 I recd. of Powley.[76]
1 7 0 I receaved of the schoole money and put it in my
owne pursse beinge toward my wages of 20^s per annum.

18   20^l recd. of Powley who had the cash in William Atkinson's
absence.

19   I came to Lowther.

20   I wente on with my brother John Lowther through Cotter-
dale and Wenseladayle; at Hardraw it coste me about 0 1 9

21   I came to Boulton Bridgende, coste me   0 2 0

22   I came to Leeds; pd. my brother the   20 0 0

25   I wente to York to my father to whom we gave the balance
of his accompte.

26   It coste me 5$\frac{1}{2}$ ounces of paracellsus stipticte playster 6^d per
ounce & 8 ounces of diacalretheos salve 2^d an ounce; in
all, & 12^d given him,   0 5 0

May 1   The firste of May beinge Munday paccked cloth.

4   It being St Christopher's Day I was compleate accordeinge
to the day of my christeninge 26 yeares olde.

6   I sett from Leeds towards Hull by York & Beverley where
it coste me firste to servantes at Leeds, Thomas Reame &
Henry Gibbens   0 2 6

---

[73] I.e. Sir Patricius Curwen of Workington, created Baronet 1626.
[74] The later Col. Richard Kirkby (1625–1685) son of Roger Kirkby and Christopher's
sister, Agnes.
[75] Pasturage, or the right of pasturage, for sheep.
[76] His servant Richard Powley.

At York as I came & Wighton[77]	0	0	10
for $\frac{1}{8}$ of a yrde of plush at York	0	2	6
and at Beverley	0	3	6

470 0 2$\frac{1}{2}$ recd. & disbursed:	466	19	0	*Page 62a*

24 Aprill Leeds 1637

My father Sir John Lowther is dr.:

To cash for spices & 4 couple of lynges & carrige home	4	7	6
For plush cloth and sattin	10	15	9
For carriage downe and a boxe	0	5	8
For the coppy of the Lyberties at St Marie's at York	3	7	0
Totall	18	15	11
Given yow[78] my note to Mr Gill	1,400	0	0
Totall	1,418	15	11

472 0 2$\frac{1}{2}$ recd. (broughte over) & d.	466	19	0	1637 May 7
Disburssed for a Gerrard's Herball in folio	2	6	3	
In petti charges beinge disburssed but forgotte to be particularly sett downe at severall tymes	2	2	2[?]	
An error in Follio 41	0	12	4[?]	

471 0 2$\frac{1}{2}$ recd. from 29 Auguste beinge in anno 1635 till 10th [May] 1637 and disburssed	471	0	2	May 10
My father per contra cr.[79]				*Page 62b*
By cash recd. of my brother C. Lo. from Lowther[80]	100	0	0	1636 Mar 2
By my father at York by him	30	0	0	9
By him more at York	50	0	0	15
By Arthur Bindlosse to be pd. at Lowther	30	0	0	
By my father at York to Mat. Foster	50	0	0	1637 Ap. 3
By my father recd. by me Willm. Lowther	100	0	0	
For woolle solde	21	14	0	
By my brother C. Lowther broughte from Lowther	20	0	0	
	401	14	0	
By 150^l oweinge at our laste accompte	150	0	0	
	551	14	0	

[77] I.e. Market Weighton, East Riding.

[78] Probably means Christopher, as this seems to be a copy of an account drawn by William Lowther, see below *Page 62b*.

[79] This account should be read in conjunction with the account on *Page 62a* above.

[80] This appears to be an account copied from Will Lowther.

Soe remayneth dew to us yet	167	1	11

	718	15	11
By my brother Jo.·Lowther recd.	600	0	0
By him yet dew to us	100	0	0
	1,418	15	11

Page 63a

Our adventure, this shipinge[81] to be about the some of	1,500	0	0[82]

In stock yet remaninge about	1,000	0	0
My brother W. Low[ther] stocke & to make up	1,000	0	0
Sir Richard Graham	500	0	0
Mr Crispe	500	0	0
	3,000	0	0

May

To send over with my brother C. L.	1,500
soe remaines more	1,500
of which suppose in debts	800
and for the next voyadge	700

August

to be charged by exch[ange]	300
returned as before	700
	1,000

Septembr.

for the next shippinge of May shippinge	1,200
to be charged	300
	1,500

Beverley's freedom in the church:
> All free mack I thee
> As harte can thinck or eigh can see

[81] I.e. shipment.
[82] All these jotted entries are in a handwriting and spelling unlike Sir Christopher's.

Page 63b

For the orderinge of our businesse there soe.[83] Betwixt 25 March and 29 7ber we have but 2 markett dayes a weeke, Wedensday and Fryday, upon which dayes we are to waite dewly either in our packhowse or at our packhowse doore and after yow have the language yow must alwayes be invitinge your marchts. to come to yow, for they are somewhat prowde and doe exspecte it, and as yow will find, some have good judgement, some little or none, soe yow must goe seeke out there disposition to apply with them, which I found the onely way to draw them to my owne ends.

Be not weary[84] of good cloth at noe tyme, nor be not discouraged[85] if yow sell not in a weeke or 14 dayes for good cloth will vent and to good men. And when yow find anie course be sure to keepe it neate and hansome, and refuse noe reasonable price of a good man.

Trust not unt[o] anie clot[h] but your remainders and trust not them but to a sure man; and where yow must stay your tyme of cmo.[86] sell them 6^l in the hundred dearer then yow will sell upon rebate.

Remembrances for Hamburg[87]

Page 64a

1. To sende patterns of the best colours.

   Pressed carsies which may here be boughte at 20^d, 22^d & 2^s per yarde which I thinck will yeelde theire 21 st., 22 st. & 24 stiver[88] per ell.
2. Sende allsoe patterns of bayzes.
3. To advize beforehande to my brother of what moneys I have remitted when I can writte more and what adventure to provide.
4. To advize whose makeinge proveth faulty, whose approved, who misse of colours & which beste by the number on the seale.
5. To marcke how John Flatherie's carsies are requested & to sende woorde.

Page 64b

Leeds the 15th of May 1637

Lovinge Brother,[89]

Although I am not worthy to advice yow, beinge more fitte to receive advice from yow, yet will I not forbeare therefore to impart what I know, that when yow come there, they may be more facile unto yow, which I desire were worthy of your desert, not doubtinge but shortly to find the benefitte that our witts wull bringe us, by God's blesseinge, which in severall wayes

---

[83] This description of trading at Hamburg (almost certainly) is in an unfamiliar handwriting which appears to be Will Lowther's, and occurs again on *Pages 63a, 64b–66a*. It may be that it should follow on after the top paragraph on *Page 66a* (i.e. at p. 205 below).

[84] Probably "wary" meaning "doubtful" or "pessimistic".

[85] [*Sic*] "discouraged"?

[86] Looks like abbreviation for "commission", although from context appears to mean "receipt of payment".

[87] This is Christopher's handwriting.

[88] Stiver—a German coin, 48 to the Rixdoller.

[89] Written by Will Lowther to Christopher who is about sail for Hamburg.

[i.e. separately] could never have advantaged us halfe soe much which union I pray God to continew unto the end, without breach or anie other appropriatinge thoughte but for each others good; each strivinge for others good more then his owne which I hope to live to see to both our comforts, credit & content, and satisfaction to all our frends.

First, for monies we take our bills for Rix dollers, 48 stivers or schilling, which Rix doller is 8 shillinges Flemish, and 3 marke lubes make a Rix doller and 16 stivers or schillings make a mark; one stiver 2^d. All our receits are most part writt in bancke which account is kept in marks and when we receive by cash most in Rix dollers, $\frac{1}{2}$ dollers and $\frac{1}{4}$ dollers, otherwayes called orts [90] tallers

48 stivers:	1 rix doller
46 stivers:	albertus dollers, peeces of eight, otherwise called ryalls, and beare dollers and other dollers as yow will be showne.
40 stivers:	called 60 creutzers, havinge commonly 60 writt on them.
32 stivers:	2 mark peece or 2 mark stuck
24 stivers:	$\frac{1}{2}$ a doller
23 stivers:	$\frac{1}{2}$ a ryall or albertus
20 stivers:	$\frac{1}{2}$ a creutzer
16 stivers:	a marke
12 stivers:	an orts or $\frac{1}{4}$ doller
10 stivers:	a copstuck which is an English shillinge
6 stivers:	an $\frac{1}{8}$ of a doller

All these coynes are in pure silver. Now every towne makes there severall coynes of small monie which are not silver.

2 stivers:	a doble shillinge
4 stivers:	
1 stiver:	2^d
1 soeflinge is $\frac{1}{2}$ a stiver or 1^d	

Page 65b For order of the bancke we have a follio in the booke, soe we come alwayes before 8 oclocke in the morninge to bancke and tell him our follio, which he looks [at] and if there be aniething writt he tells us such a some by such a man, and when we write of anie some or pay anie some in bancke, you have printed bancke settles which[91] [are?] blanck wherein yow write upon whom yow would have it writt, what somme, of what follio, the day of a month & your name, but after tenne [o'clock] yow can not give anie in.

For our show days they are betwixt 25th March and 29 7ber upon Wednesday and Fryday and in winter betwixt those dayes upon Monday,

[90] An oort was a common Scandinavian and North German coin.
[91] "Which" may be crossed out. "Settles" may mean cheques, in the sense of that which settles an account.

Wednesday and Fryday and noe goods to be showed to anie merchant but upon those dayes.

For courts, if an assistant come after the tyme appointed that the court beginne he pays 31^s flemishe.

For my advice herein my father's direction I desire may be observed; the first yeare to say little and onely to see the passage of business and to observe the nature and the disposition of all men.

For men I shall note unto yow who are good and who not, but Mr Crispe will give yow better direction herein then I kan, and tell yow whose bill will sell, and whose not, and whose debts we must ride out.

Wee are but to pay fraighte to Richard Robinson for our cloth in the *Mary Ann* for 340 *doz.*, 40 kersies & 45 bazes.[92]

		doz.	k[ersies]	b[azes?]	[?]	
	Jo. Metcalfe	20	0	0	0	*Page 66b*
5	Lee Thompson	150	0	0	0	
7	Hen. Thompson	298	20	0	114	
29	Rob. Lowther	514	120	29		
6	John Ramsden	160	0	0	0	
19	Will Busfield	413	90	0	0	
2	John Metcalfe	119	0	15	0	
19	Will Lowther	345	40	45	0	
7	Will Scotte	126	14	0	0	
		2,225[93]	284	89	114	
	Will Scotte	88	0	10		
	Will Lodge	341	40	38		
	Mr Ramsden	60	0	0		
	William Dobson	23				
	George Mitley	28				
	Mr Crew	30				
	Mr Dawson	70				
	Rich. Hillary	26				
		666	40	48		

4 tunne French wyne

RR ⎰ 1,000 doz
    ⎱   500 kersies

[92] In Christopher's handwriting. The rough manifest which is on the following page is presumably the cargo of the *Mary Ann*.

[93] Next to the total of 2,225 is a cramped entry (entr. Lapst.) with the figures 1,000 d. 500 k.

Page 67a[94]	Receaved of my brother William Lowther at my beinge at Hull the 10th			
May 10	May 1637, 5 0 0 in golde beinge to goe for Hamburg.			
11	In peti charges proprio, for 2 payre of bootes	0	16	8
11	For two payre of Spanish lether shewes	0	6	8
11	For mendeinge my olde coate	0	0	6
11	To shewmakers man	0	0	2
12	To the maister, Rich. Robinson, to put provision aboarde as he pleased	1	0	0
	My expences at Mr Mann's, five dayes & my washeinge & extraordinaries	0	11	0
12	Given in the house theire	0	1	8
	Given one of the clamorous porters	0	0	6
	My spurres rowellinge	0	0	4
	3 0 0 cash dr. to my brother William recd. of Mr William Sommerfielde charged on my brother			
	Given in foyes[95] then to Mr Sommerfielde	0	10	1
	and to Gilpin, Mosse & Jimi soe 5ˢ a peece ditto	0	15	0
13	We wente ashore at Grimsby where laid all the nighte our maister & his brother, the other maister, etc. coste	0	5	0
	Spente at two severall tymes with the maisters	0	3	0
	Spente with Mr Sommerfielde, Mr Crew, our maister, etc, other the officers of the Custome House at Southendes when I wente aboarde	0	3	0
	To the poore the 12th present when I wente aboarde	0	0	6
	For mendeinge my gloves & to a pore scholer	0	0	3
	Given in the church at Hull to the poore & when I wente to see the bells chyme with John Robinson	0	0	10
	For a prayer booke & psame boocke	0	2	0
	Prapis Medicinas & Christian Pollicies	0	5	0
15	Beinge Munday our shippe returned to Hull the wynd beinge easterly			
22	The nexte Munday we sett sayle againe but firste it coste me in expences on Mr Sommerfielde, on Maisters, Wm. Middleton & others and at dinners in wyne & beere	0	10	0

May 7 1637	Remembrances to doe before [going] over sea to Hamburg.
	1. To write to Bishoppe of Carlisle & the other gov[ernors?[96]] especially
done	aboute the steward, etc, May 10.
	2. To write to William Atkinson & to sende a coppy of the debts as they
done	stoode out at my comeinge, till I have gotten the boockes done.

[94] *Page 67a* is the last page in the sequence. There only remains some rough notes scribbled inside the notebook's back cover.
[95] [*Sic*] fees.
[96] Presumably of St Bees School.

3. To write a letter to Frances Lancaster[97].
4. To write to George Jackson.   done
5. To write to my brother Kirckby & sister.
6. To write to my mother for olde & new cash boocke [and] olde shoppe   done
boocke.
7. To write to my father.   done
8. To write to Mr Challmley for custome money.   done

---

[97] His betrothed.

SECTION FIVE

NOTEBOOK D 1643

(Set of memoranda on his estate by Sir Christopher Lowther dated 1642–1643, written in a small notebook which, judging by the handwriting of its contents, was once the property of his father, Sir John Lowther of Lowther.)

Considerations 1642/3

If it please God soe to allowe of them, to whose Blessed Will I doe alwayes refer my will.   Chr. Lowther.

When it shall please God that I shall live at Sockbridge[98] which I intende, if God permitte, at Annuntiation 1645, in which intrim I meane to builde the outside of the house that I meane to make at Whitehaven and set theire my busines in order.

It will be necessarie for me to keppe at leaste theise constant householde

to be a mason[99]

servantes theire, viz: a clerke 5^l wages per ann.; a steward 5^l; a stablegroome 4^l;
a joyner   a smith & a wrighte   a webster & cobler   a seemster
a butler 5^l; 2 plowemen 6^l both; 2 drivers or carters 3^l; a wayteinge mayde 40^s;
a knitter   a spinner
a cooke mayde 40^s; and kitchinge wench 1^l; a milke mayde 20^s; a nursse 40^s;
a shepherd 2^l; 4 lyveries once in two yeares, halfe charge per an. 4^l.

Totall of theise 14 servantes wages	44	0	0
the dyet of theise cannot be lesse then	100	0	0
the dyet of myselfe, wyfe & childe	30	0	0
the apparrell of us	26	0	0
	200	0	0
Extraordinaries for strangers, christeninges, etc, diet, wynes, spices	50	0	0
Grasseinge of sixe sadlehorsses & 4 carte horsses	10	0	0
Wynterage at 20 trayle carte full of a hay to a horsse, in toto 200 carte fulls at 2^s per cartfull	20	0	0
Otes at $\frac{1}{2}$ a bushell per horsse one with another 30 weekes at 3^s 4^d per bushell: five bushells per weeke is	25	0	0
Strangers' horsses suppose per annum	10	0	0

---

[98] The Westmorland manor that came to him by his marriage to Frances Lancaster.
[99] Presumably the functions written in over the top indicate double functions.

Coste of 2 draughte of oxen to furnish fuell: grasseinge 10 13 4; strawe 16 0 0; hay 100 carte full, trayle cartes, at 2^s per peece, 10 0 0	36	13	4
Taxes & costes of suites at leaste	23	6	8
Travelling charges	25	0	0

Coste of 2 draughte of oxen to furnish fuell: grasseinge
  10 13 4; strawe 16 0 0; hay 100 carte full, trayle cartes,
  at 2^s per peece, 10 0 0   36 13 4
Taxes & costes of suites at leaste   23 6 8
Travelling charges   25 0 0

Totall   400 0 0

Broughte over my constant annual charge at the leaste *Page 2*
  besides horsses buyeinge; houses amending, repayres of
  householde stuffe   400 0 0
& husbandrie tooles & presents to maynetayne frendshipp,
  which maybe perhapps   100 0 0
& then buildeinge and extraord. husbandrie   100 0 0

Totall   600 0 0

The reste I may save for the children.
And to dow this I must forecaste what stocke to keepe &
what lande will serve the same & what moneys to have out
of my other rentes.
For stocke:

to keepe	16	milke cowes and a bulle	65	0	0
	16	oxen for draughte	80	0	0
at a beast	6	cowes for killeinge	24	0	0
each moneth	6	oxen for killeinge	36	0	0
	12	yeareinges of the 15 cowes	14	0	0
	12	2 yeareinges	30	0	0
	12	3 yeare oldes	36	0	0
Totall	80	head of beastes	285	0	0

Sheepe at Netherdayle in Summer 400					100	0	0
Horsses:	3	breadeinge meares	30 0 0				
	3	foles, yeareinges	20 0 0				
	2	2 yeares olde	20 0 0				
	2	3 yeares olde	30 0 0				
	6	rydeinge horsses	80 0 0				
	4	woorke horsses	20 0 0	200	0	0	

Totall quicke goodes   585 0 0

Seede corne:	wheate	10	bushells	5 0 0			
	pease	10	bushells	3 0 0			
	bigge	20	bushells	6 0 0			
	otes	80	bushells	16 0 0	30	0	0

Salve, tarre, butter & tallow for 400 sheepe at 3^d per sheepe
& 1^d per peece greassinge   6   13   4

                    _____

                    Totall stocke to proffitt   621   13   4
More deade stocke: playte 100^l; apparrell 100^l; bookes
and armes 100^l; householde stuffe 200^l and husbandrie
theere 100^l.   600   0   0

                    _____

                                                      1,221 13   4

Page 3   And to beare the aforesaid stocke for to maynetayne the said porte theire muste be as much grounde rateinge (the acre of 7 yardes to the pearch: 4: in breadth & 40: in length) of arable & pasture at 10^s per acre & meadowe of the beste sorte at 20^s per acre, midle sorte 13^s 4^d per acre & ordinarie lye meadow at an angell; yet to stinte the grounde at[1] cowes & fatte beastes at 16^s a gaite & oxen & younge beastes, yeareinges, at 6^s 8^d (2 yeare oldes at 10^s & 3 yeare oldes and upwards at 13^s 4^d) per beaste & 5 fatte sheepe to a beaste gaite, and horsses: foles yearinges at 6^s 8^d per gaite & 2 yeares olde 13^s 4^d & 3 yeares & above 20^s.

				summer		winter[2]	
l.	*s.*			*l.*	*s.*	*l.*	*s.*
		28	milks cowes, bull & fatte beastes must have meadowe grounde for summer grasseinge[3] & winter hay worth at 18^d per trayle carte				
10	0		fulls getting paid at 10 carte full[s] a peece for 5 milke cowes & 5;	22	8		
			for 10 strippe milked cowes & 40 for 2 of the fatte oxen, besides strawe: 9 0 0.				

				l.	*s.*	
6	0	16	oxen for draughte must have besides straw	10	13	4^d
6	0	12	yeareinges must have noe strawe	4	0	
4	0	12	2 yeare oldes must have besides straw[3 0 0]	6	0	
4	0	13	3 yeare oldes outlyers a litle hay[3 0 0]	8	0	
5	0	10	out[l]yer horsses & foles[6 0 0]	7	6	

[1] After "at" there was written but crossed out: "10^s a horsse gait". Probably "at" should have been crossed out also. N.B. a "gait" or gate is a right to a run or pasturage for an animal in a common field or grazing ground.

[2] This portion of page three is written in a very cramped hand and the columns of figures— if there were any figures—under "winter" on the extreme right are all blotted out, perhaps deliberately.

[3] A "grassing" was either a place for cutting turves or grazing cattle, or the right to pasture cattle in a particular place.

12	0	10 horsses in the stables beside strawe	10	0		

3	0	60 sheepe for slaughter summer & winter ½	3⁴	0	2	0
17	0	400 winterage 100 hogges in the house	–	–	?	0

		50 acre for corne: 40 in corne & 10 fallow	25	0	0	–
3	0	Orchard and gardeinges & for swyne & poul-				
		trie, hay forstrangers	3	12	0	–

70	0	Totall grasseing 100 0 0 Totall:	100	0	?	–

Totall meadowe   70 0 0 besides getteing.
Grasseinge then at 10ˢ per acre 200 acres or
the grasseinge to be worth more & lesse acres,
meadow halfe at 20ˢ per acre & halfe at 10ˢ,
100: totall 300 acres & 50 more.

The foresaid stocke of 600ˡ and odde, and tenne pounde   *Page 4*
   in lyme for the grounde   10 0 0 p.a.
& grasseinge & hay grounde   170 0 0 p.a.
which with the use of the stocke is allmost   50 0 0 p.a.
besides 600ˡ deade stocke as in pagina 2

   which is in all per annum   230 0 0

saveth but towards housekeepeinge, viz:
at 3 yeares ende & soe on constantly butter, cheese &
   milk suppose   20 0 0
12 fatte beastes, a beaste a moneth   60 0 0
horsses but to make good the stocke and for rideinge &
   woorke   0 0 0
sheepe to breade a 100 lambs to make good 20 for
   death; 20 at 2ˢ per peece for drapes in harnesse & 60
   at a noble per peece for fatteing to slaughter   22 0 0
Woolle to sell about 50 stone   18 0 0
Corne: the seede stocke saved sett aparte:

Wheat 4 for one	40 bush. at 10ˢ	per bush.	20	0	0
Pease & beanes	40 bush. at 6ˢ	per bush.	12	0	0
Bigge or barly	100	at 6ˢ 8ᵈ per bush.	30	0	0
Otes 3 for one	240	at 4ˢ per bush.	48	0	0

Which corne will allowe for malte viz:
60 bushells of otes & 40 of bigge in toto 100 malte
bushells.

⁴ May be £13.

For servantes breade: bigge 60 bush.; pease 40 bush.;
for horsses otes 100 bushells and for meale and grotes
80 bush.; 20 bushell of wheate for breade, paysterie,
etc. 20 bushells to buy fish & foule weekely.
The 12 fatte beaste hydes 12^l to buy spicerie, hoppes,
etc. The 400 sheep's woolle 18^l to pay husbandrie, day
hyrelinges, etc.

Toward housekeepeing totall	230	0	0

If extraordinarily well husbanded & noe sudden losses
inflickted upon us for our sinns which wee deserve
10,000 tymes the[n] Job.

But admitte God soe blesse us as this may proceede then to this theire is yet awanteinge:	230	0	0
for wyne, sacke & extraordinaries to be supplyed in money 50^1 servantes wages constant 44 casuall wages of necessary repayres 6	100	0	0
For our owne apparells 40 Taxes and coste of suite 30	70	0	0
Unavoydable constant charge if we shall live anythinge like our selves accordinge to our place & degree & yet must be very frugall	400	0	0
But to make our houses likewise fitte for us & presents to mayntayne frendishippe or offten invitations in a hospitable way to that purposse will coste us more	200	0	0
Soe then as before the charge is still	600	0	0

SECTION SIX

MISCELLANEOUS PAPERS 1637–1644

A selection from a bundle of miscellaneous bonds, assignments, accounts, letters and agreements of Christopher Lowther which date from 1633. The first selected is dated 1637.[5]

[Document 1]

Aprill 18th 1637

Memorandum: that it is covenanted and agreed betweene Christopher Lowther, gentleman, and Henry Boylyne, ropemaker, that the said Henry Boylyne shall make into rope and cordage all the hempe and yarne which he the said Henry now haith or that shall come out of the north of Ireland unto the said Henry, which shall be sent unto him by the said Mr Chr[istopher] Lowther or his assignes, betwene this and Lammas next, and to deliver the said ropes and cordage to the said Chr. Lowther or his assynes at the tyme aforesaid; and not to sell anie ropes or cordage till the said Mr Chr. Lowther have sould the said ropes, unlesse it be of those sorts of ropes which Mr Lowther haith now lefte of unsould, and the said Mr Christopher Lowther doth promise to the said Henry to furnish him with one hundereth poundes sterling for a stock to trade in, betwene or about Martinmasse next either in reddie money or hempe worth money or at the rate as the said Henry can buy the like hempe and the said Henry Boylyne[6] doth covenant & provision to the said Mr Chr. Lowther to pay unto him or cause to be paid unto him or his assignes the some of fyvetene pounds per annum for soe long tyme as the said Henry shall keepe the said stock in his hands, viz: seaven pounds tenn shillings ster. at each half yeare after the receipte thereof, viz: at Whitsontyde and Martinmasse, and the said Chr. Lowther shall imploye noe other man in makeinge of ropes, to the prejudice of the said Henry Boylyne; in witnesse whereof we have heareunto sett our hands and seyles the day and year above written.[7]

[Document 2]

It is agreed betwixte Sir John Lowther, knight, in the behalfe of

---

[5] Documents numbered 1–3 are from an original bundle of leases and agreements 1620–1754, D/Lons/W. Misc. Estate papers, 4, D/Lons/W. Whitehaven 1. 5, 8–12, 17, D/Lons/W. Sir Christopher Lowther Misc. Bonds etc. 6, D/Lons/W. Lancaster family, Box 1. 7, D/Lons/W. Lancaster family, Box 2. 13–16, D/Lons/W. Correspondence Bundle 20. 18, D/Lons/L. Wills and Settlements, 4.

[6] Here spelt Boyleine, and later Boyline, but the initial spelling has been retained throughout.

[7] Signed by Christopher Lowther and witnessed by Richard Wibergh and Richard Powley.

Christopher Lowther, his sonne of the one party and David Bibby and Thomas Younghusband, salters, of Whitehaven, of thother party, as followeth:

First, the said Sir John Lowther doth undertake that the said salters shall have delivered at the salt pans where they now worke at Whitehaven for places of store for coles now or heretofore used for lyeinge of cole to that use, soe manie coles as they shall burne and spend in makeing of salte theire for one whole yeare after the date thereof, whereof tow tunnes to be of bad coles now gotten at Davis feild while they last and foure tune of coles theire to be gotten of new; and after the old are spent six tune there and tow tune and six barrells to be of Greene Bancke or Wooddaiegreene[8] cole grounes and soe after that proportion for all they spend, untill they have coles of the low band of Davis field or other coles in Flat feild[9] and then only to be served of those coles, or of the coles onely in the Flat feild; whereof they shall have stored reddy one hundreth tune beforehand which they are to take measured and delivered from the banckeman by the usuall barrell, or if there be at any tyme wante of coles leed, to have money to pay the leaders as coles are[10] lead to shipps theire from these places, and coles ready to be leed.

And further that they shall have the use of the salt panns, soumpes and all worke towels to them now belonging to make salt and 24[l] in money yearely allowed to pay for iron and the smith wages to repaire and mentaine the sd. pans to be pd. as the worke is wrought and what is spared thereof to remaine to the salters or undertakers. In consideracion whereof they the sd. David Bibby and Thomas Younghusband doe covenant and promise to and with the sd. Christopher Lowther, his exer[cutors] and assignes to deliver unto him or them or theire servant or servants to be appointed by the sd. Sir Jo[hn], Dame Elinor, his wife, or Christopher there sonne, for every such eight tune and sixe barrells or for every 7 tune and foure barrells of the better coles of the lowband or Flatt coles to twentyseaven measures of salt striked[11] at the panne as the salte is made and as now they are there measured of striked, and to mentaine and keepe the same panns, woorke towels, and all thereto belonging in soe good sorte as they are at there entree, provided allways that upon payment of twenty shillings by either party to tother within 20ty days this bargaine and covenant to be void; and likewise if the said salters doe neclegte there worke and follow not there laboure in makeing of salt or mending there pans continually.

In witness whereof the partys above said to these presents interchange-

8 Greenbanck and Woodagreen were later important Lowther collieries.

9 Flatt was the name of the house bought by Sir John Lowther of Whitehaven later in the century and subsequently transformed into Whitehaven Castle.

10 I.e. at the rate at which...

11 An obsolete dry measure, frequently equal to a bushel, though in some places equal to half a bushel.

ably have sett to there hands the twentyeth day of May in the thirteneth
yeare of the raigne of our soveraigne lord Charles by the grace of God,
King of England, Scotland, France & Ireland defender of the Faith, etc,
anno domi. 1637.[12]

[Document 3[13]]
   Memorandum: it is agreed betwixt Sir John Lowther, knight, in the
beehalfe of his sonne Christopher Lowther that the bargayne made with
the salters shall bee disolved & that they shall have 20^s payd, 10^s by the
said Christopher Lowther & 10^s by Tho. Lowman and Rich. Wibergh, &
the said Tho. & Rich. doe promise & agree to performe the sayd agreement
& to make the same salt with the same cole & allowance & to follow the
works diligentlye, the which, while they doe performe the said Sir John
covenants & promiseth that all shall bee performed to them that is agreed to
bee don unto the salters: and the panns to bee veiwed by two smiths & two
salters, to be left in as good repayre as they have them delivered; and allsoe
it is covenanted that the sayd Rich. Wibergh shall put in securitye for his
parte Mr Tho. Wibergh & 10^l in stocke for the use of the said panns while
hee is in partenershipp with the said Tho. Lowman. Dated the last day of
May 1637.
              Jo. Lowther   Tho. Lowman

[Document 4]
   Articles indented and agreed upon betwixt Christopher Lowther of
Whitehaven, gentleman, of the one partie and David Bibby[14], Robert
Stockdell & Patrick Card, his salters and servants of the other partie, as
followeth:
   First the sayd Christopher Lowther doth undertake that there shall be
coles ready upon the bankes at his cole pitts in Flatt fields, Davie Field or
ellse where within his Lordshippe sufficient for the use of his three salt-
pannes A, B and C where the said David Bibby, Robert Stockdell & Patrick
Card now worke at.
   Secondly the said Christopher doth consent & agree unto that the sayd
Robert Stockdell shall worke the saltpanne A & shall have allowed unto
him to burne at the said panne eight and twenty loades each fowre &
twenty howres containing two & thirty gallons at the Grove[15] for sixe dayes
each weeke if lesse doe not suffice & that his receiver Richard Powley or .
whome else he shall appointe for that place shall pay unto such cole leaders
weekly or at the least once a fortnight as the sayd Robert shall appointe for

[12] Signed with Bibby and Younghusband's marks in the presence of Richard Wibergh,
Edmund Sandforth, John Teasdell.
[13] Document 3 is written on the reverse of Document 2.
[14] Here spelt Beebie.
[15] [Sic] unexplained.

leading of such coles, according to such accompt as he shall give in for number; and for price so much as the sayd Christopher can have them led to his steere or shipping from the said pitts and this bargaine to continew for halfe a yeare from the date hereof.

Thirdly the said Christopher doth consent & agree unto that the said David Bibby shall worke the saltpanne B & shall have allowed unto him to burne at the said panne six and twentie loads each fowre & twenty houres containing two & thirty gallons each loade at the Grove for sixe dayes each weeke if lesse do not suffice and to have such other condicions as the said Robert Stockdell.

Fourthly the said Christopher doth consent & agree unto that the said Patrick Card shall worke the salt panne C & shall have allowed unto him to burne at the said panne thirteene loade of coles each fowre & twenty howres contening two & thirtie gallons each loade at the Grove for sixe dayes each weeke; if lesse doe not suffise and to have such other condicions as the forsayd Robert and David is to have.

Fifthly the sayd Christopher is content to be at such cost for repaire of the said pannes as at the sight of two honest men, one to be chosen by him, another by them, shall be thought needfull and that he will pay unto them such ordnary wages as he hath hertofore comonly used while they or any of them helpe in workeinge to repaire the same provided there be a whole day smith, waller or carpenter's worke at the time, at the least together.

Sixtly that the said Christopher shall allow the sayd salters clinching[16] or a penny a draught, & further that they shall have the use of the sayd salt-pannes, sumpes, & all woork tooles to them belonging to make salte & twentiefive pounds yearly allowed to pay for iron & the smith's wages to repaire & maintaine the said pannes to be paid as the worke is wrought, in case the said Christopher shall neglect to cause the same to be done, & that it may encourage the sayd salters to be more carefull & not willfull to spoyle the pannes what may be spared of the said five and twentie pounds yearly the sayd salters to have it according to the proportionable allowance of the pannes that each of them worke at viz: Panne A two fifths, Panne B two fifths, and Panne C one fifthe.

In consideration whereof the sayd Robert Stockdell, David Bibby & Patrick Card doe covenant & promise to & with the sayd Christopher Lowther, his heyres, executors & assignes to deliver unto him or them, or his or their servant or servantes to be appointed for oversight of the sayd salteworkes in forme following, viz: the sayd Robert Stockdell fowerteene bushells of salte with one shake as is now used for each day & that for sixe dayes in each weeke one with another, whole dayes of repaire excepted only; and to pay two fifth parts of bryne, winding blowers, dressing shovells, creeper and battle shaftes & coles measuring at Groves if he likes

---

[16] Or "clincking", second letter smudged; sealing material?

not to trust to James Willon; and the sayd David thirteene measures of salte for each day & sixe dayes for each weeke & for all other things as Robert Stockdell; and the said Patrick Card fowre and thirty of the said measures or bushells of salte for each weeke & in all other things to be at one fifth part charge with the said Robert & David & to have & doe as they have & doe according to his proportion, and if they shall chuse rather to have the five and twentie pounds[17] for repaire of the pannes then that the sayd Christopher shall repaire them himselfe, then that each of them shall keepe the pannes appoynted to them with all worke tooles & all else therto belonging in so good repaire as they are at present, provided allwayes that upon payment of twentie shillings the either partie to the other at the end of seven weeks from the date hereof this bargaine & covenant to be voyde & likewise if the salters doe neglect their worke in makeing of salte & mending their pannes continually, in wittnes whereof the parties above sayd to these presents enterchangeably have sett to their hands & seales eightenth day of February 1637/8.[18]

[Document 5]

The 18th of February 1638/9

It is bargained and agreed betweene Christopher Lowther and Roger Fleming that the said Roger Fleming shall get or cause to bee gotten and delivered at the porte of Whitehaven to Christopher Lowther or his assignes the quantyty of tenne roods of blew slaite such [as][19] he slayteth his owne house at Kirkby-in-Furnesse, for largnes and goodness, the roode to contayne, beinge layde on the houses, sixe and a halfe yeards square every way —slayter's measure.

And the said Roger shall have liberty till midsommer next for the deliverie of five roods at Whitehaven as aforesaid and that Christopher Lowther shall pay five nobles for each rood of slaite soe delivered upon the deliverie thereat & to bynde this bargaine they have given to each other six pence by assumpsitt & have interchangeabley sett to theire hands the daye and yeare first above written.[20]

[Document 6]

To Mr Richard Fallowfield, Esq.　　　　　　　Sockbridge 1st Nov. '39
Worthy Unckle,

My beste respects salute you. My mother in lawe, my Uncle Tankerd[21] and Dr Dawes have moved an agreement touchinge the good of my sisters for theire preferment, which I have ascented to upon the assurance of

[17] There is an interpolation sign here and in the margin: "they refuse the five & twentie pounds & leave Mr Christopher to repaire the pannes."
[18] Marks of Bibby and Stockdell and Card but no signature from Christopher.
[19] Damaged.
[20] Signed by Roger Fleming, witnessed Rowland Jackson, Richard Powley.
[21] Variously spelled, possibly Tancred.

Wayteby and Penrith to me and some other moneys, but herein we have neede of your helpe and advice to which ende to satisfie my Uncle Tanckred of a knowne ende before he departe we intreate you to be here toomorrow by 9 of the clocke and you shall theirby oblige,

My deare Unckle,

Your loveinge nephew Chr. Lowther,

to be your servant in a greater matter.

[Reply written on the same folio:]

Good Cosen,

I am right gladd that things ar in so good a way amongst you of which I nothing doubted because I knowe yow all discreate and loving one to another, but I am sorie yow putt me to such a short exigent of time which I cannot possibly observe, and I am the more sorie in respect that I have a true zeale to contribute my poore indeavors and industries in my love to yow all; therefore if Mr Tankard for so good a worke as the setling of the interests of his sister and her children can dispense with his occasions and stay ther till Munday I intend to be ther with yow on Sunday in the afternoon. If not yow may drawe articles of your agreaments which may be perfected afterwards, so with my best respects to yow all I rest,

R. Fallowfield.[22]

[Document 7]

Penticoste 1640

Directions for my man John Wilkinson.

1. Firste buy to make a salve on for the horsse one pynte of musterd seede & grinde it; nexte 4[d] in brimstone beaten, 3[d] in tabacko shredd smalle, nexte 3 or 4 spoone full of tarre & put all theise in a quarte of trayne oyle such as shewmakeres use to which adde some urine & put theise in a pan or earthen potte over or neere the fyre soe that the salve may in 24 houres space be gently boyled downe till it be as thicke as sheepe salve, & lay it on the horsse, sheddeinge the hayre where theire is neede but not cutteinge it & some what rownde about farther then it needeth & rubbe it well and the skin with your hande & renew it once in three dayes but first lett him bloude a day before, but put not his owne bloud upon the horsse as many doe.

2. Get a gallon of tarre sente up into Patterdayle againste clippeinge tyme.

3. Buy a goode stronge carte such as I directed with reasonable hye wheeles & a carte sadle & hayrnes.

4. Buy a hatchet to have over about with thee.

5. On Wednesday next goe & cutt & sortte wood at Lowther New Parke & get William Wilkinson with thee & take a length of thy balke trees & consider for all husbandrie uses.

[22] This letter was found at D/Lons IV, Lancaster Family, "Settlements" 1559–1664. The "sisters" would be sisters-in-law.

6. On Thursday be at the ponde, on Friday at New Parcke againe though but thyselfe.
7. On Saturday to Appleby with the three fatte cowes & the reade one as directed.
8. The nexte weeke follow wood leadeinge & dike makeinge till it be done.

Page 2

Mother, I pray yow dayly aske John of all thinges & knowe how my directions are followed.

9. Appoynted my mother to let John have what money as   1 June
     he need it for my use   0   5   0
     For a carte   0 15 0
     For carrt hopes 2^s; for a rig rope 12^d 3   0   0
10. Remember bloudinge the bay horsse and salveinge him which thou has   6 June
neglected.
11. When the wood is led from Lowther (which leade with the 2 horsses in the carte when the other horsse cometh) and that the hedge is made thou may be finishinge the higher ponde theyselfe & make the gutters to them.
12. Blowe a litle ginger graited into the Irish slott eye, it is one of the leaste & the left eye as I remember.
13. I thincke it not amisse on Wednesday morneinge or Tewsday come a seavennighte when thou goest into Patterdale to carry those ewes that have loste theire lambes with thee & forget not the tarre & a litle salve, for on that Wednesday will I be at Hartsoppe & on Thursday with thee at the clippeinge.
14. If water wante firste drive one company of the beastes & nexte another & dresse every morneinge the well.
15. Pade to two men for dicking 12^d.
16. On Tewesday carry the bay Whitehaven nagg to Dick Wilkinson to ride or woorke while he seeketh the lost beastes if yow heare not of them in the intrim.

Page 3
Repd.

Pd. to John Wilkinson, he pd. to Lanty Wilkinson for
     hedging for Mr Lowther   0   1   6
17. To gett hay in firste thinge that is done.   Sep. 22
18. Then to fetch the lambs downe on Michaelmas day.
19. To gett halfe a dosen braken shearers, some heere[23], some about Whale, to get braken in Lowther Parcke.
20. To hyre Edward Lancaster lad to looke at beastes when thou art away.
21. To carry a butcher to buy a score of the beste weathers & a score of the woorste ewes when thou goest for the lambes & sell them as John Harrison, shephard, & thou thinkest them woorth though at to mid-

---

[23] Presumably the manor of Sockbridge.

sommer or lambing nexte upon a goode bonde which get Will Lancaster to take.

Pd. out
of Parson
Twine's
fine.

22. Let William Lancaster have twenty shillinges of the feaste money to that 13^l which he hath.

23. Goe over to Richard Wilkinson of Lowther & take his opinion & knowe of him what is fitt to sell of every y ... [yocke?] of beates [beastes?] with day [delay?][24] to midsommer or lambing nexte & then enquire both thou & he for chapmen to buy them.

24. If any soldiers come within 7 miles & that yow feare any disorder from them drive to Whitehaven both beastes & sheepe.

25. So lett out what beastes to draughte as yow can which yow cannot sell.

[Document 8]
Worshipfull Sir,

Affter my humble servise and dew respecte presented unto youe, hopeinge that both youe and my mistress be both in good health; if it please youer Worship to take notice I beinge without money, haveinge none at this time, and haveinge coles comeing in apace now; we thought it good to get as much lether as to put up the two other paire of bellows that we might have all the 4 harths goeinge this somer currant; then I expecting to get some of Mr Davis came heare to Carrickfergus and stayd heare 3 dayes goeinge to him morneinge, nowne and at night everry day and some times more, and when all was downe that I could not come to speak to him; then I took paper and did write my minde unto him and sent it to him by one of his men but to this time, which was 12 [h]owers after could have noe answer at all from him, but went my way home without one peney of money; not to delay any time but to goe & get some lether a trust of some taner or another, that we may get all the 4 harths to woorke, which I hope if we doe we shall get cleare or at least neare hand with Mr Sandis; yeat before Christanmas nexte I desire youer Worship to write to Mr Davis about that money for I doe feere the getinge of it greatly; unles that youer Worship will either be pleased to take of that wine which I sente youe; or els tobacco for the foresaid money; there is yeat behynd 30^l and as I hope to be saved I could get none at all of him; then I haveinge such a great occation for money at this tyme heareinge that Will. Hinde was at Belfast, soe when I came there he was gone to Strang Millis to deliver his coles, but money I could get none; therefore I intreat youer Worship to send us by the next return some good store of minde[25] and money, for I am in good hopes that if we get stocke as he doth endever himself all he can for coles, that we shall get cleare with Mr Sandis this yeare.

I would have sent $\frac{1}{2}$ tun of playts & $\frac{1}{2}$ tun of barr iron along with this

---

[24] Smudged and partly damaged.
[25] I.e. iron ore, "mined".

beerer but that it is such an unloucky time heere with shouldgers[26] that I could not get it carryed downe if I would have given $\frac{1}{2}$ the price of the iron; but by the nexte return, God willinge, I hope to have 2 tun or 3 to send youer Worship. Thus haveing nothinge els for the present but desireing God to bles, guyd and direckt youer Worship in all your affaires, I humbly take leave whoe is,

Youer dewtifull and obedient servant in his poore till death,
Strangmillis the 27th of Maye, 1641.   Richard Powley
Anthony Herman haith written for some salt as I perceave. I thincke he will pay for it at the receipt of the salt 7^s 4^d if youer Worshipp please to send it, but he is yeat dew of his last bond above 2^l 10^s.

[Document 9]
Knowe ye that I Christopher Johnston, merchant, doth acknowledge and confes myselfe to be oweing and indebted unto Thomas Wilkinson for anckarrige and kaige[27] being due to Mr Christopher Lowther the sume of 1^l 14^s 10^d which I promisse to pay att my returne upon demande as witnes my hande this 10 day of June 1641.

Christopher Johnson
Witnes here of: Jo: Gurnell
                  Robert. Hodgson

[Document 10]
Ever loveing and my good maister,
Time will not permit me that I can write unto yow my full mind, we ar put to such a straite heare in the country; all men paseth away and leaves us heare in this woeful case and amongst the rest our hamer man for to sucker and save his wuife and children flyeth amongst the rest;[28] and as your worship haith put me in trust with some parte of your estait in this kingdome I will either get something to come home unto youe both for youer proffit and my credit, or els I will end my dayes among my enemys. I doe owe our hamer man Georg Elyson some 3^l or there abouts, not much more nor lesse; therefore, good maister paye him if youe please what is dew to him, be not any way offended at me but with tears desireth that God my bles both youe & youers, I rest youer poore & trew servante in what I may,
Mainewater the 26 of October 1641   Rich. Powley

The 12th day of November 1641[29]
Recd. the day and yeare above written from Mr Christopher Lowther of Whitehaven the some of twenty shillinges sterlinge beinge now in distresse

---

[26] I.e. soldiers.
[27] I.e. anchorage and keyage.
[28] The Irish rebellion had broken out in Ulster on 23 October.
[29] On the same sheet of paper.

which I promisse to allowe in the reckoninges which are betweene me &
Richard Powley servante to the said Mr Chr. Lowther as witnes my hande,
George Ellison, Hammerman his marke.

[Superscribed:] George Elison, hammerman of Maynewaters, recpt. for 20ˢ
pretended to be paid and allowed in Rich. Powley's accounts by the said
Geo. Ell.

[Document 11]

Sir,

I have received your tune of irone from the hands of Mr Hudlston,
clarke, the number of the ends is fifty and fower. I have brought it downe
to Hugh Brockbancks house at Laydyhall in respect it is near, if youe cary
it by water, whereit will be in safe costody untill you fetch it; and when you
send for it I doe intreat you to send me some coalles & allso a not[e] under
youer hand both of the price & who I must pay the money to, and so with
my love & duty remembered, I rest,

Your servant to use,

Frome Thwaits this 14th of Aprill 1642   John Wennington

[This letter was addressed to the right worshipfull Christopher Lowther,
Esquire, and endorsed in a different hand "To the worshipfull Christopher
Lowther, Esq., at Meaburne Hall their, hast, hast. Christopher Woodburne
I pray yow send this letter as yt is directed with all speed."

[Document 12]

Ryght Hoble. Sir,

My love and service remembered to yow and all you love. These ar to
shew you that I have taken the boldnes, being short of Ynglishe money to
continew the payment of two pound to my over-comyng, which God wylling
shall be shortly and yf your honr. neyd any more pouder or pepper, indago,
synamont, clovis, mase or gynger or sope, what is neydfull send me word
and it sall be sent over with the first. I heir thair is some comodyties
comet[h] hence so that I houp the 6 pair of puttrynells is come hence so this
shall be as sufficient as is star[30] and bill so rests comitting you all [and] all
ye love to the protectione of the almichty God.

Yours to the utemost of his power,

Johne Johneston, merchant of Dumfries

Dumfries 4 of May 1643.

[Documents 13 to 16 are four letters from Roger Kirkby of Kirkby-in-
Furness, M.P., to Christopher, his brother-in-law, during the summer of
1641. Kirkby was member for Lancashire in the Long Parliament and
subsequently a Royalist. He died in Ireland in 1643.

[30] A bond.

[Document 13]

Sir,

Yow may well thincke it longe since yow writt your letter to mee and that yow have harde noe thinge from mee, but somethinge yow may imagine hath beene in it. The truth is noe thinge hath beene soe uncertaine as the tyme and manner of keepinge the assizes, the charge against the judges being sent upp but yesterday and what the effects of it will prove verie uncertaine soe that yett I cannot write yow certainly who will be your judges.[31] Neither could wee well tell what to resolve conserninge those thinges yow writte for, yett nowe wee have adventured, and bought such things yow apoynted, findinge the tymes inclininge to peace, and hopes of an end of theis trobles. For your leveries wee have bought yow onely for thirtie, as yow may perceive, which is a number as large as any frend I could meete with thought convenient. The House of Commons haveinge declared that it is not fitt that soe much luxurie should bee used by sheriffs in their entertainements and attendants and that noe sheriffe should give any intertainement to the judges, nor fees or gratuities to the judges' men, and this declaracion my Lord Keeper is to acquainte the judges withall before they goe in their circutes, and the House is resolved to proceed to make an accte for the prevencione of such inconveniencies in the future. However, this is a fyne opportunitie to doe both yourselfe and your contrie righte. This I thought good to give yow notice of as tymlye as possiblie I could, it beinge but the motione of yesterday; and soe yow may fitt your occasiones, and if theare bee any alteracion yow shall have as soone intelligence as I can by any meanes procure, the rest of your things will bee sent yow by the next convenient carrier, and in the meane tyme I hope yow will excuse our delay, consideringe it did not proceed from any neglecte of your busines, but the uncertaintie of the tymes.

Yesterday I must tell yow thear happened a little rubb in our proceedings which is much feared by many and what effects it may produce is to bee feared indeed. It was thus: wee hadd prepared 2 bills, one for the extirpacion of the Starr Chamber, and regulatinge the Counsell Boarde and another for the takinge away the High Commissione Courte. Theis wee hoped should have passed with the greate bill of Poale[32] money but His Majesty gave his assent to the Poale bill, and tooke tyme to consider of the other 2. This hath begotten verie much discontent amongst men especially in the Citie, soe, as it is thought, the money will not bee paid unlesse those billes passe but what will bee the end noe man knowes. This greate somme is to bee received by all the sheriffes of England and some are to returne the money

---

[31] I.e. the judges of the Cumberland assizes. Christopher was now Sheriff of Cumberland and apparently had written to Kirkby for advice on the entertainment, perquisites, etc. the judges would expect of him, and also for liveries for servants to meet and wait on the judges. Kirkby had been Sheriff of Lancashire in 1638.

[32] The Poll Tax Bill which fell with a graduated scale of payment upon men of different ranks of society.

to York and some to London; I have sent yow hearwithall a cattaloge of the somes imposed, of the particulare men as they are qualiffied.

For your busines conserninge your costomes Barronett Curwen and I have attended that committie verie dilligently and are in some hope to reduce your costomes upon our coast to 12^d per chaldrone coales for all exported to noe other then His Majesty's subjectes but the truth is the wante of money for the disbandeinge of the armies, and the jelousies amongst men begotten by theis plots and conspiracies, and discontents about the Courte hath put a delay and a stand in all other busines, and yett wee have sitten everie day both forenowne and after even till 8 or 9 of the clock at night. The busines nowe in hand is the charges against the Bishopp of Canterburie and the judges, the disbandeinge of the armie and the futher discoverie of Percie's plott, which by some men is much more feared then by others, beeing veriely thought by many it will end in noethinge.

This day the King hath passed the 2 billes and all are well pleased soe that nowe theare is noe talke but of peace, disbandinge and the King's goeinge into Scotland. Sir, I am hasted, but yet never soe as to neglecte my frends and soe rests,

Your verie loveing brother to serve yow,

Roger Kirkbye

July the 5th 1641.[33]

[Document 14]
Loveinge Brother,

I writt yow by the last post but feareinge the certaintie of that letter's comeinge unto your handes I thought it fitt by this bearer, Peeter Mawsonn, to certifie yow howe things stand heare and what wee have doone conserning your busines. Tempora mutantur: the world is nowe growne to that passe that it was a longe tyme before wee could resolve what to doe at the last. Least wee should bee to late wee adventured and have bought yow lase for 30 liveries which by my last letter I did conceive to bee a competent number, and am still of the same mynde, for the same reasonn I thear gave, for the house of Commones continewe in their resolucione conserninge the intertainements of judges and the exorbitant fees and gratuities challenged by their men. Thear is a bill in the House which hath beene twice redd against this abuse, and for the present theare is a comtee. appoynted to drawe a declaracione to that purpose, whereof I am one. This day wee are

[33] The letter is addressed to "his much hond. brother-in-lawe, Christopher Lowther, Esquire, High Sheriffe of ... Cumberland ... Hast, post hast! Leave this letter at Mr Banister's house in Preston to bee sent to Lancaster and soe as directed." In Christopher's hand: "Mr Brother Kirkby about judges & our coles impost & custom. Letters about Sheriffe's busines—litle woorth."

to meete about it soe that I cannot write yow soe fully as I would, but sure I am it will proceede.

I have received your letter by Pearsonn and because I perceive by it, and by Gyles Moore that yow have provided cloth for 50 cloakes wee have resolved to send yow lace for 20 more, soe that nowe yow may doe as yow please, and howesoever yow resolve, thear can bee noe losse of any valewe in that commoditie.

For the judges wee heare of none spoken of yett for our circute but Serjeante Whitfeeld alone, but as yett it is not certaine, but when wee knowe certainly I shall advise whether or noe or howe to addresse myselfe unto him in your behalfe.

For the rest of your things we have bought some allreadie and shall goe about the rest as fast as may bee, but truly wee have a greate want of my brother William, for I for my parte am soe ingaged by reasonn the House sitts soe close everie day both forenowne and after as that in truth I can hardly gett soe much tyme as I could wishe to doe yow that servise which I doe desire, but my sweete sister spares noe paines and I doubt not but we shall send yow all things downe in good tyme.

For newes I must refferr yow to the last, only this: the Kinge hath made his manifeste conserninge the Quene of Bohemia, his sister and her children, and the House of Commons have aproved of it, and that it shall bee published to all the world to this effect in shorte: that His Majesty hath beene longe enuffe deluded by the Spanishe treaties that both hee and his Parliament are sencible of; and that nowe once for all hee hath sent his embassadores to the Dyett at Ratisbone, wheare if such an honorable conclusione bee aggreed upon as fitt (verte) both for the restauratione of the dignities and estates of his sister and nephewe in the Pallatinate or elsewhere, it shall bee well pleasinge to him; if otherwise hee will delay noe longer but will by his owne force and the strength of his allies compell that justice to be doone them by force of armes, which otherwise would not bee.

For your Poale money yow will have full directione from the knights of your shire, soe that I need say noe thinge, and for the armies I doe believe yow have as good intelligence as wee can give yow.

For the Bishops' Bill which is nowe the greate worke in agitatione, and it is a greate worke indeed, for the settlemente of the government of the Church doth depend uponn it, is as yett but under comittment in our house and hath many rubbes, goeinge with much difficultie on; soe that, if it passe, as it is thought, it will goe offe with much oppositione, and then what will be doone in the Lords' House bee easilie imagined.

For the Booke of Rates it goes one thinge after another farely on and yesterday morninge wee hadd yor coales in agitatione, which is settled by Comtee.[34] at 12^d per chaldron exported to Ireland, and the Isel of Man, but for Scotland Mr Secretarie Vane would by noe meanes give way soe

[34] Abbreviation for Committee?

Barronett Curwen and I doe intend to trie the Scotishe Commissioners to see if they will recente it and labor to have that kingdome as the rest of the King's dominiones.

Sir, I am hasted and thearfore crave your pardonne for my shorte relaciones. Hartelie gladd to heare of the healtth and wellfare of my sweete sister and yourselfe but as sorie to heare of my litle cosin's death which I doubt not but your wisdome will take patiently.[35] Thear is more riches in that cabinett from whence hee came.

Wee are all heare verie well, and busie and carefull to accomodate your desires and soe rests.

                          Your loveinge brother and readie servant,
July the 10th 1641   Roger Kirkby

[Document 15]

Sir,

At my cominge downe from London I intended to have geven yow a visite at Whitehaven, but meetinge with soe uncomforthable a wellcome home I have diverted my purpose, my cheefest comforth in your partes is taken from mee and the joye of my harte in this world is in apparent danger soe that if I should seeke it, my content in this world is nowheare to bee founde. I have sent yow by this bearer a sworde which I hope will give yow content; my sweete sister and I did our best to accomodate yow with all those things yow writt for, which I hope before this tyme yow have recived.

Sir, I beseeche yow, if I may serve yow in anything, command mee for thear is noe man liveinge that enjoyes soe litle of himselfe; that is more willinge to bestowe that litle of his frend, then myselfe. Send mee worde, I pray yow, whether yow keepe house of yourselfe, or yow hould your purpose of keepinge an ordinarie[36], which in my oppinione is the better waye; if yow please to imploy any servants of myne, lett mee knowe that they may accomodate themselves accordingly.

For your judges, Sir Robert Heath is to bee your only judge. Hee will come from York to Apleby and soe to Carlisle, which will bee the 2nd of September. I was with him and did present your service to him, but for [the] matter of his intertainement did not medle because the House of Comones was still in hande with their declaracione, conserninge those things, but was not finished when I came downe. It is good to bee provided and yow may heare what is doone at York and soe yow may resolve. I heare in severall partes of the kingdom it is intended to lessen those intertainements verie much.

---

[35] Evidence that Christopher and Frances Lowther had at least one child, who died in infancy, prior to the birth of John Lowther in 1642.

[36] I.e. to entertain the judge and his suite in an inn rather than in a private house taken for the purpose.

Good Sir, comande mee and myne and soe I shall conclude yow love mee. Present my service I pray yow to my sweete sister, your loveinge bed-fellowe, and assure yourselfe noethinge shall bee more acceptable to mee then an happie opportunitie to expresse myselfe,

Your most loveinge brother and faithfull frend,

August the 12th 1641[37]   Roger Kirkby

[Document 16]

Noble Sir,

The declaracione I formerly writt to yow of is nowe comme to my handes, and I have hearinclosed sent a copie of it to yow. I doubte not but yow will receive one signed with the clark's hand from some of the members of your owne countie, yet I thought it not amisse to give yow as tymely notice as was possible that yow might dispose of your busines accordingly, and thearfore I have purposely sent this bearer to yow to knowe your comandes, for hee is not worthye the esteme of a frende that at such a tyme as this will not be readie to testifie his forewardenes to expresse his love, with the best service in his power. If yow intend to make use of Nan; Radcliffe shee shall bee readie for yow, or any other servant or thinge that I have but I beseech write mee your mynde by this bearer, that wee may accomodate ourselves soe as may bee moste for your service and their creditt.

My mother, if yow have any occasione to send to her, I beleeve will bee all this weeke at the least at Kirkbie, for my wife is soe verie weake and ill, in this foule disease, as that she will not leave her till God send her some better mendes.[38]

Yow may relie of a brase of Buckes from mee, and if yow bee not fitted with a peece of fatt beeffe, I doe verilie believe I shall bee able to furnishe yow.

Wee are all sent for to the Parliament soe that I knowe not whether I shall have the happines to waite of yow or noe. However, I intende by God's grace to see my poore wiffe in some better dispositione of her bodie before I doe stirr from home.

Sir, God blesse yow and prosper yow in all your undertakings and make us all soe order our course heare, as that wee may raigne with him in glorie hearafter and theis bee the daylie prayers of,

Your entirely loveing brother and servant,

August the 15th 1641   Roger Kirkby

I have sent yow the originall order itselfe, signed with the clark's hande. Yow may take a coppie and sent it mee againe.   Farewell.

---

[37] This and the succeeding letter were both presumably written from Kirkby. It was received on August 15th.

[38] Probably Lady Eleanor Lowther, Christopher's mother, Roger's mother-in-law, is meant.

[Document 17]

A lease from Sir Christopher Lowther to Lady Eleanor Lowther, William Lowther and John Lamplugh of his lands in Cumberland in trust.

This indenture mayde the 12th of February in the nineteenth yeare of the reigne of our soveraigne lorde Charles by the grace of God of England, Scotland, France and Ireland, Kinge, defender of the faith, etc,[39] betwixte Sir Christopher Lowther of Whitehaven in the countie of Cumberland, Baronet, of the one party and his mother Dame Elinor Lowther of Meaburne, his brother Mr William Lowther of Leeds and his nephew John Lamplugh, of Lamplugh Esquire,[40] of the other party, witnesseth that the said Sir Christopher Lowther for the love and affection he beareth to his sonne and heire John Lowther and such other child or children which his wife the Lady Frances Lowther is in all likelyhood conceved of, for his or theire better maytenance and preferment, nowe when by losses at sea by piretts, the rebelles in Ireland, and the vaste charges of theise warlike times at home, and purtchise of land, his personable estate is reduced to lesse then what he thinketh fitte for his or their preferment, his estate considered, hath revoked all former estates and wills by him revocable, and hath demised, granted, and to farme letten, and by these presentes doth demise, grante and to farme lett, unto the saide Dame Elinor Lowther, William Lowther and John Lamplugh all his mannores, measuages, landes, tenementes, rectories, mills, tythes, penciones, cole mynes, salt pannes, proffites and heareditaments of and in the County of Cumberland (excepte his rentes and lands in Penrith) to have and to hould all the said measuages, landes, tythes, rectoryes, hereditaments and premises with theire appurtenaces, excepte before excepted, to the said Dame Elinor and William Lowther and John Lamplugh, their heyres, executors, administrators and assignes from the day of descease of the said Sir Christopher Lowther untill such tearme of yeares be expired as that his heyre be of the age of one and twenty yeares, in trust to rayse such somes of monye out of the profitts theirof and in such manner as hearafter followeth:

First, to pay shuch debts as he the saide Sir Christopher Lowther is oweinge and legacies which he shall give by his last will and testment in writinge wheare his personal estate will not amount to pay the same, his wife's thirdes and legacies being first taken forth, and likewise to rayse fifthy pound starlinge yearly for the maintynance, attendance and education of his sonne and heyre John Lowther till he be fitt for the universcety or Ins of Court, and a hundreth pound yearely after while he shall be at the Ins of Court or university or in travell and allsoe five and twentye pounds by yeare for the maintaynance, attendance and education of such other

[39] I.e. 12 February 1644.
[40] John Lamplugh of Lamplugh's first wife was Jane, daughter of Roger Kirkby of Kirkby, and therefore Christopher's niece. He was destined to marry Frances, Christopher's widow, as his second wife.

younger childe or children which he hoopeth his wife the foresaid Lady Frances Lowther is conceved of til he, shee or they be fitt for the university or education at London or elsewheare abroade, and after fifty pounds starlinge while he, shee or they be fitt to be educated abroade untill he shee or they be of the age of one & twenty yeares. Further to rayse out of the said lease towe thousand poundes starlinge for his said younger childe or children, if God shall blese him with any, for all portions and other demandes out of his estate to be paid to him, her or them, at the age of one and twenty yeares, if he, she or they live soe longe.

And lastly after his debts paid, legacies discharged to be given by his last will and testement and the foresaid somes likewise satisfied and payd, then to imploye the surplusadge of the profitt of the leases to be putt forwarde for his foresaid sonne and heire John Lowther and to be imployed in somme purchase of land for him free from all questions in lawe suties, or tythes, though the land cost dearer, provided allwayes that if the said Sir Christopher Lowther, Barronet, by his writtinge under his hand and seale shall revoke the presents or any part therof or lett for years or life any parte theireof for soe much theirof shall be revoked or leased this lease shall be voyde. In witness whearof the partyes to theise presentes have interchangabeley sett to their hands and seales the day and yeare firste above written.

Sealed, signed & delivered in the presence of us by John Lamplugh, Esquire: John Lamplugh, Eilinor Lowther, Francis Hechsetter, John Studdert, Lan. Relffe, [on the other side it notes: "sealed, signed and delivered by the within named Lady Elinor Lowther in the presence of: Rich. Kirkby, Frances Lowther, Agnes Braithwaite her mark." Further down it notes: "sealed, signed and delivered in the presence of us by ... William Lowther" but no signatures follow.]

[Document 18 Sir Christopher Lowther's Will, unsigned and unsealed, dated 14 February 1643/4[41]]

In the name of God. Amen. The 14th day of February in the of our Lord God 1643 I Christopher Lowther of Whitehaven in the County of Cumberland, Baronett, being Collonell of a Regiment under the comand of his exellency the Marques of Newcastle and daily comanded on service not knowing but that it may please God to call me out of this world very suddenly as many as are especially in these times of war, do make this my last will and testament in writeing revokeing all former wills and testaments;

first, I comend my soul unto Almighty God, my Maker and Redeemer, not doubting but through the merritts and mercy's of Jesus Christ, my

---

[41] Jackson deposes that this will, which he knew of but had not seen, was never proved, and quotes Sir James Lowther, Christopher's grandson, who possessed this copy, as saying that he did not know if it was a true copy for he had found no evidence of probate, Jackson, *opus cit*. Vol 2, p. 96.

Savaiour, to have my sins forgiven and after this mortall life ended to be an inheriter of his heavenly kingdom for ever with his saints and angells and I will that my body be disposed in such seemely manner as my own mother, the Lady Lowther, and my wife shall think me worthy of and as touching my lands, my will and desire is that my wife have all my lands in Westmorland and rentes at Penrith and the tenement bought of John Harrison, dureing her life in full of her dower out of all my lands, hopeing if my son live or the child or children which I believe she is withall who is to inheritt the same after her decease, that she will make the house at Sockbridge a convenient and fitt house for such of my children as may live to injoy [it], the better to do which I give to my said wife a tun of lead lent to my brother Sir John due upon demand;

for all other my lands, tythes, tenements, and hereditaments in Cumberland I give them to my son John Lowther and the heirs males of his body to be begotten and for default of such issue to my right heires for ever, and for my personall estate I do thus dispose of it:

first, I give all hewne stones or stones quarried, wooden stuffe and all iron implements for either house or husbandry, a brass pott at Sockbridge, my golden signett and mine and my wives pictures to my son John and his heires as heirloomes for ever saveing the use of the same for what is either at Sockbridge and Hartsop to my wife for her life;

for my shipp, Christo[pher] if ever she be recovered from the rebells at Wexford I give her to my servants John Wood, George Wood, Richard Powley equally to be divided between them, which if God send peace, I believe they may easilie gett, hopeing by their service to my wife and children they will meritt the same;

Item, I give to my wife over and besides the third parte of all the remainder of my personall estate due to her by law one of my best saddle horses, the bull and four of my best cows;

Item, I give the custody of my son and heir to my wife while she liveth unmarried desireing he may be carefully educated and brought up a Protestant according to the settled descipline of the Church of England with allowance of 50^l by year for him for his dyett, apparell, attendance and educacion till he be fitt for the university and 100^l per annum while at the university or Inns of Court as being sufficient till such time as he be of the age of 21 years or marry, which I desire may be with the advice of my executors and overseers of this my last will and testament if they or any of them be liveing;

Item, I give the custody of my other child or children which I hope my wife is withall while she liveth unmarried unto her my said wife with halfe allowance that my son and heir is to have for his, her or their keeping and if it happen my wife to marry then I give the custody of my children with the former allowances to the execators and overseers of this my last will and testament or as the major parte of them shall advise;

and, I confirme the lease by me made to my mother, the Lady Ellinor Lowther, my brother William Lowther and nephew Mr John Lamplugh to help raise these summes by me given in that lease, and the will being the same and not divers, soe farr as in the lease is mencioned where my goods, chattells, debts and mortgages shall fall short and not be sufficient to performe the same amongst which I mean not but that Sanwith and Coutherton tythes or the money for them shall goe to my son and heir, but for the mortgage from my couzin Senhouse of Seascale and my couzin Senhouse of Netherhall also Alneburgh[42], those I account of as amongst my personall estate toward payment of my debts and legacies;

Item, I give to such younger child or children as my wife is with child withall at this present two thoudand pounds sterling to be paid unto him, her or them at the age of twentyone years if he, she or they live soe long and after my debtes paid and legacies herein given, I give to my son John all my other mortgages, debts, goods and chattells and the surplusage of the profitts of the aforesaid lease to be put forward for him and imployed in some purchase for his use by the said leasers;

Item, I give yearly to the leasers and overseers of my will at their to perfect accounts once every year ten pounds amongst them that are then there equally to be divided;

Item, I give to my servant Tho. Beacroft Towerson horse or five marke in money; to George Hewetson the Scotch mare and 20^s in money; and I give to Richard Chappelhow his indentures of apprenticeshipp and 40^s in money;

Item, to Robert Bradley, my late servant, to build him a house at Whit[haven] 6 13 4 being that my father in his will did give him soe much, which he is not likely to gett, thoug[h] in marrying without my privity he doth not deserve it;

Item, I give a hundred pounds to build ten alms houses for ten aged, lame and decripitt colliers or salters of mine or my heirs to live in dureing their life rent free and my heirs to repair them and I give 100^l the use thereof lett out or imployed in lands to be for ever to one that may be a reader of prayers at Whit[haven] and teach schollars;

and I make execators of this my last will and testament my most dear virtuous wife Frances, my mother the Lady Ellinor Lowther, my [brother] William Lowther and nephew John Lamplugh, Esq., and I make my said mother, brother and nephew and allsoe my sister Agnes Kirkby and brother-in-law John Dodsworth supervisors thereof. In witness whereof I have hereunto put my hand and seale the day and year first above written.

[42] Alneburgh or Ellenborough Hall is an alternative name to Nether Hall, at Maryport, Cumberland. The Nether Hall Senhouse was probably either Peter Senhouse, former Sheriff of Cumberland, obit 1654, or his heir Captain John Senhouse, Royalist officer, obit 1667, which is more likely.

Sealed and delivered in the presence of us: Lanc. Lowther, Chr. Hare, Geo. Wood, Tho. Beacroft.*

[Ten weeks and three days after the date of this document, on the 27 April 1644, Sir Christopher was buried at the church of St Bees. No tomb or inscription seems to have been erected over his grave. No record of the cause of death has come to light so far.]

---

* N.B. these are all written in the same hand which drew up the will. They are not signatures, nor is the will signed or sealed by Christopher.

APPENDICES

[Appendix A: A document the first part of which is in the hand of Sir John Lowther of Lowther, father of Christopher, and the second part almost certainly in the hand of Robert Lowther, London merchant, his younger brother, concerning the possibilities of Ireland which Robert is to visit (or is visiting).[43]]

Inquistiones to be made, considerations to be had and remembrances for my brother Rob. L.

1. First how money is lett to use by a permission of state without question in law, in the cyties and contries everie where severally.
2. How land is sowlde by the yeres purchase to be letten agein for money, and what measure of land and how it is in value proportionable to ours.
3. Thirdly let the inquirie be near the port towns joiening upon our coste and consider the dannger, of men, and beasts, and the civilitie their, and the wayes to vent and exchainge and how to be served by laborers, and tradesmen and inquier what things of valew are to be soulde, and how often, and let one precedent be noe generall rule in ainie thing with you.
4. Inquier out their comodities and how they be vented moste where, the rates of corne, and cattle, the wages of servants, the power of the lords of their undertenants in their owne opiniones and usages.
5. And principally consider upon the power of the law, civill and marshall, their preheminence and present use, and whoe serveth one the other and the certeintie that may be established without their extrajuditiall controll or help, and the taxations imposed.
6. How the rate is in Dublin for vittales in the Markett, for howse rent, and other provisions.
7. Inquier by my Uncle[44] the valew of the Attorney's place, and how it riseth, and if ten yeres and a halfe will purchase it; let him make a stay and I will presently come over if it be 500^l by year and above. Inquier how it riseth, the use and service in circueits with the Deputie or otherwise of it and how I am served if I have it. You know my losse in my

[43] D/Lons/L. Letters "Enquiries about economic prospects and investments in Ireland *c*. 1620". An endorsement "Letters from Sir Christopher Lowther to his son at the Temple" suggests that the paper may have been used as a wrapper at some time. The Sir Christopher Lowther referred to is Sir Christopher of Lowther 1557–1617.

[44] Probably Sir Gerard Lowther, a justice of the Common Pleas, who died in 1624, as there is a reference to "my Uncle G." later in the document. He should not be confused with Sir Gerard Lowther, Chief Justice of the Common Pleas in Ireland, who is frequently referred to by Christopher.

liveing in my practise heer and the moneys I disburse, and let it be above all or not, as I have informed you.

8. Inquier your owne fitnes for an office toward the law their, the certenitie of it, the service, the valew and the meanes to gett it, and the valew of other eminent places fitt for me, which I have towlde you of.

9. Tell my Uncle G. because I wish that we let noe good fortune fall that we all cowlde attein to, that if Ireland be not fitte for me, that yet if he like it since he hathe bestowed money their, that if he may make double profit he shall have my money and bestowe it for me or if he like to sell it all together I shall take his English land in exchange or for securitie.

10. If any commoditie be their neglected or useful for us, and the means, charge and rediness of passage, and retorne thither and hither, and if their be anie new plantated[45] inquier the place how it stands and precisely observe the nature of the soyle.

[There follows in Robert Lowther's hand:]

A note what I have gathered and learned concerning the premises above written.

1. Use for money is no more in Ireland, by permission of staute[46], then in England, but all men which puts monie to that use, doth make 20^l at 100^l in the cities and in the countries more, for as yet it is not striklie looked unto.

2. Land is sould at 13 yeares purchase within the English paile and maie be leten to that raite againe. Their measure is greater then ours, and with out it is cheaper but all is according to the seat and place.

3. I cannot se any good can be done with any kind of merchendize out of Ireland in to England, for all is sought out that there semeth to be anie kind of profit in, the countrie is plenished with all kind of tradesmen, but they are deare. The land is secure enough from spoile but there impost and costoms is so greate and the carrages hither and thither so dere it takes away som of the whole stok beside gaines, but corn and linnen cloth are tow of the best commodities.

4. The price of cattell is uncartane, somtimes hier and some tymes lower, but the comon rate is 20^l a score fat and leaner chep, there wheat a barrell 14^s and there pecke 11^s and great barle 7^s and small corn 6^s, there ots 3^s, there peck is our bushell and more by one of our p[ecks]; a plowman's wages is 40^s, a sarving man 4^l. The power of the lords of there undertennants is verie greate, they maie use them as they will, but most ar tyed to this custem to give them there yearely rent in money, besides this: for ever[y] cow they kepe 16^d and vi quarts of butter, 3 daies plow in wheat sede tyme, 3 in ot tyme, harres all[47],

[45] I.e. "plantations".
[46] I.e. "state", see above p. 233, question 1.
[47] Could be harrs., possibly contraction of harrows?

reapes all, ledes all, gets all they furrus. [furnish?] and gives them tow daies a weke worke, and a fat hog a gaine Christenmas, and hens, cand[lemass?] carrages, in some more in some less.

5. The Marshell law is quite ablolished[48], and the civil law in great power, all is in peace and saiftie in Ireland, the kernes[49] all gone, a man maie live as secure in Ire[land] as In Eng[land] if it kepe as it is. Their taxations is but as ours in England, only paye the rent which the king has resarved of the land. When subsidies and feftens are, then they must paie them.

6. For house rent it is verie greate in Dublin 20 m[arks] and 20^l all according to the goodness, and vittales reasonable in the market, but at ordinaries deare, but in the countrie a man maie kepe a house verie chepe.

7. The attourne[y's] place is above a 1,000 m[arks] by yeare, there is 200^l standing fee, and the rest is in giving pattans[50] for plantations and the sarvise is [no]t[51] greate for he goes no sirkutes, it has beane a 100^l a yeare, but Sir Robert Jacob lokes for it.

8. My unkle is contented to let you have the land in Pen[rith] but no more as yet; as fur as I can parceive, he wood have no greater man of the name here then himselfe, for he semes as he would have a greater place in Eng[land] and so would he have you too, and howsoever he would not have you to purchas in Ire[land] unless you managed[52] heare a while yourselfe.

9. There is no profit heare neclected that we could make any of, but mo[re] there is 2 plantations [at?[53]] Conwarth, the one in the County of Longford, the [other?] in the County of Linforth, the Scots has beged th[em of ?] the King, but they will sell them againe as I he[ar? two or three words missing] is good. But in those parts there be the M......[54]

[48] [Sic].

[49] Kern, a troop or band of Irish footsoldiers.

[50] I.e. patents.

[51] Damaged.

[52] A contracted word squeezed at the edge of the page, perhaps a letter or two missing. Could be contraction for "manage".

[53] The paper has a substantial piece missing hence the conjectural reconstructions of certain words in this sentence.

[54] Large gap here with only a few words surviving which seem to make the phrase "....I will have no being unle[ss] ...... be heare and under you."

[Appendix B: the transfer of the St Bees–Whitehaven estates from Sir John Lowther of Lowther, Christopher's brother, to Christopher Lowther, on January 5th, 1638/9.][55]

This indenture made the fifth day of Jenuarie in the fouertenath yeare of the raigne of our soveraigne lord Charles ... betweene Sir John Lowther in the Countie of Westmorland, knight baronet[56], one the one partie and Christopher Lowther of St Bees in the countie of Cumberland, Esq., and brother of the said Sir John Lowther on thother partie, Witnesseth that the sayed Sir John Lowther as well for and in consideration of the performance of the last will and testament of Sir John Lowther of Lowther in the countie aforesaid deacesed, father of the said Sir John Lowther, knight baronet, and the said Christopher Lowther, as alsoe for and in consideracion of the performance of an award made by Sir Richard Diett, knight, and one of His Majesty's Right Honourable Councell established in the North Parts, betweene the said Sir John Lowther, partie to these presents, Dame Ellenor Lowther, mother of the sayed Sir John and the said Christopher Lowther, and other the children and legatories of the sayed Sir John Lowther, deseased, beareing date the tenth day of May last past, haith granted, assured, conveyed and confirmed unto the said Christopher Lowther and to the heires males of his body all that the Mannor, Rectorie, Parsonage, Sell and Scite of St Bees, with all its rights and members and appurtenances and all houses and buildinges, barnes, dovehouses, stables, oarchards, gardens, milnes, messuages, lands, tenementes, meadowes, feedinges, pastures, commons of pasture, rents, reversions, services, woods, underwoods, tythes, oblasions, pencions, obvencions and other paroichiall duties and waies, waters, fisheinges, moores, mosses, waistes, court leets and profitt of court leets and view of franke pledge, and whatsoever to a court leet doth or may belonge, and all coole mines and other mines, quarries, salt panes, faires, marketts, customes, anchorages, keyages, wrecks, weefes,[57] straes fellons goods, fugitives liberties, priviledges, commodities, profittes and hereditaments with the appurtenances whatsoever as well spirituall as temporall of what kinde or nature or by what name soever the same be knowne or reputed, scituated, lyeinge, being, renewinge, comeinge and groweinge in the townes, fields, parishes, or hamblets of St Bees and Enderdaile[58] in the County of Cumberland or elswhere whithin the said Countie of Cumberland and Yorkshire to the said mannor, rectory, sell of St Bees any wayes belonginge or appertaininge or as members, parts and parcells therof, had knowne, taken, used

---

[55] D/Lons/W St Bees 1/41.
[56] Possibly a later transcript for Sir John's baronetcy of Nova Scotia is usually dated 1640.
[57] waifs.
[58] I.e. Ennerdale.

and reputed, and alsoe all the colemines in Corkikle, otherwise Corkegill, within the said parish with all waies, easments, profitts and appurtenances whatsoever theirunto belongeing or there withall used, occupied or enjoyed whereof Sir John Lowther deseased was at any time seased, being parcell or lyeinge within the said mannor rectorie or sell or parish of St Bees or elswhere or to the same belongeing or there withall used or enjoyed as part, parcell or member thereof, and all dedes, writinges, and evidences which the now said Sir John Lowther haith or any other to use or may lawfully cum by without suite in law, to have and to hould the said mannor, rectory, parsonage, sell and site of St Bees and all and singuler the aforesaid messuages, lands, colemines, other mines, salt pans, tyeths and heridaments and all the before granted premisses with the appurtenances whatsoever unto the said Christopher Lowther and the heyres males of his body to the onelie use and behoofe of him the said Christopher Lowther and the heyres males of his bodie, and the said Sir John Lowther, knight baronet, and his heires all the before granted premisses unto the said Christopher Lowther and the heires malles of his body, against him the said Sir John Lowther, knight baronet, his heires and assignes will warant and forever defend by these presents, and the now said Sir John Lowther for him, his heires, executors and administrators doeth covenant, promise and grant to and with the said Christopher Lowther, his heires, executors and assignes that the said Christopher Lowther, his heires, and assignes shall and lawfully may at all times and from time to time quietlie and peacably have, hould, occupie, posses and enjoy all and every the before granted premisses without any lett, suite trouble, eviction, expulcion, interruption, charge or incumbrance whatsoever of the said Sir John Lowther, his heires or assignes or from any other person or persons haveing or claymeinge any estate, right, tytle, interest, clame or demande whatsoever from him, his heires or assignes or by his or their meanes, assents, defaults, privitie or procurements, and further that he the said Sir John Lowther for him, his heires, executors and administrators doeth covenant, promise and grant to and with the said Christopher Lowther his heires and executors administrators [and] assignes that he the said Sir John Lowther and Dame Mary his wife, and the heires of the said Sir John Lowther, partie to these presents, shall and will at all times and from time to time hereafter dureinge the spase of seaven yeares now nexte ensueinge doe make, doe knowledge, suffer and execute or cause to be done, knowledged, suffered and executed all such further or better assurance, assurances, estate or estates, conveyance or conveyances of all and every parte of the before granted premisses unto the said Christopher Lowther and the heires males of his body at his and theire cost and charge in law, as shall be reasonably devised, advised or required, be it by fine or fines recoverie or recoveryes feofment, ded or dedes, indented or not indented, inrolled or not inrolled, by all or any of the said waies or meanes or by other waies or meanes whatsoever sow that they be not compelled to travell above 30 myles from the plase of theire abode for the doeinge thereof at the tyme of such request made all which [assur]ances shall be to the use of the said Christopher Lowther and the heires males of his body

In witness whereof the parties abovesaid have to these presents inter-changeably sett theire hands and seales the day and yeare first above written.

John Lowther[59]

Sealed and delivered in the presence of us:
Matthew Richardson
Jo. Gowlinge.

[59] Sir John's holograph signature.

INDEX

Alternative forms of surnames given in brackets; an alternative spelling bracketed with a query suggests a possible error in the original or the transcription. Where the text gives no Christian-name, but uses a style, e.g. "Mr", this is reproduced in the index. For named ships, see under "ships".